D1623010

LONDON PUBLIC LIBRARY
WITHDRAWN

Mystery Stories

Mystery Stories

DAVID HELWIG

The Porcupine's Quill

LONDON PUBLIC LIBRARY

Library and Archives Canada Cataloguing in Publication

Helwig, David, 1938 –
    Mystery Stories / David Helwig. – First.

Short stories.
ISBN 978-0-88984-337-0

    I. Title.

PS8515.E4M97 2010   C813'.54   C2010-903543-7

Copyright © David Helwig, 2010.
1   2   3   ·   12   11   10

Published by The Porcupine's Quill, 68 Main Street, PO Box 160,
Erin, Ontario N0B 1T0. http://porcupinesquill.ca

Readied for the press by Doris Cowan.
The cover and all interior photographs are by David Helwig.

All rights reserved. No reproduction without prior written permission of the
publisher except brief passages in reviews. Requests for photocopying or
other reprographic copying must be directed to Access Copyright.

Represented in Canada by the Literary Press Group.
Trade orders are available from University of Toronto Press.

We acknowledge the support of the Ontario Arts Council and the Canada
Council for the Arts for our publishing program. The financial support of the
Government of Canada through the Canada Book Fund is also gratefully
acknowledged. Thanks, also, to the Government of Ontario through the
Ontario Media Development Corporation's Ontario Book Initiative.

Canada

Ontario
Ontario Media Development
Corporation

Canada Council   Conseil des Arts
for the Arts   du Canada

ONTARIO ARTS COUNCIL
CONSEIL DES ARTS DE L'ONTARIO

To Bill and Haide Aide

Contents

I.
Young and Old

Missing Notes   11
Red Barn, Interior   27
Prophecies for April   41
Adam on the Art of Dying   47
Wakefulness   55

2.
Domestic Arrangements

The Steps   67
Stitches in Air   80
Housebound, 1969   112
An Act of Oblivion   130

3.
Late Hours

Where Is He Now?   165
Flight   176

4.
And Variations

La Rue du Chapeau Perdu   205

I.

Young and Old

Missing Notes

Hugo heard a voice speaking to him, would have said that, although he could make out no words. It was like the insistent noises at night in the empty house. Hugo didn't believe in ghosts of course – he sees a dim figure reflected in the old TV set as he crosses the room, and that's ghost enough for him – and yet when he heard the voice, he would not have said it was imagined.

At the time this took place, he was alone in a church. It was one of those white wooden Prince Edward Island churches, old-fashioned carpentry still plumb and level, well kept up and freshly painted, and when he tried the door, it was open, and he walked in. It was the graveyard he'd come to see. He was not, in the usual way of things, interested in genealogy. It had always appeared to him a sad pastime, a hopeless, primitive attempt to find a place in the cold universe, but he remembered his Aunt Claire telling him how many of their ancestors were buried in this field, and it was just along the road, and when he arrived here in the cold early spring and carried his bag into Claire's house, he found that he wished, in his solitude and confusion, to make a gesture of filial piety. He walked past the flat white stones set upright in the green grass, perfectly tended, the grass luminous with spring. He didn't care which were the ancestors, only to walk the earth over their bones. Rose was here somewhere. Was that the reason he'd come? He looked past the bare branches of a birch tree, the buds swollen but not yet open, to the frame church, the white walls caught in momentary pale sunlight, shining against a background of rolling grey clouds, and he was drawn to it. He didn't expect the door to be open. The light shone down on the plain walls, the waxed wood of the floor and the pews, the pulpit from which some early Scots preacher had made the fierce assertion of John Calvin's creed. In the shed behind the house, he had found a framed motto, handwritten in ornate letters. 'Flee from the wrath to come,' it said, and below that, 'How shall we escape if we neglect so great salvation.' He stood still, and the silence sang in his ears until he heard whatever voice it was and looked around him, and there was nothing but the light and the flow of time.

As he walked back down the road to the house, he reflected on the nature of ghosts. The voices of other times, the past, the future, the voice of desire, plain and hidden, the fears which were desire in dark clothing.

2

When he found the small figure in a box in a closet, the figure of a naked woman in dark brown wax, he knew who it must be. The long neck and rather wide flat breasts, the wide hips, it was his cousin Rose. Years before, Rose had gone away to study art. In Boston. Though all that was forgotten when she came back from away, found a government job and settled down to ten years of responsible work. He held the small naked figure, perhaps two feet tall, in his hands and thought that it must be something that Rose herself had made, probably in art school. Had stood in front of a mirror and her fingers had shaped this portrait of her young body. The figure was crudely enough done; Rose had not been greatly talented. He remembered the handmade Christmas cards she would send. The last time he recalled seeing her – on a short visit with his mother, who was recovering from some disaster and wanting the reassurance of her old home – he was nineteen, and they had talked mostly about the early summers they had spent together here.

He looked at the naked figure and tried to remember if he and Rose had once undressed for each other in one of the small back rooms of the house. He thought so. It was perhaps at the end of the summer, when he was about to leave, and they both understood that he might not come back. Two small white bodies shivering and staring at each other with the same blank awareness. Adam and Eve knowing everything, nothing. He left the nude figure in the closet. Already he was too aware that this should have been Rose's house, that it had only been left to him because of her untoward death in that car accident five years before.

It was only later that she began to come to him in the night.

3

After his wife left, Hugo had quit his job as a music teacher in a good private school, left behind the house on Long Island and moved into the city, where he found an apartment in the Village, small and too expensive, but he needed the noise of the city, the traffic, the danger. The living world, city streets, cars and crowds, they made him real. He watched from his window as his neighbours passed by. The print seller going to his small shop. A man with AIDS being walked to the corner by his friend. Hugo would go out in the streets and watch the unemployed young black men playing a fast pickup game of basketball at a small court on a corner at Seventh Avenue. Himself, he could make a living of sorts editing and proofreading musical texts. When he was in university – in Toronto that was, another stage of his wanderings – he had supported himself as a copyist. He was careful and had a good hand. Now it was done on computers. It was all but unknown for anyone to copy musical text by hand, but there was editorial work to be done, and he did it well.

Until A. announced that she was leaving, he would have said he was a happily married man. As evidence, not once in the fifteen years of teaching music to adolescent girls in a private school had he been indiscreet. A couple of times there had been pupils who were too intense, perhaps a little mad, who made gestures toward him, and each time, at the first hint, he went to the school's principal and explained the situation, made sure that she sent him a memo acknowledging the discussion and the fact that he had initiated it. He was not going to be destroyed by some hysterical girl. Early schooled in the consequences of heedlessness, he was a prudent man. He was proper and respectful, but of course he was not innocent. He had never once touched a student, had never spoken an indiscreet word, but he had looked at the girls who were coming to the peak of their physical beauty, had watched how they moved in the provokingly sexy school uniforms, the short skirts and long socks, long bare legs – Julie Christie in *Doctor Zhivago* – breathed their smell, caught the scent of a new soap or shampoo, had in fact spent all those years in the grip of a fervid erotic awareness. A hungry soul in a garden. His manner was formal, but he was sure that at some level the girls-becoming-women knew him for what he was. His classes were all the better for the soft buzz of desire in the air. A string didn't produce music until it was stretched to a very high tension. Janet Yetkind, the school's art teacher was, he suspected, much like him in this way, a lesbian who adored her disciples but kept a discreet distance. Neither of them ever had discipline problems. During his last week at the school, he had been tempted to go to Janet Yetkind and discuss the matter with her, for old times' sake, more or less, but he decided against it.

A. had brought all this up – speaking in her small, now hardened voice – when she announced she was leaving. She told him that he came home every night smelling of adolescent sex. Well, he might have said but didn't, she came home from the city smelling of ritual slaughter. That was how he thought of it, her work in the brokerage, as bloodshed. A. – well brought up in a decent family – loved danger.

The end was calm. Over the years, A. had borrowed money from him to invest along with her own savings, had even got him to borrow against his salary and pension for her, and she had made herself, if not rich, at least safe from immediate disaster, and she had paid back his loans with interest, given him the house and gone away. He was set to learn the rules of a new life. In the morning he lay in bed, cold and shaking, and he began to suffer from spells of dizziness, nausea. He avoided friends out of the fear of becoming dependent and tiresome, and he managed to silence himself each time he was on the point of telling his students what had happened to him. Every smile troubled him; the freshening girls were no longer mere leaves and flowers. His fingers had wishes, he would find himself beginning a class with tears in his eyes or sitting behind a desk to conceal a persistent erection. He knew that he couldn't go on like this for long, and so he resigned before he got into some pathetic mess.

4

How he came to spend those childhood summers on the island: his parents had been ahead of their time in their devotion to marital disaster. Back then people stayed married, but not Ralph and Lou. They met during the war. If he had used that phrase – during the war – to his students, they would have been puzzled, but when he was growing up in Canada, even though various wars were to continue, it was understood that there was one real war, in perhaps the way that as a child he'd believed there was one real Santa Claus, in spite of the variety of department stores, each with a jolly old man. During the one real war, Ralph, who was an American sailor, got himself to Halifax where Lou was training to be a nurse, and against all sense, they had got married, Lou pregnant with his older sister, Linda. This was only the first evidence of Ralph's fecklessness When last heard of, Ralph had been moving to New Mexico with his third wife, and now he was missing, as they said in the one real war, and presumed dead. Hugo owed to this vanished father his early musical education (by the time he was born, his father was closing out a stint as a military bandsman), a very careful nature (who not to be like), and his absurd name. His father wanted to name him after Hoagy Carmichael, his mother didn't, and somehow they compromised on Hugo, which gave Hugo, in spite of his careful nature, a dim view of compromise.

He always tells stories about his childhood in this tone. It is safest to think of it as a kind of comedy, and perhaps true.

It was in periods of maximum disorder that Hugo got shipped to the Island to stay with his mother's sister Claire, and he and Rose, much of an age, had been the closest of friends.

5

He sat down at the piano and his fingers tried to play a Beethoven bagatelle, but there were keys that didn't sound, others out of tune, and the bass had a loose vibration, as if the hammers were at the wrong distance from the strings. There were spaces in the sound and extra rattles, but he played the piece through to the end, with a certain delight in its strangeness. The spaces where the notes were silent made room for other, unwritten notes.

He was a little out of practice – he kept an electronic keyboard in his apartment, but didn't often play it – and his fingers were cold. The old furnace used a lot of oil, and he kept the thermostat turned low. Claire had let things go in the last years, probably in a kind of despair after her daughter's death, though she had taken the trouble to correct her will, leaving him the house – the farmland had been sold off years before – while her small nest egg in Canada Savings Bonds went to the church. She had called him once to tell him what she'd done. He wondered if it was a reward for the fact that he had got here from New York, a long day's exhausting trip by car, to attend Rose's funeral. When he heard the news, he climbed in the car and began to drive. Claire had recognized him instantly when he walked into the church, and she had left a circle of cousins to come to him and take his arm and lead him to the front pew to sit with her.

When Hugo heard from the lawyer in Charlottetown, a letter to tell him that he had inherited the house, he thought that perhaps Claire expected him to move to the Island and live there, and he himself had given the idea some consideration. He was alone now, with nothing to keep him in New York, but the Island had never been his home, not really, and for all his delight in its beauty and the astonishing quiet, the way he could hear the sound of the slightest breeze, the soft piping of a chickadee somewhere far off, it wasn't a place to settle. Certainly not to settle alone.

He had a phone number in his wallet, one of his former students he'd met at a concert at Lincoln Centre. Valerie Quinn: a tall elegant girl who sang alto. When he thought about her, he pictured her in her school uniform, not in the slightly military black outfit she'd worn to the concert. Recently, he'd taken to looking at the personals in the *New York Review of Books*, and the absurdity of that made him feel that it was time he did something about himself. He would sit in Central Park, watching a trim aging woman riding her rollerblades with narcissistic abandon, and he'd think that she might be one whose brief notice he'd looked at, now just as glad he hadn't answered. Did he have the courage to start over? Dating, all the embarrassment. It was a comic muddle, this business of arranging life. Better to be in the power of the ghosts.

6

He couldn't move, and he wasn't sure whether he was awake or asleep. Something in his throat was preventing him from breathing properly, and the temperature of his body altered from cold to hot every few seconds. There was someone in the house, and yet he could see only empty rooms and doorways. The figure of the wax sculpture drifted through the rooms, in a kind of invisibility that he ought to understand but could not. There was a weight on his body, an impediment to his breathing, and yet he felt that if the waxen ghost would come and lie with him, the weight would be eased. The figure would melt against him and he would be safe. But it didn't come any further than the edge of his vision. If he could call out her name, she might come to him, but he was too choked to speak.

The house was shaking in the wind, and there was no hope of safety. All he could do was wait, and there was a happy sense of inevitability, he was calm, and the noise of the wind stopped, and everything was perfectly still, while the figure of the naked woman stood in the empty room. Rose was watching him. There was something she had to tell him. Then he heard a voice without speech, and she was gone. The house made a soft groaning, then a clicking in the walls, then there was the creak of a floorboard. This was the natural world calling out for the return to it of all that had been made.

7

He stood at the edge of the garden looking down at the first dark green of the strawberry plants appearing from under the fallen leaves. A cold breeze shook the trees, a wind coming off the water, still the feeling of winter. He had never known the Island in winter. Always summer and sun as the two children sat there between the rows and picked the red berries. When Rose found a very fat juicy berry she would give it to him and watch him crush it in his mouth, the acid sweetness of the juice touching his lips and making them darker red. He couldn't understand this, how she gave him the best ones. At home with his sister Linda, he had to fight for his share of everything, had to make deals to ensure some level of fairness. Linda was fierce and determined and full of anger and cunning, and it took all his cleverness not to be defeated and become her slave. But Rose always liked to see that he had the biggest serving, the sweetest berry.

The strawberry leaves grew in sets of three, like giant serrated clover, dark green against the rusty-coloured earth between the rows, and he could feel the heat of the sun through the straw hat that Aunt Claire had given him to wear. He and Rose were putting the fruit in little wooden boxes, and when a box was full, one of them would take it in the house. When there were enough boxes, Aunt Claire would make jam. The air was full of the sweet smell of the hay that Uncle Ethan was cutting in the next field. Rose was giving him another berry, but he shook his head. Her face, pink with the heat of the sun, was freckled over her nose, the eyes, blue of sky or of forget-me-nots, bright and intent, and puzzled.

'Don't you want it?' she said.

17

'We have to pick them.'

'There's lots and lots.'

She held the berry out to him again, and he took it, and her face showed her pleasure as he ate it. He lifted his head, and he could see the window of the little back room where he slept, the room next to Rose's, down the low hall under the sloping roof. When he wasn't there, the room was empty, waiting for him, the book he'd been reading spread out on the bed. He felt someone watching him from that window. Tonight when he went to bed, he'd look out here and see the berry patch.

When they'd finished picking the berries, and maybe helping to make the jam, they were going to play their duet on the piano. He played better than Rose, but her parents said she had to practise anyway. Music was something Ralph did, and Hugo wasn't too impressed with anything Ralph did; if Hugo was clever at music, he might turn out to be like Ralph, who was no damn good. He turned and watched Rose's face under the straw hat, the way she picked the berries, carefully and with concentration, as if they could feel her fingers touching them and must not be frightened. Sometimes he would look, and find she was studying him, and then she would declare that she knew what he was thinking. He didn't dare challenge her to read his mind for fear that her claim might be true. Though he was almost sure that it wasn't. Almost.

Hugo stood alone in the yard, and the cold spring wind made him shiver as he wondered about the truthfulness of his memories. Did those things really happen? Something like that. Certainly all through the season, the two of them would be sent out to pick berries, and they would eat them for dinner and help Aunt Claire make them into jam. Later in the summer, they would drive to the blueberry barrens. It was part of the old life of seasonal necessities, a life that was gone now.

8

How he met A. and came to get married: Hugo was a music student at the University of Toronto, and A. was at Smith, but came to Toronto on a one-year exchange, and they met through a woman friend of his, a church organist who was also a don in the residence. A. was small and had a little voice, a sexy whisper that reminded him of old Marilyn Monroe movies, and her American accent took him back to places he'd lived with Ralph and Lou when they were still together. At that stage Ralph was somewhere with a second wife, and Lou was living in Oshawa and working as a nurse in one of the car plants.

Hugo never had any doubt about who was in charge. A. was. She was a virgin when they met, but it was soon clear that she had selected him to be her first lover, perhaps only because he had a basement room with its own entrance, and that allowed a certain amount of privacy. Maybe it was because his father was an American. He never knew. What he knew was that virginal A. had put herself on the pill, and then put herself in his bed. Hugo had been planning to go down to the Island after his graduation, perhaps to look for work there, someplace safe and familiar, but he and A. couldn't keep their hands off each other, and before he knew it, he was checking on whether he could work in the States. Because his father was American, it was surprisingly easy.

Two years later, they were living in a small apartment on Long Island, and he was teaching while A. was a messenger for a brokerage house, a job she got because her father knew one of the partners.

Hugo can never find the appropriate tone for that story. He's never been quite sure whether it is a comedy and if so just what kind of comedy. Once A. left, he felt that he should be able to see it all in a new light.

9

No matter how he tried, he couldn't get warm. He had two sweaters on and a scarf around his neck. He didn't own long underwear. He stood by the back window of the room where he'd slept when he was a child here, and looked out over the long grass of what had once been a lawn, past the tangle of the overgrown garden, last year's plants with a hint of green here and there. The woods beyond were misted with a light rain. Some of the spruces were dying, the branches bare, covered with fungus of a beautiful grey green. It was a haunted, ruinous landscape now, until the leaves came. The leaves were usually out before he arrived on the Island for the summer, though he was once taken out of school before the end so that Ralph and Lou could set out on some hopeless adventure, as cook and bar manager for a resort in upper New York State, something that wouldn't work out and would give them subjects for argument for the next several months. Linda would be sent to Ralph's mother and Hugo to the Island to Ethan and Claire.

His Uncle Ethan was a silent man, probably not unkind, it was hard to tell. Hugo knew that Claire and Rose liked having him visit for the summer, and he always hoped that Ethan didn't mind. If he'd been a son, rather than a nephew from away, Ethan would have started to teach him farming, but as it was, he was left to the women. He read books and played the piano, and on Sunday they all went to church. Hugo listened to the organ and wondered what it would be like to play it, but he could never bring himself to ask Mrs MacDonald to let him try.

The raindrops were heavier now as they struck the glass of the window and hung there or slid down, and the woods were dim through the wet pane. In the ghostly grey light between the bare trees, he saw something move then disappear behind a tree. He leaned closer to the glass to try and see more clearly, then glimpsed it again for a moment, a woman, who stood and looked back toward the house, her eyes lifted to the window where he stood as if to observe him. She was dressed in something dark, like an overcoat, and he couldn't make out her features, and then she walked away into the dead forest.

He was shivering as he waited to see if she would return, but there was no sign of her; there was nothing but the rain and the wet trees, so at last he turned away, went down the narrow back stairs to the kitchen and plugged in the electric kettle he'd bought and made some instant coffee. The fridge didn't seem to be working, so he was using a jar of whitener. With his hands clasped around the cup for warmth, he went into the front room. Put aside the cup and sat down at the piano. He let his hands settle on it, and he began to invent a little melody that avoided the missing notes, and as he played it through, it seemed to have words, the words of an old hymn he'd been taught in the Sunday school in that white church up the road. The odd tune shaped around the missing notes provoked equally odd harmonies, and when he had it worked out, he took a piece of paper and sketched a version of it so as not to forget. He'd never written music except arrangements for his students to play or sing. As he scribbled the last notes of a figured bass, he heard a knock at the front door. He set aside the piece of paper and went to answer it.

He didn't recognize the woman who stood there facing him. She was his age with thick blond hair and eyes of a very pure blue. There was something familiar about her face. She wore a dark overcoat, and he wondered if she could be the same woman he'd seen in the woods behind the house.

'There's something I have to tell you,' she said. 'It wasn't the way they said at all.'

'I beg your pardon?'

'The way she died, it wasn't an accident.'

'You mean Rose?'

'You can't believe what people will say. They never understand.'

The wind was blowing the cold rain into his face.

'Would you like to come in?' he said.

'No,' she said. 'One thing leads to another. It's just that you're here, and someone should know.'

'Are you talking about Rose? Is that it?'

'You can't believe everything you hear.'

'She died in a car accident five years ago. I was here for the funeral.'

'What's an accident?' she said, her eyes looking at him and then past him into the house, as if she expected someone to appear from behind him. 'Who knows what was going on in her mind, what broken promises?'

'You know about that? She told you something?'

'I've said my piece,' she said, turned and walked from the door out the road, turned left and began to walk through the rain, her head down, the water soaking into the cloth of the black overcoat. It was like a coat his mother wore when he was very young, the same colour and cut. There was no sign of any car that might have brought the woman here.

'Can I give you a ride?' he shouted after her, but she didn't look back. He closed the door and went back to the piano, glanced at the notes he had written, but they seemed to make no sense. He decided that he couldn't leave the woman out there getting soaked, ran out to the rented car that was parked beside the house and drove down the road, but he couldn't find her.

When he got back to the house, he thought about Rose, the last disastrous seconds before her car hit a bridge abutment, the woman's hints. Broken promises. Hugo didn't make promises.

10

What Hugo sees when he wanders through the house, looking at things: in the front room was an old stuffed chair, upholstered in a dark red fabric that he remembered from his visits to the Island as a child. The fabric was heavily worn, the nap rubbed off in places, but the cloth has never worn completely through. It was the chair where Ethan would sit after dinner and sometimes doze off for a few minutes. Over the back of the chair was a crocheted cover in an orange and black pattern, colours that clashed painfully with the colour of the chair. Across the room was the small black and white television set, on a long coffee table and beside it a lamp with a glass shade. On the side wall was the old mahogany piano. Behind the front room, the dining room with its heavy oak table and chairs, too big for the space, and the glass-fronted cupboard full of dishes.

In the kitchen, there was a mark on the linoleum where the old cook stove had sat, and a stovepipe hole in the chimney behind, covered with a round tin cover held in place by light metal springs. The replacement was an electric stove, with various marks and stains from Claire's later days, when she wasn't in any state to keep things in order, not strong enough. The old cupboards were painted in a pale green that had faded towards grey. In places the wallpaper had pulled away from the plaster, and in others it had been glued back but with creases and wrinkles. There was a brown water stain in the shape of a bird. A church calendar hung on the wall near the back door, and on the wall a print of Banff National Park, a lake of an unnatural blue and snow-covered mountains.

On the stairs, the rubber treads were ripped, and at the top the hall was dark. The bulb in the overhead light had burned out and Hugo hadn't changed it. The top of the high veneered chest of drawers in Claire's room was crowded with family pictures. Hugo liked to study the one of Claire and his mother when they were girls, the two of them side by side in front of a farmhouse, an unknown man by the far corner of the house, staring with what might be curiosity or hostility.

The room that had been Rose's when they were children was

empty, except for a narrow bed and a small blue-painted chest of drawers with nothing in it. There were pictures of her in Claire's room, but here there was no trace.

Hugo had chosen to sleep in the back room where he always slept when he was sent here for the summer. There were clean sheets on the bed, as if it had been prepared for him, though there were also cardboard boxes filled with folded rags, old copies of *Reader's Digest*, odd dishes. Propped against the wall was the framed motto he had found in the shed. 'Flee from the wrath to come. How shall we escape if we neglect so great salvation?' The words went round in his head and made as little sense as a nursery rhyme. When he stood at the window, he saw the garden and the woods beyond. Just outside the bedroom door was the narrow stairway that led down to the kitchen.

Hugo knew that to sell the house – and that was the only thing to do – he should empty it out and leave it clean and ready for someone to move in, but he couldn't bring himself to change anything. He camped out here, in the rain and fog of a maritime spring, as if he were waiting for something, perhaps for the leaves to come out, the wild cherry to blossom, the bed of strawberries to flower and bear fruit.

One evening, in a light rain, he walked up the churchyard again. He'd found an old slicker of Ethan's in the shed, and he wore it, but the rain blew into his face. Still he kept walking, as if he might have an appointment there, as if the anonymous ancestors were waiting for him. When he arrived, he moved among the graves that rose from the wet grass, the old white stone pitted and pocked. He stopped in front of one of the taller stones and read the names. Four children of the family had died within a period of two years, between 1892 and 1894. Little figures lying in the dark, a mother or father watching by the yellowy light of an oil lamp. A child died, a child died, a child died, a child died. What had that woman said? Broken promises. Hugo had no children. Sometimes he thought his students were his substitute, a hundred daughters, he the lustful patriarch watching their growth into beauty. They were gone now. Everything from the past was gone, and as he looked across the grass that shone in the rainy light, he was one of the dead. He saw himself, standing here among the graves, a ghost, a figure trapped between the world and memory, light shining through him, a quiet old man searching the past. Rose's grave was here, but he didn't look for it.

The rain was cold on his face and was soaking into his trousers. As he walked back to the house, he hummed the tune he'd made up, but he couldn't quite remember the words of the hymn that went with it.

II

She had come to him again. In the doorway, with the empty rooms beyond her, and with a promise of peace and calm. The body wavered between a dark figure of wax and a white figure of flesh, and he was confused about which one would come and lie with him, but he longed for her to come, and yet he was unable to move to go to her. He was paralysed, and the figure did not come to him, yet he thought that she was speaking and that he could almost hear a strange babble of words, or perhaps not words, perhaps only the soft crooning of desire. Then he knew it was not that either, but that she was telling him secrets, offering him knowledge of death.

'Tell me again,' he said, though the words were not spoken aloud.

'We are many,' she said. 'The wax is formed then melted and remade.'

He was at first moved by the words and then disappointed. A formula, motto from a homily.

She was lying on top of him, and her body was soft against his, sighing as she vanished, the wax soaking into his skin, as she became part of his body, and he was heavy and yet full of happiness. He knew that she would never come back to him.

Hugo is awake, or believes he is, and remembering. The two children are on a beach. The sand of the beach is dark red and, above, the cliffs are a flatter more intense shade of the same colour, and the grass has a tint that is luminous, blue-green, bright. The sun is shining down, and the two children play at the edge of the cold water, and if they look up, they can see across the choppy water to the horizon, where somewhere northeast across the gulf, Newfoundland rises. Down past the beach there is a small lighthouse, and a harbour with fishing boats. The two children are building forts or castles out of the sand, and they are dreaming of the future.

'I know what you're thinking,' Rose says. 'I can tell.'

In the morning, he will drive to town and talk to a real estate agent, put the house on the market. There is nothing else to be done.

There is nothing to be done with the past except to remember it; or to forget.

12

Hugo back home in New York: he stood by the window of his apartment and watched the man with AIDS being taken along the street by his friend. He moved very slowly now. Soon he was going to die, and his progress, step by step, was an act of fierce determination. His face was all bone, with a thin wrapping of skin. Coming the other way was a young black woman, short, with heavy breasts and hips, and it was as if she might have been deliberately set there as a contrast, an icon of the fullness of flesh.

When Hugo arrived, there were three messages on his answering machine, one from A. to call her if he wanted a valuable tip on the market, one from a music publisher offering him work, and one from Valerie Quinn, who said she had just heard somewhere that he was living alone – he hadn't explained anything when they met – and suggested they go out for dinner. A tall elegant girl who sang alto and would wish to make him happy. So there it was, three calls: offering him money, work and love.

The two gay men had reached the corner and were coming back. Another, older man had joined them, and Hugo thought that he knew him from somewhere.

13

His last day on the Island, he went back to the graveyard. The church – still dedicated to its imperious but now much-abandoned god, kept up by his loyal rearguard, a place to listen for some transcendent voice, a place of decency and vengefulness – shone white at the end of the lane, and he stopped to look toward it through the delicate half open leaves that hung from the drooping branches of an old birch. In the morning he will leave, but this evening he has come along the road, his coat held tight around him to keep off the wind. The house was more than ever full of noises, voices crying out to him not to forsake them, but it has been put up for sale, and it will go to a stranger, and the old life will be taken from it and some new life will come.

In a week, if the weather is warm, all the leaves will be out. Already there is a dust of pale gold brushed over parts of the woodlands, but now he is in a hurry to be away. He will not wait for the beauty of the leaves. He has come here once to pay homage to the ancestors, and then he will abandon them.

Now he walks between the graves, his eyes catching a name, a date, aware of a hundred stories, untold and lost, and for a moment he has a certain sympathy for the genealogists and their brave, sturdy attempt to salvage a fact or two from the great silence, a chart that puts names in order, abstract and arithmetical, but an act of saving all the same. A country graveyard reminded you of the old cycle of life, the rebirth of the natural world in the sap that plumped the buds, the grass that would be wild over all this if it hadn't been regularly trimmed. Yet it was trimmed, and the names were cut into each stone, the human record kept in order.

When he looked up, he saw there was another figure in the churchyard, close to the edge under the low branches of a large tree. The man was looking toward him, not so much toward as past him, as if he could see something beyond, and Hugo was convinced that the man could see Rose there, behind him, that she had returned to Hugo from another time, and that she was reading his thoughts. As he studied the man, who was partly hidden by the bare branches, Hugo heard a voice speaking to him, but the words were inapprehensible. All he can hear of the voice is the tone, the lost music.

Red Barn, Interior

Carl leaned against the wall as he watched them bringing out the painting. His back was aching, and he couldn't find a comfortable position. A terrible thing that it was no longer possible to stand and watch an auction without pain and awkwardness. He looked at the painting as they put it on the easel. Of all the Sachs paintings, this one was closest to him. The figure had never really left his mind since the first day.

'The next lot is number 34,' the little grey auctioneer said. 'The Red Barn, Interior, by the Canadian symbolist Reuben Sachs.'

The light on the outside of the barn, the bright painful sunlight on the freshly painted red walls, the whole texture of daylight on the back of a barn swallow that perched on the edge of the door, the grass stems rising beside the open doors that disappeared out of the sides of the painting with a slight distortion of perspective that was more real that any right perspective could be.

'What am I bid to start?'

Remmnant turned toward Carl, looked at him for a couple of seconds and then winked. Carl turned away. The auctioneer was recording bids, soliciting higher ones. Carl tried to see who was doing most of the bidding. Bernard Webber would likely buy the painting. He bought most of the Sachs paintings, but he wouldn't buy them privately from Remmnant; he was never sure of the value of anything unless he'd bought it at an auction and knew that someone else wanted it almost as badly as he did. Sometimes he might pay more that way, but it satisfied him.

'Do I have another bid? A very fine painting, ladies and gentlemen.'

The umber dark interior, dark, yet with the filtered sunlight of a barn, the light coming in through the walls, so that there was a kind of reflection on the back of the horse that stood there looking out of the painting. And on the clothes of the man.

'Is that your final bid? Anyone else? Once, twice, sold. The next

27

lot, number 35, a landscape by the English artist Thomas Parr, dated 1837.'

Remmnant crossed to where Carl was standing.

'Webber again,' Remmnant said.

Carl just nodded.

'Listen,' Remmnant said, 'that guy from the Art Gallery has been at me again, how he wants to talk to you about Reuben Sachs. He's got Bernie Webber all excited about the idea of a book, but he can't do much unless he talks to you. He wants you to set it up for him to talk to the sister.'

They were taking the painting down now. Carl stared, fascinated, at the figure of the man in overalls, hanging upside down from the barn beams, dead but with his eyes open. Astonishing.

'How about it?' Remmnant said. 'Will you talk to him?'

Carl shook his head and walked away. He was tired and angry, and he wanted to get out on the street again and see the sunlight, the way it shone on the bricks of old buildings near his home. He went down the steps of the auction gallery as fast as he could and started walking west, thought again about the inverted figure in the painting, the way the trousers hung. He remembered once watching Reuben paint a pair of trousers that he'd thrown on the floor of the small barn where he worked. Carl tried to recall the details of that painting, the colour and shape, but it wouldn't come back.

He walked across Bay Street without waiting for the light to change and heard someone honking and braking, but he didn't look. He was too old to care how he missed dying, so long as he missed it. When he got home, he thought, he might do some nudes. Remmnant was always happy to get some. Carl had a small reputation for his drawings, especially his nudes, but he was better known as the man who had grown up on the same street as Reuben Sachs, who was the intermediary between Nellie Sachs and the public, the man who could talk Nellie into parting with one of Reuben's paintings now and then, putting it on show or even selling it.

All this because of the hours he'd spent in that barn watching Reuben paint. From 1914 until Reuben's death in 1919.

Carl walked quickly, and already he was nearly at Spadina, and he was able to find, here and there, the kind of old brick walls that he needed to see. A few blocks more and he'd be at the factory where he'd worked, first as a machinist and then as night-watchman for twenty years, and where the walls were so dark and lovely and worn that Carl could stand for hours and watch the changes of light.

At the time he started work in the factory, he'd lived far from here, in a small house near Cherry Beach, but when he'd decided to leave, he'd made his way to the neighbourhood of the factory and found an apartment with a big sun porch he used for a studio. He wondered if his wife was still alive, still neatly present in that little frame house. When Carl left, she probably brought out doilies to put on the arms of the chairs, to make them just like the chairs in her mother's house back in the town where they'd both grown up.

Would this man who wanted to write the book try to see Nellie Sachs on his own? If Carl refused to talk to him, he might. Tomorrow he should get the money from Remmnant and drive up to see Nellie.

When he had reached the factory, he stopped to look at it; a man came out the door and waved to him. It was Jim Meyers, foreman back in the days when Carl had worked there, now part-owner and half retired, coming and going as he pleased, observing, complaining, making himself important. He wasn't looking well these days, and Carl noticed as he got in his car that he moved slowly, as if he could only just control his muscles. Everyone was getting old now.

The afternoon sun was shining across the factory walls at an angle; here and there, patches of shade from the Manitoba maple that had grown wild in the bit of yard beside the factory door. The texture of the wall, the direction of the light, and the pattern of light and shade were so intense that Carl thought a blind man could feel them with his fingers. He walked over to the wall, closed his eyes and put his hand on the surface, trying to feel the slant of light, the pattern of shade. Sometimes he thought he could catch it.

He opened his eyes, looked at the wall again and then walked away and went toward home. He hoped that the children in the apartment upstairs didn't have the television set on. He wanted it to be quiet. When he walked in the front door of the house, he stood still to listen. No television. He was pleased, and when he opened the apartment door, he was hoping that Anna would be there and not too busy to pose for him.

She spoke to him from the big armchair where she sat with a book.

'Did it get a good price?' she said.

'Not bad.'

'You want some tea?'

'Come into the studio. I want to do some drawings.'

'I'll put the kettle on first.'

Carl walked into the studio and began to get himself ready. As he moved around the room, surrounded by light and the green of the grass and weeds and trees in the yard outside the windows, he began to relax, and as he did, he knew how tired he was. He hated going to the auctions, but he felt he must be there. He got out paper and charcoal and moved a table close to him for the tea that Anna was making.

'Bring the whole pot of tea, Anna. I'm a little tired.'

'Maybe you shouldn't work right now.'

'I want to.'

He sat and waited for her to come. While he was waiting he thought again of the day he'd watched Reuben paint a picture of the old trousers. He'd thrown them on the floor, but then he'd picked them up and hung them upside down over the workbench. That's what he'd painted.

Anna came in with a pot of tea on a tray with two white cups, plain china cups from Woolworth's that had always struck Carl as very beautiful as they sat on the wooden tray with the dark brown teapot. There was a row of white cups in one of the Sachs paintings. Anna poured the tea and put the tray on Carl's table. She took her own cup to the other side of the room and set it down on the trestle table while she took off her clothes. Her big breasts with their pink nipples hung at a slant as she turned to one side to unfasten her skirt.

'Wait,' Carl said. 'Can you stand just like that?'

'If it doesn't take too long.'

Carl took a quick mouthful of the hot tea, burning his tongue with it, and then picked up a stick of charcoal and began to draw. He had drawn her a hundred times, but with luck could find, even yet, a movement, a pose, that made it as good as the first time. She was strong and patient and made a good model. He was excited now about the shape of her body, the way her arm pressed against her breast, the crease at the side where she had turned. He used the skirt spreading out from her as a way of letting the lines disappear downward. He worked quickly, happily.

First thing in the morning, he must definitely get the money from Remmnant and drive up to see Nellie, just in case the Gallery man did decide to find her on his own.

When Carl finished the first drawing, he stopped to let Anna have some tea and to have some himself, and then he had her pose again, still wearing the skirt, this time sitting down on a long bench in front of the trestle table. He finished the second drawing and began a third, posing her so that her body was strangely distorted, looked shorter and heavier than it was. Though Carl had drunk three cups of tea by this time, he was still aware of being tired, and after the third drawing, he put down the charcoal and wiped his fingers clean on a rag. Ordinarily, he would have taken Anna to bed and made love to her, but today he was beyond that. He worried sometimes that she would leave him for a younger man, but she never showed signs of restlessness. Carl wondered why.

He stood up. He was a little dizzy and not very steady on his feet as he moved across the room.

'I think I'll go to bed,' he said. 'I want to drive up and see Nellie Sachs in the morning.'

Anna came and put her arm around him, to walk with him to the bedroom. Carl climbed onto the bed with his clothes still on, and Anna lay beside him, holding him against her big soft breasts. As he moved toward sleep, he was talking to Reuben Sachs and trying to remember a painting of black-eyed Susans.

He dreamt a lot during the night, but the dreaming was confused, chaotic, events disappearing and then coming back. Then there was a dream in which he was looking at the painting of the red barn again, but this time the figure of the man was the figure of Reuben, and he was not dead, but hanging inverted, alive, telling Carl that he was preparing himself to paint. Carl wanted to get away, and he was aware of trying to bring Anna into the dream to help him, yet he was aware at the same time that the dream was taking place in the past and Anna was not yet born.

When he woke from that dream it was morning, and then he remembered that early in the night Anna had wakened him to undress and get under the covers. He could hear her in the kitchen, preparing food and singing. We should always wake to hear someone singing, he thought. When he began to climb out of bed, he felt a little sick, but he sat on the edge of the mattress for a moment, and then he felt better. At first he couldn't remember what duty it was that this day held in store for him, but he remembered the trip, and for a moment could feel the two presences, the Sachs house and the barn, linked, but quite separate, as they always were, for the few feet of grass between them was a greater separation than years of time and worlds of change. The house and Nellie: the barn and Reuben: from the moment that he remembered he was to go there, it was all present in his mind, sounds and smells and feelings, the time that once was.

He put on his clothes, the same ones as the day before, for he was superstitious and knew there were days when he shouldn't change his clothes. He went into the studio to look at the drawings he had done the day before; two of them, he thought, were good. He sprayed them so the charcoal wouldn't smear and rolled them to take to Remmnant when he went for Nellie's money. Remmnant would frame them and sell them within a few weeks.

Carl put them down and walked into the kitchen where Anna stood in the old blue flannel robe that she always wore in the mornings. The sight of her right after looking at the pictures moved him. He put his hand on the back if her neck and squeezed gently. She looked toward him for a second then went back to measuring out the coffee.

'I'm going to drive up and see Nellie Sachs today,' Carl said.

'To take her the money?'

'I'll stop and get it from Remmnant on the way.'

She nodded without speaking. A moment later she looked up.

'Do you think you'll be bringing back any more paintings?'

'I don't know. I might.'

'You still look tired,' Anna said. 'Why don't you wait and go on the weekend?'

'No. I have to go today. There's somebody who wants to write a book about Reuben and might go and see her.'

'That man at the Gallery.'

'Yes.'

'Have you ever talked to him?'

'No. I'm not going to.'

'You think he might go up to talk to Nellie?'

'He might.'

Anna served out breakfast, soft-boiled eggs, toast and coffee. Carl didn't want to eat, but he knew if he was going to be driving, he'd better have something on his stomach. It took well over an hour to get to Nellie's place, even if the traffic getting out of the city was reasonable.

Nellie had given him breakfast once when he was there. A cup of tea and a piece of toast with ancient-tasting marmalade. She never went out, and when she needed food, she'd send a neighbour's boy down to the grocery with a note. She had old-fashioned ideas about what was available at grocery stores and never bought anything that wasn't there in the years when she'd still been in the habit of going out to do her shopping.

'Would you like me to drive up with you?'

'No. She doesn't like meeting strangers.'

'I could stay in the car.'

'I'm not so old that I can't manage to drive the car.'

'I know, but I've always been curious about her and that town. I'd like to see where you grew up.'

'It's the same as all the other country towns.'

'I suppose.'

She was silent for a moment.

'How long is it since Reuben Sachs died?'

'Forty-nine years.'

He thought of how the years right after Reuben's death were different from those before, more real or less real, depending how you used the word. Carl had lived his life once again among ordinary things. He'd played hockey and lacrosse, hunted and fished, taken a job, and after working for a few years had married a local girl. And then suddenly, after his marriage, he had needed to leave, and he'd taken his wife to Toronto and equally suddenly and much to her surprise, told her that he was an artist. She'd never seen him draw or heard him mention drawing. Now in the middle of her first pregnancy, he'd demanded that she strip herself naked and pose for him. They had fought long and hard over that, and once or twice, tense and grudging, she had posed for him, but she was so tense that he couldn't draw properly, his arm stiff and awkward, and he had given it up. But he had drawn and painted, begun to exhibit. A few years later, he took the job as a night watchman because it would give him some free time during daylight when he could work.

Anna offered him some more coffee, but he refused and stood up, ready to go. She kissed him on the cheek, and he touched her on the side of his head with his fingers, went to the studio to collect the new drawings and walked out through the dark hallway. He could hear the television set on upstairs. He left the car in a neighbour's garage off a laneway around the block. It was an old car, but he never drove it very far or very fast, and it was good enough for a trip up to Nellie's. He drove slowly through the streets leading to Remmnant's gallery. He had to park two blocks away. When he walked into the gallery with the drawings rolled up under his arm, the secretary at the desk smiled at him. He saw Remmnant near the back of the gallery holding the elbow of a middle-aged woman and talking intensely to her. Carl went across the soft rug to the back, where the framing room and Remmnant's office were to be found. While he was waiting in Remmnant's office, he opened the drawings and looked at them. The first of them was the best, the breasts heavy and fleshy, the pose suggesting that the figure was on the point of movement.

In a few minutes Remmnant walked in.

'Good price for the barn, eh? We got to get some more out of the old girl.'

'I'm going to see her today.'

'Can you get any paintings?'

'I'll see.'

He held out the drawings to Remmnant.

'Beautiful,' he said. 'Great stuff. To tell you the truth I like these a hell of a lot better that that morbid stuff of Sachs'. But the newspaper guys can't find such smart things to say about them. They are what they are. We'll get these framed and sell them.'

'I want to take Nellie the money,' Carl said.

'Sure. I'll just get Myra to make out the cheque.'

He walked out of the office. Carl followed him, for the little room was beginning to make him sweat and make his head spin. The young secretary took out a cheque and made it out in Carl's name. He put it in his wallet.

'What kind of split do you make with the old girl?' Remmnant said.

'None. I give it all to her. I don't need the money.'

'Hell, you should be taking a commission,' Remmnant said. 'You earn it.'

Carl had nothing to say.

'How do you sort it out with the income tax people?'

'I don't tell them anything about it,' Carl said and started toward the door.

'Good luck,' Remmnant said. 'Next time I see you, I hope you have a painting for me.'

'I think I will,' Carl said, and suddenly he felt that was true. He walked out of the gallery and back to the car. Driving slowly and systematically, he made his way north through the city and out to the highway that led northwest to the town he'd left forty years before, where Nellie had stayed all her life. Once or twice on the way, he pulled off the road and took out the little sketch pad that he kept in the glove compartment and made a quick sketch of a building or the shape of a set of fields and fences that intrigued him. There were many sketches in the book now, and Carl noted that he'd soon need to buy a new one.

When he arrived at the edge of town, the summer sun was so bright that he couldn't lift his eyes away from the road, and even the black asphalt reflected light at him. He stopped at the bank then drove down the quiet, familiar streets that led him to Nellie's house.

It hadn't been painted for thirty or forty years, and the blinds and curtains were drawn, but the lawn was kept trimmed by one of the neighbours, and in the back corner of the yard, near the spot where years before Carl had crossed over from his parents' yard into the Sachses', there was a bunch of black-eyed Susans growing wild. Carl went to the back of the house and knocked loudly on the door, waited, then put his mouth close to the glass.

'It's Carl, Nellie.'

He heard her inside and stood where she could see him from inside. The door opened.

'Come in, Carl.'

He followed her into the house, and the smell of the place, of a place closed but kept clean, some vaguely feminine smell, as if there were rose leaves far off in the upstairs rooms, made this visit continuous with all the others. Nellie walked down the hall in front of him, a big-boned woman becoming gradually smaller, thinner, more bent with the passage of the years.

'Reuben's out in the barn,' she said. 'Working day and night. He's got himself a little cot out there ... but I suppose I've told you that.'

35

'How are you, Nellie?' Carl said.

'Fair, Carl. Just fair.'

She was sitting in an old rocker and had picked up a piece of red glass, a small cream pitcher, from the table beside her. A Souvenir of Buffalo, 1898. She was turning it around in her big fingers. The whole room was full of old glass and china, everything dusted, everything always in the same place. On each visit Carl saw them poised in the strange light of the room behind the drawn blinds.

'Does anyone ever come to see you, Nellie?'

'I see Jessie Knoebler from time to time.'

'Has anyone ever come to ask you about Reuben?'

'No. Why should they?'

'About his paintings.'

'I don't bother my head about them.'

'If someone came to talk to you about them, I think it would be best not to see him.'

'I don't usually see people unless I know them well. I've just lost the touch of meeting new people.'

'I suppose that can happen.'

They sat quiet for a moment. Nellie put down the red pitcher and began to straighten a mat on the table beside her chair.

'I brought some money for you,' Carl said. 'From one of the paintings.'

'I don't need any money, Carl.'

'I put it in the bank for you. In case you're ever in need of it.'

'You've done that before, haven't you. Put money in the bank.'

'Yes, there's quite a lot there.'

'In my name or Reuben's?'

'In your name, Nellie.'

She stood up.

'Would you like a cup of tea?'

'Yes, I think I would.'

'I'll put on the kettle.'

She went out of the room. At first Carl thought to follow her, but he stayed in his chair. From the street outside, he heard the sound of two teenage boys shouting at each other, and the sound made the silence of the house more complete, more oppressive. Carl looked at the little red pitcher and wondered who had brought it here. Nellie's mother likely, having gone to Niagara Falls and Buffalo for a rare holiday, bringing back the pitcher to prove that she had been away from the town.

The silence of the house made Carl think of the different silence in the barn, a male silence, Reuben's silence, a silence of dying. Carl remembered the fire in the corner of the yard, and Nellie coming from the house behind him, her clothes rumpled, for she and Carl had been lying on a couch, kissing and fondling, holding one another, touching, when suddenly Carl had moved a little and seen through the window the pile of canvases burning. All his life since, Carl had wondered. What was the final thing? Was it Carl and Nellie, together like that? Reuben had known without appearing to have known. Carl had thought Reuben wouldn't care about it, that it had nothing to do with him really.

Nellie came into the room with a plate of biscuits, an English kind that Carl hadn't seen for years. He took one and ate it. For a moment he wished that he'd let Anna come with him to protect him from the flood of memories. It was the same each time he came, but each time they seemed to get stronger, as if the past were coming closer and closer, pursuing him, on his heels, about to throw a great dark bag over his head and proclaim an end to all but itself. A few events, a few years of time: he was their prisoner.

Nellie brought him his tea.

'Thank you, Nellie.'

'I'm always pleased to make tea for an old friend.'

'Yes. I know.'

They drank their tea, not speaking. Carl ate a biscuit, and the sound of his chewing was loud in his head. He wished this to be over so that he could go out to the barn and make his visit there. Finally the tea was gone, and Carl put down his cup.

'Thank you, Nellie,' he said. 'I think I'll go out to the barn now.'

'Of course, Carl,' she said, but she didn't look at him.

Carl took the key from its nail beside the back door. As he walked across the few feet of lawn, past the lilacs to the barn door, he held the key tight in his hand, as if it were a talisman to get him safely in. It was like this every time. Even when he was a boy and had looked in the door on his way to school, he'd been afraid, at first, of the man inside, who stood there so concentrated on his work.

It was usually morning at first. Carl would go out the back door of his own home, always the back door, for he wasn't allowed to go out the front past the parlour. He'd eat his breakfast at the kitchen table, smelling the yeasty odour of bread and buns set to rise which would be put in the oven after he'd left for school and perhaps eaten for lunch if there weren't some older and staler available. It always annoyed Carl to be given a stale crust for lunch when he could smell the fresh bread that had been put away in the cupboard, but his mother was convinced that young boys were provided by God for the virtuous disposal of stale bread and buns, and until the stale bread and buns were eaten, Carl would not see the fresh.

One morning, entirely by accident, Carl had gone out the back door, planning a shortcut to school, and on his way through a backyard had found the barn and Reuben Sachs. He had noticed that the door of the little barn was open, and he could see the figure of a man inside. Curious but half afraid, Carl walked close to the door and looked in. The man inside was stocky with fat fingers, and in those fingers he held a paintbrush. That was how it had begun. Carl felt it all again as he unlocked the door of the barn and stepped inside.

The barn was the same as ever. Nellie had told Carl to lock it the day after the funeral, and no one but Carl had been in it since.

It was only a few months after the door had been locked that Nellie began to refer to Reuben as alive and working in the barn. There was talk of sending her away. People in town said that neither she nor Reuben had been right since their mother died years before, leaving them alone together. It was easy to find a dozen remarks of Nellie's, even the fact of Reuben's paintings, his death, that could justify suspicion and fear, but Nellie's old aunt, the only relative she had left, had defended her and insisted that she was harmless, and the town learned to forget her. She became a kind of ghost, a presence seldom seen. The children called her place 'the haunted house', but the town grew accustomed to her strangeness.

Carl sat down on the little stool in front of the easel and breathed in. Still the same smell as on all the days when he watched Reuben work. Five years. Reuben never talked much, but Carl had known that he liked to have him there. Once or twice he had used Carl's shoes or his legs in paintings, but he never drew or painted his face. Carl wondered why but never dared to ask.

Carl got up from the stool and reached over to the cupboard beside him to take out brushes, oil, a box of paints. He spread them on the white table and got a canvas from the corner of the barn, one of the many on old-fashioned stretchers that Reuben had prepared but never used. He set the canvas on the easel and took another deep breath, the smell of the barn and the paints carrying him back.

It was only in the last years of their time that Reuben had encouraged Carl to draw, but once started Carl had become excited by the power of his pencil to make a thing appear on paper, and instead of watching Reuben paint, he would sit in the corner of the barn and sketch what he could see through the door or what he saw hanging on the walls, his pencil moving faster as the excitement of it gripped him. Reuben would seem to work faster too, his strange, almost misshapen face glowing with energy.

Minutes, hours, days, weeks, months. The two of them in the barn. Carl would sometimes stay away from school so that he and Reuben could be together, and for a while his parents spoke of forbidding him to go there. Carl promised not to miss school, but there was always a look on his mother's face as he went out the door that suggested how little she approved of his pastime. Carl never cared. He wanted nothing but to be there with Reuben, unspeaking, everything silent except the tiny sounds of their work.

Carl could no longer remember how it was, or when, that he started to become interested in Nellie. She was older than he was, and he had come to notice that she was a woman, with a woman's shape and gait. One day he had left Reuben at work and gone into the house to draw a picture of Nellie. When it was done, Nellie had been pleased with it and had taken it to the barn to show her brother. Reuben stood holding it in his thick fingers, then announced it was no good and tore it in pieces, and Nellie had turned on him, told him Carl had more talent than he did. Reuben didn't speak, only went back to his painting. It was the one with the white cups in it, Carl remembered that clearly, and Reuben had worked away, stolidly, deliberately, ignoring what Nellie said to him until finally she turned and walked out of the barn, and Carl followed her, like a puppy that is confused and follows its mistress because it can think of nothing else to do.

It was in the week after that day that Reuben painted the red barn picture. Carl had praised it highly, absurdly, trying to make up to

Reuben for what Nellie had said, but Reuben ignored his praise. It was a few weeks later that Carl caught that glimpse of fire and jumped up to run from the house, knowing that the fire was a holocaust of Reuben's paintings, coming out the back door to see that there was nothing left of them, nothing of his work but hot ashes. They had gone to the barn, he and Nellie, afraid of what they would find. Wondered how they had failed to hear the gunshot. No one, as it turned out, had heard it. The barn, the body, the hot ashes: once again Carl reached the end of the sequence of memories. The others were unimportant, the funeral, the other events, not quite real.

Now that he had reached the end of his memories, Carl looked around him. It was starting to get dark outside, and he had to strain his eyes to see the painting on the easel. The sunflowers, the wild sunflowers. He stared in astonishment at the way in which the flowers seemed to be becoming faces, yet weren't. It was hard to see it in this light, but he knew it was right. It was Reuben's painting. Sometimes Carl wondered about them. Once or twice he had thought that he could no longer remember Reuben's paintings, that he might have imagined them all, imagined the whole five years, but as he looked at this one now he was sure.

He closed his eyes. Later he'd go into the house to see Nellie, but first he must rest. He wished Anna was beside him. It seemed to him that he was more tired than he'd ever been in his life.

Prophecies for April

It was raining. That wasn't surprising, considering the season, but it made you stop and look out the windows. Don't you agree?

He's been at it again, Sylvia.
The same one?
Yes. I know the voice. And he said the same things.
The same as he said to me?
The same as he said to me before.
To both of us.
Maybe he thinks we're the same, that there's only one of us here.
We don't sound a bit the same.

It was raining. I believe it had been raining all day on that street in that city.

Again today?
Yes.
Same?
Yes. Same words.
As he said to you before.
To both of us.
If they are the same.
We discussed that.
Not the words.
We did.
Not the exact words.
I told you precisely what he said to me, and after a moment's thoughtful hesitation, you told me that he had spoken exactly those words to you.

More or less the same.

It was a side street of fairly old (not very old) brick houses near what used to be the edge of the city. It had been raining all day, and there were many puddles.

To me he sounded very gentle. Frightened almost, but determined to say what he had to say.

It can't be the same man.

Well, he may never phone again.

It took several days for the puddles to dry. The air remained cool and damp, and nothing was seen of the sun.

The Professor was coming to tea. He would eat three arrowroot biscuits and drink three cups of tea while he explained once again the reasons for the difficulties between him and his wife.

Why don't you marry the Professor, Sylvia?

I don't find him at all attractive.

It would be a kindness. The story of the difficulties between him and his wife is becoming a little boring. He ought to have a new story to tell.

About me? I prefer not, Anne. Really, I prefer not.

Perhaps it's the Professor who phones.

The Professor and his twin brother.

Does he have a brother?

No.

Soon after the puddles had dried, it rained again. The twigs of the poplar at the side of the house were wet and shining.

You still insist it's two different men?

Of course. It seems obvious to me. One dangerous and one harmless.

And the dangerous one phones you?

It seems so.

The Professor, once he had taken off his tweed suit, proved to be something of a surprise. He no longer seemed old. In fact he seemed very young. When she found herself in his arms in the backyard long after midnight, she was less astonished than she would have expected.

Answer the phone, can't you?

I'm washing my hair.

If I leave this on the stove it will burn.

Let it ring.

What if it's the Professor?

He'll call back.

He called this morning. I told him you'd be here later.

It seemed for a while that the rain might go on forever, but in April that's to be expected.

I think it is the Professor who calls.

Why?

Last night as he spoke to us, his voice was familiar, and then something he said.

He must be the harmless one.

There is only one. We hear him differently. Haven't you read enough stories to know that?

What?

That the difference is an illusion. It shows the relativity of all human perception.

It shows there are two men phoning.

I can't quite imagine what either of the girls looks like. Also I confuse their names. I think of Anne as Sylvia and Sylvia as Anne. That's because Anne speaks first and mentions Sylvia's name.

Perhaps we should invent an appearance for each of them. Sylvia (Anne really) is elegant, the larger of the two, but it's Anne (Sylvia really) that I find the more attractive. In spite of the fact that I can't imagine what she looks like. If I described her I would give her features I find sexually attractive in a woman. I could describe her body in detail.

Imagine the description. Imagine the scene. Male fantasies of course. For women readers I should describe ... what? The surprisingly youthful body of the Professor? Or perhaps only his eyes and the way they drew something out of her, breath, blood, the gaze of her own eyes ... you see I try to understand.

As for the rain, it is occasional. It was that time of year. Soon the poplars would be in leaf.

Is the Professor moving in with you?
Yes, do you mind?
Won't it be a little crowded?
Perhaps.
Especially if I ask someone to move in with me.
Do you have anyone in mind?
Yes.
Who?
The man on the phone.
But that was the Professor.
No. The other one.
You can't invite him in here. He'll kill me.
He won't really. He's quite harmless.

Then there is another woman who is physically and spiritually all the things that the one we imagined is not.

Are you happy with the Professor?
Of course.

Why are you happy?
Because when I lie with him I don't notice that he's there.

Perhaps you would rather have someone else in the story, a man or woman that you can picture more easily. But you should be careful, for the story happens in the future, and it is dangerous to give a man or woman too much freedom.

The Professor and I are parting.
Why?
He was cruel to me.
In what way?
He made me listen while he made improper phone calls to my best friend.
Did you consult a psychiatrist?
My best friend insisted she didn't need one.

You see at this point the story is getting entirely out of hand. However, it has reached this stage without (and this is remarkable) becoming merely a sexual fantasy.
As to the Professor, he is gone now, and his identity is known to only three people: Anne (Sylvia), Sylvia (Anne) and myself.

Let me take a picture of you.
For what purpose?
I promised the Professor that I'd send one. For his scrapbook.
I don't like having my picture taken.
Why not?
It weakens me.
He wants it very badly.
I owe the Professor nothing at all.

The leaves are out on that street now. I could describe them, the

45

little twisting buds, the green subtlety of the colours, the sudden un-furling of the leaves like a million suns bursting into light.

Imagine the two girls in bed. Together. No, this is not the collapse into sexual fantasy, for I knew, you knew, from the beginning that they cared about each other more than about any man.

The phone's ringing.
Shall we answer?
Might as well.
All right.
Put it on the pillow between us.
So we can both hear.
Both speak.
My love.
My love.

I hadn't meant to write this, not really, but once begun it had its own necessity.

What did I wish to imagine?
You?
You?
No.
The trees, the street, the rain.

Adam on the Art of Dying

The Reverend Graham Lund woke from a dream. He had been in a church that seemed to resemble the small town church he had attended during his adolescence. The dusty organ pipes rose in ranks like long heads with gold lips. The pulpit was in front of him and to his right, and it was not clear whether it was occupied. Or the choir loft either because all his attention was drawn far to his left and upward, where a woman stood, somehow raised above the congregation, as if standing on the seat of her pew. A thin hard woman, probably in her forties, her hair cut short. She wore a dark coat, and she was holding up a book for everyone to see. The last moment of the dream came with his knowledge of the book's title, *Adam on the Art of Dying*.

He lay in a half sleep, the room still dark. It was winter. It must be close to morning. This was the day he was to visit Miss Malcolmson on her hundredth birthday.

Then he remembered the last moments of his dream. It was seldom that he remembered his dreams, and his life often seemed to him strangely opaque, as if the depths of his being were even more unknowable that the depths of other men. Sometimes he thought he didn't dream at all, but here in his hand now was a secret dream, held, not lost. The woman in his dream (who was she?) was hard. Graceless. He reached out across the bed and touched Janice's sleeping body, his fingers sensitive to the rough flannelette of her nightgown. His fingers followed the long curve of her back.

There was no Christ in the dream. The world was unredeemed, there was only the art of dying, the chill, reluctant dignity of stoics who lived to be the audience for their own performance of life.

Who was it spoke to him? A loose electron wandering in the brain like a firefly in the wind? The unlearned wisdom that was a grace in the body? The figure of the woman. She seemed hard, but that might be a disguise to make him listen, so that he wouldn't be seduced by her, would attend to her instead.

Sleep was distance, and everything was becoming farther away.

He turned so that he could feel Janice's hips warm against his own. Fell.

When he woke again, Janice was coming back into the room. She closed the door behind her, went to the bureau and took out a pair of underpants and put them on. Her period had started, the first flow always dangerously heavy, and always painful. She crawled across the bed, her long straight hair hanging across her face.

'Are the cramps bad?'

'Getting pretty bad.'

'Want me to get Laura off to school?'

'Would you mind, Gray?'

'No.'

He put his arms around her, held her breast in his hand, the nipple, covered in flannelette, between his fingers.

'Is it time?'

'Not quite. She better have a bath. I forgot last night.'

'Okay.'

He let himself sink into the warmth of the bed again.

The alarm roused him, made him turn in the covers like an animal trapped in a net. He got one arm free to reach the clock and stop the noise then lay on his back, tempted to drift off. He wished Janice would decide to get up after all.

In a series of awkward gestures, unrhythmic like a film showed at the wrong speed, he threw back the covers, got out of bed, wrapped a dressing gown around himself and walked to the bathroom. As he stood at the bowl to empty his bladder, the smell of sex, which had clung to him through the night, rose to his nostrils. The paper wrapper from a Tampax hung over the edge of the wastebasket, almost ready to fall out. He reached down and flipped it into the basket.

As he watched the bathwater run into the tub, he envied Laura, wanted to get into the tub himself and lie there while his body gradually moved toward being awake, in the light that would grow brighter soon, even in the small bathroom. He woke Laura from the cocoon of her sleep and went downstairs to put on the kettle for his coffee.

It was a freeze-dried brand of instant coffee that Janice had bought for the first time, and he liked it. He carried the mug, green leaves on

48

white, as he went upstairs to watch Laura in her bath. He sat on the toilet seat and let the strong odour of coffee drift into his face.

'Daddy,' Laura said, 'are there any cats with feathers?'

'No.'

It was quiet for a moment, and she looked up again.

'Daddy.'

'Yes.'

'Are there any birds with fur?'

'I don't think so.'

'Why?'

'I guess a bird with fur couldn't fly. The wings wouldn't be right.'

'So God gives them feathers.'

'Yes.'

He looked down at the child who floated in the soapy water, her young face still a little soft and unformed.

'You look like a dumpling in a soapy stew,' he said.

She didn't look at him. She was thinking. She was somebody else, not his.

'You'd better hurry,' he said, 'or you'll be late for school.'

Her round little fingers were holding the washcloth, and she watched water dribble out of one end of it while she squeezed.

'I want you to get out of the tub now.'

'All right,' she said, agreeing to come back from all the futures that were in her mind. She looked at him, as if to show him she was back now.

'Will you dry me?' she said.

He took a towel, and as she stepped out of the tub he wrapped it tightly round her and rubbed his hands over the rough texture, holding her against him and rubbing his hands down her back and legs. He hugged her little body against him.

'Caught by a bear,' he said.

She wriggled.

'Can I have Cap'n Crunch for breakfast?'

'If you have something else as well.'

'What?'

'Orange juice and toast.'

'With peanut butter?'

'Okay.'

49

He finished drying the child, took another towel and wrapped it around her. There was always a draft in the hallway from a storm window that didn't fit properly.

He went down to the kitchen and began to make breakfast. There was a little new snow in the backyard, a line of white emphasis on each dark branch and twig. The stalks of zinnias stuck upward, dead and stiff, but now flowering with snow. The early sunlight was pale. Laura came into the room, dressed, but with buttons undone where she couldn't reach them. She sat down at the table and concentrated on the cereal that looked like wrinkled pellets of orange plastic.

'Do you know what I'm going to do this morning?' Graham said to her.

She shook her head.

'I'm going to visit a lady who's a hundred years old.'

She looked up, startled.

'Is she going to die?'

'Sometime. She's still pretty healthy.'

Laura returned to her cereal. Graham looked out at the snow. Silence crept through the room. As he presented Laura with her food, she would look up, meet his eyes and then return to her eating. She was a stranger.

Breakfast over, he let her watch TV for a few minutes while he collected her coat and scarf and mittens and boots. The only mittens he could find were a brown wool pair, matted with use and still damp from yesterday's snowballs.

'My mittens are wet,' she said as he helped her put them on.

'They're the only ones I could find,' he said.

She looked at him, as if considering whether to say anything more, then accepted the damp mittens in silence. She was a secretive child, so disciplined and self-contained that he was left wondering what she felt, who she was. He kissed her goodbye and watched her walk down the steps to disappear behind a snowbank and a hedge. Then there was just the snowy emptiness; the street was childless.

For a moment he stood by the door and listened to the sounds of the house then went upstairs to wash and shave and dress. Washing, he enjoyed the splash of cold water on his face, shaving, the scrape of the blade against his cheek. He hadn't bothered to turn on the light, and his broad face was dim in the mirror, his nose, crooked from a break in a minor car accident, gave him the look of a boxer or football player. An illusion. Tennis was his only game, and there was little violence in his nature.

Shaved, washed, brushed, his identity reassembled from the wreckage of sleep, he went to the bedroom for his clothes. Janice was asleep, her head turned sideways and her mouth a bit open so that he could see the slight protrusion of her upper teeth that was somehow the essence of her beauty. Yet her face looked inhuman. Graham had noticed it before, that people sleeping were mere things, collections of features. She was white teeth, skin a pale ivory, straight nose, curving forehead.

He moved around the room on tiptoe. He wanted to touch this woman, to wake her and see the change in her face. Sometimes he would do things like that, just to see, to know her in a new way. It was like an anger at her separateness.

Why wasn't she pregnant? It had been three months since she'd stopped the pill, but each month she had this day of cramps as the lining of her womb tore away, unused, and the dark blood poured out. The semen from last night's loving lost in the waste of blood.

The room was almost dark with the drapes drawn across the window, and the light that came through them was a dark wine colour. As if he were in the red darkness of her womb. Janice moved and gave a slight groan. She must feel the cramps even in her sleep. The world went on inside the sleeping body. An idea for a sermon in that somewhere. His own dream came back to him, and it seemed that he was drowning in mysteries, the deep flow of Janice's sleep, his own, the blood that poured from her; it was as if, suddenly, he knew that this was a different life, that he was already dead or twice dead, and all the solidity of earth was a deception.

He wanted to see his wife's blood, to feel the cramps in her stomach. He was drowning. He dressed quickly and walked on tiptoe out of the room.

Outside, sweeping the snow off the red Datsun, he breathed deeply the cold air that shocked his lungs into a kind of brightness. He unplugged the car. When he turned the key, it started quickly, with a comfortable chugging, the engine sounding small and personal. He had driven the car for two years, and he was fond of it. He backed out of the driveway and drove off down the street toward Mrs McGarvey's house, where her aunt, Miss Malcolmson, sat at the edge of her century.

The house was large and ornate, brick with dormer windows and dark green trim. At the door, Mrs McGarvey took his coat and scarf, and together they walked up the dark staircase toward the old woman. Down a long brown hall with an odd assortment of old prints hanging on its walls. Graham caught a glimpse of a green English field with cattle.

As they entered the old woman's room, Mrs McGarvey introduced him, and Miss Malcolmson's eyes made some small adjustment, to see him or acknowledge him. He stood beside the bed.

The window near the bed cast the chill of a cold snow light on her face, a face that had the wonderful purity of bone and forgetfulness. She was so close to being nothing, to being only a part of God. And her eyes looked as if she might be sure of that, hardly blue any more, hardly any colour at all; no longer possessing the world; no longer wanting to see. Only letting in whatever light might fall on them.

Graham looked out the window at the empty yard, the snowdrifts and dead branches, aware of his own lust to see. Desire, even for the snow, even for the empty branches.

He turned toward the old woman again and reached out to put his hand on top of hers.

'You've come a long way,' he said.

She turned, acknowledging the pressure of his hand but perhaps not knowing what he'd said.

He smiled and nodded, not as one did to those who couldn't understand but as one smiled and nodded to one who could, one so close that no words were needed.

Sister in God. The old-fashioned expression became suddenly real for him. Sister in God.

Holding her own hand in his own, he thought how close she was to breaking, always. If he squeezed too hard a bone would crack. Like a frozen thing in winter, no longer limber; sister in God, yours is the beauty of winter, the light at the edge of death.

'She doesn't hear much,' the niece said.

'I think she hears what matters,' he said, knowing that he could not say that she heard the angels, saw their light shining through her own skin.

Graham could feel Mrs McGarvey behind him, an old woman too, but one who hadn't yet given in to age, hadn't yet become free enough to let her body be only itself, a dying thing. She expected Graham to speak, to pray, perhaps, and to leave, but what he wanted was only to sit there and look at the ancient woman, at the only just living bone and skin.

Her hand moved a little under his own. He took his own away, and she slowly drew the dry fingers back toward the body. She spoke. Graham could make nothing of the thin notes; they sounded like Chinese spoken by a dying sage. The whisper of snow falling on snow.

'Just here on the table,' her niece said. She walked to the table beside the bed, her footsteps heavy.

Graham watched her as she reached the table, wondering what meaning she had been able to find in the old woman's whisper. She picked up a book and turned toward him.

'My aunt wondered if you had ever seen her book.'

'No. I haven't.'

He opened the book. It was a collection of short essays on rural life in Southern Ontario, first written as columns for a Toronto newspaper, then reprinted in a volume. He looked at the date of publication. The book had been printed when Miss Malcolmson was already over seventy.

Graham looked at a couple of pages and got a sense of the book's style, vigorous, but with a self-conscious feminine lyricism. It was odd to read the words, look up and see the old woman who was no longer of any sex, just human, not even that, a clever insect with a shrill whispering voice. Graham thought of his own flesh, Janice's, the room that was dark red, a mirror of her womb.

'That's very fine,' Graham said, giving back the book.

Miss Malcolmson's eyes followed the movement of his hand.

'Did she write the newspaper column for a long time?'

'Nearly twenty years. After she went into retirement. My aunt was one of the first women in Canada to write for the newspapers.'

'I didn't know that.'

'She became quite well known for the stories she wrote from France during the First World War.'

Fifty years ago, that war, to be followed by another in Europe, and now the strange American adventure in Vietnam. Graham saw her in a kind of illustrator's dream of the time, young officers in neat uniforms, trousers tucked into puttees; the clear-headed fellowship of young men, the whole war first conceived as a lethal recreation for the English officer class, the Canadian woman journalist moving among them, a mature woman, daughter of an old and respected family, at once stern and gentle. She had been one of the new women making a career in the public world.

He wondered if she had been religious or if religion had been imposed on her by the piety of her old-fashioned relations.

Sister in God, he had called her, this woman who might have been an atheist for all he knew about her. Sister in God still for the absolute of her age; her body was one of the names of God. All man's struggle was to make sense of disparate names, of warring vocabularies, but in the ultimate grammar was no contradiction.

Graham looked at the ancient woman in her bed. Her eyes were closing. He stood up.

'I think she's tired now,' he said.

'Yes. She tires easily.'

They moved to the door of the room past a large mahogany chest of drawers with a coloured cloth lying on top. Above it was a print of a little girl in a swing. The girl wore a long pink dress, and her hair hung in curls and had a pink bow in it.

As he reached the door, Graham turned again and looked at the woman in the bed. Her eyes had closed, and her head sunk to one side; her mouth hung open, making a small dead hole in her face. That was how she would look when she died.

The round body of Mrs Garvey went ahead of Graham to the door. She said goodbye to him there.

He walked out into the cold day holding his scarf tightly around his neck – as if to keep his head from falling off.

Wakefulness

The old man is dreaming. He has a name, Edgar, but for the most part we are nameless in dreams, and the laws of our being, gravity, identity through the onward movement of time, are suspended. In the dream he is flying, and when he looks down, he recognizes the shape of certain islands, the long curving snake of water, the smaller serpents that come to meet it. The old man knows that what he observes is Venice, and he knows that this vision is one of the miracles of the intricate baffled world of dreaming. Edgar was blinded in his early years, and in the dream he remembers this and rejoices in the perfect miniaturized image of close-packed buildings, the gondolas on the canals. In one of the gondolas someone is waving to him. It is a woman, naked and splendid. She lifts her breasts and offers them. Then he is awake. Beside him his wife is silent, asleep. Now the visible world is once again inaccessible, though he has a certain ability to invoke dim memories of sight. What he observed long ago. It is a winter night, and he can hear the wind hurling itself against the bedroom window, and out there in the darkness is a young man, alone in the windswept avenues, walking.

He never saw Venice, though perhaps he once saw an antique map which offered a source for his dream vision. He was already blind when Milady took him there. And they had not flown, but travelled by train, a slow blundering train creeping through cities that were slowly repairing themselves after a war. The war that had blinded and almost crippled him. At Lyon, she told him, there were four men in brown overcoats, one man wearing eyeglasses with darkened lenses, and all four were staring at her. Past Avignon, a boy tending a goat was seated under an old twisted olive tree. One of the factories at Mestre was a burnt-out hulk. He did not need to know these things, but she wished to tell him, and she recited these, his lessons, through the much-interrupted train journey. Now I am seeing hills of white rock, now the sea. We are approaching the mountains. She did not tell him of the grey and shattered state of London as she left it, but he guessed. The trip to

Venice was her gesture toward a past that was gone, all its ways and habits vanished. They had played farce, in her large intricate house in Richmond, she and Edgar, Sir Robert and his ballerinas, irresponsible children of the *entre deux guerres*, and now, after the general shipwreck of the continent, the two of them came ashore on these ancient islands, among the maze of streets. The sound of wings, boat horns, voices, water lapping against the stone sides of the *rio*, the conversation of pigeons. Some had been caught by the tide and drowned. He didn't try to understand it, what led the woman to seek him in the nursing home where he was recovering from his wounds, lost among the incoherent signals that the nerves of his destroyed eyes were sending to the brain. He still believed, for a precious deluded moment now and then, that his vision was returning, that in the night there were shapes moving in the blackness of the halls, a patient climbing from his bed to go to the end of the hall and light a cigarette, staring into the night, where the starlight picked out the shapes of the bare trees, the coal at the end of his fag growing brighter as he drew air through it into his lungs. It was just over a year since he was wounded. The war in Europe had been over for a year, and he was inclined to believe that the Canadian army had lost him in their files as he went from one hospital to another, then from one nursing home to another, survived the terrible winter, waited to be sent home. Nothing but time could heal him.

He was listening to Sergeant Brett, who lay legless and one-armed in the next bed. The sergeant, who spoke broad Yorkshire, was explaining once again that he had been dead for two days before life returned to his broken body. 'Tha' can hear 'em,' he would say, 'them voices, but tha' mun't answer till tha' coom again.' Perhaps Edgar understood the experience that Sergeant Brett, in his visionary way, was describing. His own last thought, in the moment of awareness as the explosion took place, and before the pain, the loss of consciousness, was that he was dying. Then somewhere else he was alive, in a cascade of light and darkness and crying out. Perhaps he too had been dead. The Anglican chaplain appeared to take Sergeant Brett at his word and hoped to learn from him some details of the afterlife. Edgar had heard the story enough times by then, and he was not displeased when another voice interrupted, though it took him a moment to know who it was speaking his name. The previous day a nurse had read to him a letter from his mother in which she mentioned a plan to send his sister Elizabeth to England to rescue him and accompany him on the voyage back to Canada, and at first he wondered if the woman's voice he heard might be Liz – though they had never been close, and Edgar couldn't believe that she would stir herself to take ship for England on his behalf. For the briefest of moments he thought this might be his sister's voice, and then he knew precisely who it was. The voice, though unheard for some years now, was one he knew in a very particular and intimate way. Speaking softly, always a slight throatiness, it was a voice meant to be heard from close by. An instrument for a small room, like the virginals. She told Edgar that she had discussed his case with those in charge, and since he was now passing the afternoons walking in the grounds of the hospital, within a week or two he might be strong enough to go with her on the trip she had planned for them.

It was she who chose Venice, though she knew no Italian; she disapproved of foreign languages. Edgar knew a little of the language from the period of his musical studies, and with his tongue and her eyes they would make their way about the city. In those days he was out of touch with the things of the world, but in later years when the blunt arithmetic of cash had become real to him again he wondered how, in that bleak time after the end of the war, she was able to make the arrangements. He had no idea how she got the funds out of England in that period of postwar shortages and rigid restrictions on foreign exchange. Collecting overseas debts, something in that line, or borrowing against a future when it might again be possible to move money abroad. She supervised the achievement of immigration documents, the permission for his official leave. She had great charm and knew everyone. He had once spoken of Venice, she said, in their time together, told her the story of how Petrarch left his library to the republic of Venice, which promptly lost it, the tale of Casanova's prison break, and she had taken note. Sir Robert was dead, crushed in a building that collapsed during a bombing raid, but Edgar assumed she was able to use her husband's European connections to get dollars or lire into her hands and pay their way. Perhaps she chose Venice because money was available there. Even then he knew that the world of banking rises above borders to achieve the elision of difficult political events. No one was a fascist now, or ever had been. Yet as they left the train station he imagined eyes watching him, the enemy.

57

It was spring. Venice, she told him, had survived the war almost untouched, though there were shortages, many of the hotels were empty. His strength was returning, but he often needed to rest. He slept badly, pain, nightmares. On their first day she found a small park a few steps from a canal, and he heard the gardener's broom, twigs brushing the grit of the pathway, stroke, stroke, stroke, and there was a faint scent of tobacco, dry footsteps moving along the gravel closer to them, then going away from the bench where the two of them sat, not touching. Birds somewhere above, the breath of wind on his cheek, its tiny whisper against branches which, she told him, were beginning to show a thickening of the buds, with here and there a tree in blossom. She reached out to take his hand. She had brought him to Venice in the mistaken belief that she could heal him.

The old man has long since concluded that he understood very little, that young soldier, hurt, encased in bitterness. He did not find her altogether real, and while they played farce, climbing in and out of beds they never made, she had encouraged such an attitude, had presented herself as a goddess and he accepted that. Every young man wishes to be taken in hand by Venus.

Mars to follow: camp, orders, the world of men and machines. He was beautiful, or so she had told him, and now he was blind and his face was raw with wounds, and he was weak, and limped, but some of the strength would return, though the limp, conquered, would recur in old age. The old man who is lying in bed beside his wife has difficulty turning from side to side. It was his habit, in those first months of dealing with wounds and blindness, to blame everyone for what had been done to him, and yet the woman was familiar, and he could be easy with her companionship; they had been shipmates before the wreck. She was widowed, and she was rich. Or was she? The house at Richmond was to be sold. Her address, when he returned to Canada to study, practise law, take up a sort of life, was an apartment in Knightsbridge. After a few attempts he stopped writing to her. He was not comfortable dictating in his raven's croak the letters he sent. He could tell nothing that might be truth through his amanuensis, the capable young woman who became in due time his wife and now lay beside him in the winter night; outside, the wind and snow, the night walkers.

Each day they strolled through the narrow Venetian alleys. He smelled the fish that was for sale in a market at the edge of the Grand Canal, the scent sharp and penetrating, a gabble of talk between the men selling and the women buying. The smell was rich and good, and then it made him sick.

'I can't bear the stink,' he said. 'Take me away.'

She took his arm and led him off, and he was ungrateful. He knew she would soon lose patience with him now he was damaged and ugly.

He told her she must show herself the great paintings. She reported on a scene with a soldier, a fat naked girl and a baby and on a portrait of a toothless old crone with white thinning hair. He heard the sound of a cane passing a trattoria where they ate, tap, tap, tap, another blind man. (How had he lost his vision? Blind from birth.) What was she thinking? He remembered her face, a certain illuminated look.

Spring, it was spring, and they entered a small church where the air was as cool as the marble walls. She found him a place to sit, moved away. He could hear her breathing, further off, then further still, and he was certain that she would go out the door and leave him there, alone with the wonder-working painting of the Virgin. She might wish to be rid of him, the corpse of an old desire, now lost to her. They slept in separate rooms. Perhaps she was ready to stride away, confident that he would save himself. He had survived a war in France and Holland and Germany, he would survive abandonment in an old church in Italy. He heard a door open and close, and he knew that she was gone, and he listened to the lambent silence flickering on the marble walls. For him, lost to all light, what is called silence had a multiplicity of textures, a varying thickness, and it flickered with the inaudible as it crept toward perception. The touch of the chill on his skin was mingled with hints of hearing. He ought to plan how he would go on alone. Once or twice she had warned him that he was wandering too close to the edge of a canal, and proceeding alone he might easily fall in, but such thoughts, the practicalities, though they were perhaps present in some dark alleys of the brain, didn't move into the lens of awareness, not yet. Tiny murmurs from far away sang to him. When at last he stood up, held his cane a little in front of him, searched for the place where he had heard the door open and close, someone took his arm and began to mutter, gently, in *dialetto*, soft incomprehensible sounds. Edgar would have taken an oath that he was alone in the church, but now the sacristan, giving off a rich, sweaty, garlicky smell, was beside him, with a grip on his arm, leading him out of the church, and as he stepped into the outdoors, afternoon sunlight was warm on the parts of his face that were still able to perceive such things, and her familiar voice spoke his name. She was waiting, he was not abandoned, and what he felt at first was something like disappointment at being saved from the absolute, and fumbling in his pocket, he found coins to hold out to the sacristan, who let go his strong hold on Edgar's elbow and refused the money, mumbling phrases about war.

There was a hint of a sourness coming from the *rio* at the side of the church, and under the wind of late afternoon, water lapped against the foundation of the buildings, and they stood apart, in the little square, and he waited for what would come next. He was still young. He was young and he was ruined. He walked with a cane, he was blind, disfigured. From far off, he thought he could hear the sound of the *vaporetto* in the Grand Canal. Nearer, the sound of the communal water tap pouring against the stone drain at the edge of the square. It is possible that if he took a few steps toward the place where he heard the ripple of water in the breeze, he might have plunged in the little canal, drowned. He was young. He heard the brush of wings, the dim throaty mumbling of the pigeons. Soft voices, like hers. He was young, and he had been betrayed. The old man, as he recalls this, knows that his soul was saved by such anger, but still, he would prefer not to remember it.

Back at the hotel, they separated, to rest. Church bells clattered over the narrow streets. Later they went into the cool evening. Canaries, set out when the owners returned from their labours, were singing happily. Is a caged canary happy when it sings, or simply unable to act against its nature? Who is to know? Then he slept, dreamed that he was buried, fighting to breathe, woke into the night's tranquility, lay there, wondering if he could find his way to her room. And then? A cat moaned, scrabbled across a roof. The sound of a bird calling out into the last darkness before the dawn, one bird, then another further off, answering. The previous morning, after they had taken their coffee at a small bar near the hotel, they had walked north into Canareggio and to the end of the *fondamenta*, and she told him about the mountains that could be seen far off across the water, the Dolomites, snow on the peaks. No doubt a kind act, sharing the beauty of her world with a man who could no longer see it, but he did not take it as a kindness. That hoarse caressing voice, that voice for small rooms, offering a vision of the far mountains, the pale blue shapes that were always cold, that reached upward to an unending winter. They turned and walked back into the city. There is a particular set of echoes in Venice, each narrow street, each bridge, each square, covered passage. The sound in mist one day, the sound in sunlight the next.

That evening as they were returning to their hotel through a damp passageway, the walls close and damp, the oncoming chill of night, he heard beside them the sound of a stream of water splashing against a wall. The sharp smell of urine. A muttered apology, and a door closed as the man – a cook from one of the restaurants, she said – went back indoors. In the mornings they heard the incantatory voices of children playing, the words of old men gossiping about politics, and these came each time differently. One morning they had stopped in a small square where a woman's voice from above, at a window he supposed, was speaking loudly to a neighbour standing on the cobbles beneath. She was holding his arm. He stopped and turned his face toward her. He wondered if she was looking at him.

'Tell me a lie,' he said. 'Tell me a beautiful lie.'

'I can only tell the truth,' she said.

She always told the truth, and she always kept her promises to him. She had arranged a concert for him at Wigmore Hall in the last days of peace, for the clear baritone voice that many admired. He performed *Winterreise*, stood onstage in his tuxedo and black tie, at the piano a small man with pale blond hair and thick glasses. The first bars, the marching rhythm, open fifths in the left hand, and the accompaniment lifted him through six measures of introduction, as he prepared his first word, *Fremd*, 'Stranger'. He came a stranger and now departs a stranger, the flowers of May replaced by a snow-covered road. The lines sang themselves in his head in the silence. A quietness startling to one who had spent years as the companion of loud tanks, the deafening great guns. Now he lay in the night that was becoming morning, heard the bird call once again. An answer. The two signalled back and forth, perhaps preparing to mate and raise young. He heard the door of his room open, and he tensed himself. Put a hand against the rough plaster wall. One of the *fascisti* had seen him and come for vengeance. Once again, as in his dream, he couldn't breathe. The door closed. Bare feet on the bare tiles. He could smell her, the soap she has always used, and he heard the sound of some soft garment moving against her skin, falling to the floor.

'You can't heal me,' he said, in his broken voice, grudging, vengeful. 'The damage is done.'

'Hush.'

He felt the bed sink as she sat on the edge of it.

'Touch me,' she said, and in spite of himself he reached out. Her skin was warm and dry as he moved the tips of his fingers along the neck and back. She was trembling. Her body was softer, heavier than he remembered.

'Pendulous,' she said. 'Fallen.'

His hand was lifting the soft flesh of the breast. The sagging, the looseness of the flesh pleased him. Slack, imperfect, doomed. His fingers were hard and insistent.

'We used to play farce,' he said. 'You were the cruel goddess of love.'

She began to tell him a story, whispering, the words coming slowly, the small, poorly sprung bed sagging beneath them, about the Venetian hero Marcantonio Bragadin, who, after losing a battle with the Turks, was tortured for ten days, tortured and revived, left to hang from the yard-arm of a ship for hours at a time. Finally he was chained to a stake and slowly flayed alive, his skin to be tanned, stuffed with straw and sent to Constantinople.

His finger gripped the flesh of her belly, probing its textures, exploring. The old man, remembering all this in the night, knows that if he had not wakened, if his dream of Venice had continued, he might have seen them far beneath him in one of the tiny rooms, the wounded soldier and the woman, what they did, the postures, the cries.

Morning came, laughter from the boats passing in the canal beneath their window. Again that day they walked and just as they were about to cross a bridge, she held him back, and they waited. She wished to remain there, she said, until a group of nuns crossed the bridge and walked out of sight. Out of a superstitious respect or perhaps a distaste she did not wish to be close to them.

'You are another kind of nun.'

She didn't respond. The tide came and went, and she would describe to him the reflections moving in the canals, like the shimmer of feeling passing over flesh. They rested in a square, and the sunlight struck his face, though where the scars were thickest, he could not perceive its heat.

The blind old man lies in his bed, wide awake. The footsteps of the music go steadily on, in his mind or elsewhere, the winter journey ending with the hapless organ grinder winding out his little tune, barefoot in the snow. Beside him his wife stirs a little, breathing out, sleeps. She has never visited Venice. Shortly after his visit he was repatriated, and he never went to Europe again. They had tried to kill him, and he did not wish to return. Now it was a different world, modern in its style, pragmatic reason in triumph. Venice was an old illusion, built where no city should be. It ought to have fallen into the ocean long since. Napoleon was an early voice of the new order, and he hated Venice. Petrarch's library was never found.

Edgar can feel the slight sway of the boat as the gondolier's oar propels it forward. There were gondoliers still, in those days, at work, not merely an entertainment for the tourists, back before everything in the canals became motor traffic. He can remember the long echoes in the square in front of San Marco, a wind from the Adriatic. A slow walk along the sand beach of the Lido where Byron and Shelley rode on horseback. In his letters Byron tells about the menagerie he kept in his palazzo on the Grand Canal. Edgar remembers that the woman spelled out a poster for him to translate, the Communist Party exhorting Venetians for vote for progress into their version of the modern world.

2.

Domestic Arrangements

The Steps

Old now, a widow who was ready to leave the house where she had spent her life, Mildred sat in her usual spot on the stairs – fourth from the bottom. For all the forty-some years of her marriage it had been her place to sit and think when she was alone, though she couldn't quite explain why. Just the feeling of it, a habit she'd got. Perhaps when she'd moved here with her new husband, the stairs were neutral territory, possessed by no one. Always passed by, not a place where she sat in the usual way of things, or Jack sat, or her mother, visiting. So one day, alone and musing, she plopped herself down here, to have a good think. You could see a fragment of the lawn through the window in the front door, part of a tree. Now in her age she could look all those years back; 1919 was the year they bought the old place. Mildred was old enough now – creaky in the knees – that she knew she would have difficulty when she wanted to get back up to her feet. Pull herself up with the banister, that would be the ticket. No hurry. Just rest here for now. She was a widow, and she was moving out. Her son Bob had gone off to town with a truckload of her furniture and boxes of pots and pans and clothing, and it was true enough what he said, she could have gone along with him, but she was firm that she'd wait for Penny to arrive after work. That had been the plan, and she'd stick to it, not mere pigheadedness, though she could be a stubborn old woman, she knew, but more that she wanted some time in the house that had held her life before she left for good. Say goodbye to it all, not that the old walls and ceiling and floors would give a care.

Jack had this house rebuilt for them, hired the carpenters and plumbers and electricians, and they'd turned a derelict log cabin into a proper house with two floors, bedrooms upstairs, a kitchen added on the back on a stone foundation. Jack himself had built the little front porch the second year they lived here. Even now when she thought about it, she could smell the sharp bitter odour of the creosote he put on the wooden posts that were dug into the earth. It hung around the porch for weeks afterward.

The porch was still standing. What Jack had built was still in use, but Jack was gone, and now she was moving out – to an apartment in Kingston, not far from Penny's little house. It made sense; she would be isolated if she stayed out here on the island all winter, Bob and Penny both settled in town. The island held nothing for her but memories. She wasn't a sentimental woman, but she thought there ought to be some loyalty to all those years of life, a recognition that those years were the life you'd been given or had chosen, the days and nights passed in these rooms. She could look at any corner of the house and know its history. She glanced at the light fixture that hung down in the living room over the round oak table, and she saw the kids sitting there on a Sunday afternoon playing cribbage with her and Jack, the four of them putting down their cards in order – the little pegs marching their way along the board until they reached the end. It was at that table that Mildred would sit on Sunday afternoons and write her letters to Jack every summer when he was on the boats. Just in front of it, beside the front window that looked toward the bay, lay the wire from the aerial that Bob put up on the roof, a few years back now, when Jack first decided he wanted a TV. Bob raised a tall ladder, and with Benny helping him, he put the aerial on the roof, and Jack watched the hockey games on Saturday night all that winter, and Don Messer during the week and Ed Sullivan on Sundays. The next summer, Jack's final year on the boats, Mildred turned on the TV in the afternoon once or twice when she was feeling lonely, but she found it didn't help. The last years Jack worked locally as a deckhand on the ferry, until he had the first heart attack.

On the sideboard behind the round table she'd been staring at was a pile of cards, condolences from when Jack died. Almost a year ago now. Sixty-seven, he was, not very old, and Mildred was younger, and she knew there was every chance she'd live on for years without him. She'd be an old lady living in an apartment in the north end of Kingston, pulling a little wheeled cart along the street to bring home her groceries, maybe bowling in a league once or twice a week.

That lighting fixture over the table, with its pink glass shade: Jack had brought it back with him in the fall, the second year they were married. That was when she was still getting used to the arrangement of things, Jack leaving to take ship in the spring, returning in the fall, the two of them settled in here for the winter months, Jack taking on a few odd jobs for people on the island. She got used to that shape of a life, even if it was different from most of the lives around you, him away half of every year. She remembered the times of strife and how the government brought in that Banks man. They said that the Canadian Seamen's Union was run by communists. She didn't suppose Jack was a communist, but he kept his own counsel about it all. A tight-mouthed sort of man. When the fights started in the ports where the freighters came in to load or unload, she'd read about it in the papers, scared that Jack would be wounded or murdered by the thugs. Once she dared to mention it to him that winter, when the shipping season was over, and he shouted at her, maybe the only time in their lives, said she didn't know what she was talking about. Maybe he was right; it was often a puzzle to her, politics, the way men organized the world, or believed they did, voting and governments, communists and liberals and conservatives. It surprised her when women got involved – Agnes McPhail and Charlotte Whitton and that Judy LaMarsh – how they understood it. Mildred voted, just because it was there and she could, making her mark for the man who sounded most decent.

The pay on the boats was better after the new union took over. They sent Banks back to the States, and things were quiet again, but she believed that Jack had been hurt by it all, hurt somewhere inside. At his funeral a stranger came up to her and introduced himself as from the old union. That was what he said; I'm from the old union. Jack was a good man, he said. Looking at the man, thin, pale white hair, you wouldn't have known he was a communist, though she supposed he must be. Maybe Jack was as well. If so he was a dead communist now. Either way he was a man who'd done the best he could. Now and then Mildred remembered Jack's brother Herbert, but not too often.

Penny knew a real estate agent in town who was going to put the house on the market. Penny said he'd get them a good price. A few more people were starting to move to the island, going in every day to work in town. According to the talk, Des Stettle, who had rented a couple of fields from them, might buy it for the land and just try to sell off the piece with the house.

You could spend hours of time thinking about the past, but there wasn't a lot of point to it. Gone, the lot of it. She'd sat here long enough. What she would do was check over the place once more to make sure she wasn't leaving anything she wanted, then pick a few flowers out of the garden to take to town with her, to put on the kitchen table of her new apartment. She'd go from room to room. Penny asked about the attic – needed a ladder to get up to the trap door – but Mildred said there was nothing up there she planned to take. The floral piece from little Doris's funeral stood in a dim corner, unless Jack had put up a ladder some time and taken it away, but she didn't think he would do that. Maybe other things there she had to leave behind; it was all done with. Sooner or later the house would be sold, and the ones who lived here would know nothing about it, about her and Jack, the life they had made. Doris's ghost would be left alone here, the spirit of a solitary child, pale and weak. Mildred thought of young people buying the house, changing things, maybe putting in new windows or doors, their children sleeping in the small bedrooms upstairs. She wanted to know these people, but she couldn't find them in the centuries of non-existence that lay ahead.

Another hour and Penny would be here to fetch her, deliver her to her new apartment. Mildred wasn't quick to make friends, but she hoped that the people around her apartment were neighbourly. Someone to speak to on the street.

2

The house was quiet, except for a creak now and then, the aches and pains of the old wood, Mildred in her quiet place on the stairs, alone in the house as she had been every summer for thirty years, darkness outside, Jack off on the last of his boats, or he said it was the last, though he might stay with it for a couple of years, if it was a good crew. Bob had moved to town this morning, got an apartment to share with his pal Benny, not far from where the construction yard where he worked. Now only the two of them would live in the house, and Jack was away for the summer months. Mildred wondered, now and then, if it might have been different if Jack had been here every night, summer and winter, for all those years. Thirty years now. She didn't have words for how it might have been altered, the shape of their marriage. At first, when she was young, and it was all new, she was almost glad of his absence. It took a while to get used to a man, to his ways, and for the whole summer she could do whatever she wanted. After Penny was born, and the two of them spent their time in the garden behind the house, Mildred planting and weeding while Penny fussed over the rag doll that Mildred's mother had sewed up for her. At night, alone in bed, Mildred thought of where Jack might be, and now and then a picture of Herbert came to her mind, Herbert as he was when the two of them had just left school. Herbert was one of the casualties of war, and so perhaps was she. She had gone from being young to something else, not exactly old, but accommodated to things, her girlishness expended and forgotten.

That summer, if Penny woke in the night, Mildred would take her into bed and cuddle her until the child fell asleep, and Mildred would lie very still, not to wake the child, and in the morning Penny's voice would wake her, demanding breakfast. Then Doris was born, and one day Mildred was talking to the baby as she changed her, said, 'Don't roll that way, sweetheart,' and she heard Penny's plaintive voice, 'Is she your sweetheart too?' And Mildred said, of course, that they both were, that she had two sweethearts now. But she knew that the little girl was heartbroken; Mildred hadn't let her come into her bed when she was big with the baby, and the child was bereft. Nothing she could do to help. Penny had just begun to accept that the new sister was part of the family when the winter came, and Doris was so sick. Jack carried her from room to room, the doctor did his best, but it wasn't enough. The child grew weaker, and then in that two-day storm when they couldn't get out, she died. Mildred was torn apart and wept and wept, and then she was angry with everything, everyone. Rage, just all rage. She blamed Penny for hating the new baby, though she had the sense to keep her mouth shut, but she knew that she had grown cold with the child. Jack did his best, quietly cried his own good tears, and Mildred hated him for his decency.

Last year when Mildred had bronchitis, she asked her doctor, the new one, a bright young man, whether penicillin, if they had it back then, would have saved Doris's life. He couldn't say for sure, of course, but he gave her to understand that it probably would have saved the baby. A door closing. Doris didn't need to die, you'd say, and yet the miracle drug wasn't available, so she was doomed. Born too soon.

Mildred thought that perhaps it was never the same with Penny after that. Nothing that was ever spoken, but some coldness or distrust. Penny knew that Mildred was not perfect, that beyond a certain point, she couldn't protect her children. It made her grow up too soon. Then Bob came along, and Penny became his nurse and protector. Penny married young, but they had no children, not yet. Mildred wanted to know if there was a problem or if they didn't want to have any, but she couldn't bring herself to ask. Her own daughter, and she couldn't enquire about something so important. The coldness was still there. She thought about the questions she wanted to ask her own mother and never did.

Strange knowing that Bob wouldn't be back, that he was grown up, settled in town. She looked at her watch. Too late for *I Love Lucy*, which she watched sometimes on the TV. She wished that Jack would phone from some port where they were loading freight, take her mind off these things. She'd wait ten minutes, just in case he might phone, though he did that only two or three times a summer – it was expensive to call long distance – and if he didn't phone she'd scrub the kitchen floor. It was late, but that would get her good and tired out, and then she'd have a warm bath and sleep soundly. No dreams of past or future.

3

What Mildred was happiest about was that Bob was too young for this new German war, and Jack too old. Whatever Hitler got up to she didn't suppose he'd be attacking the lake boats, and she knew that the transfer of goods up and down the Great Lakes would have to continue in much the same way. So Jack would have work, and nobody would be trying to kill her family. It was dark outside, and right now the children were in their bedrooms, though they shouted back and forth now and then. As she sat in her spot on the stairs she could hear them, mostly Bob, who was supposed to be going to sleep. Penny was listening to the radio. She insisted that she was going to quit school this year at the end of grade twelve, and Mildred didn't have much argument against it, though she figured she might get a better job if she stayed on and completed the final grade. She'd taken a commercial course, and chances were good that she could get a job in town. When Mildred tried to tell her why she should stay on, she wasn't altogether convinced by her own arguments, but it was her duty to say these things. What she really believed was that Penny would manage all right whatever she did. She had a good head on her shoulders, wasn't boy-crazy like some of her friends. What about Mildred herself? Had she been boy-crazy? Well, a little crazy for Herbert, she supposed. Him going away to the war, so young, changed things. Everything went from silly to far-too-serious just overnight.

Jack was due back in the next couple of weeks. What Mildred should be doing was peeling and cutting up the box of apples that she and Bob had picked from the two apple trees that grew at the edge of their property, just down the hill. They were old trees, and they didn't get pruned or sprayed, but even if they were small and warped, the apples had a sharp taste that was perfect for apple jelly. She could leave them until tomorrow, or she could stay up long enough to cook them and set them in the jelly bag to drip over night. Yes, she'd best do that, but she could sit for a couple more minutes.

'You going out with Steve Larush?' Bob shouted. Penny didn't answer.

'He says you are.'

Again no answer.

'He says you really want to go out with him.'

Silence.

'He says you think he's cute.'

That did it.

'He's about as cute as a sick pig. Now you shut up and go to sleep.'

They were good kids, Mildred told herself. She was lucky to have them. And Doris? Well, that was just what happened sometimes. Or that's what she tried to keep saying, that she was lucky to have Penny and Bob. Something Jack had given her, and she was grateful. She wondered how long it would be until she went through the change of life. Not for a while yet. And after that would she and Jack still do things in bed? It had never been all that important to her, with Jack, but she had the children. You got some things and not others.

The newspaper lay downstairs on the kitchen table with the news from Europe, how Hitler had invaded Poland. Mildred didn't know anything about Poland, and not much about Hitler. He was a silly-looking man, and she could never understand why the Germans wanted him for a leader, but she had to admit that Mackenzie King wasn't exactly a heart-throb. Not exactly Clark Gable. Maybe she and

73

Jack could get to see *Gone with the Wind* when he came back. Jack wasn't that keen on the movies, but he'd take her if she asked. Mildred liked the movies, but it meant a trip into town to see one. He was a handsome thing, that Clark Gable.

Mildred shook her head. Here she was, a grown woman with two children, sitting on the stairs thinking about movie stars when she should be peeling apples.

4

Summer was coming on. Her second summer here in the house. As Mildred sat on the stairs, trying to put things straight in her mind, she could see, through the thin white curtain that covered the glass panes of the door, the shape of a tree at the edge of the lawn, a cottonwood that was beginning to shower down its white fluff, the way it did in the late spring. The white cotton would be blown in the lightest breeze, and last night she'd noticed the pale fuzz floating on the dark water of the pool at the end of the swamp.

Mildred hadn't been to a doctor yet, but she knew she was pregnant. In the fall Jack had come back from the boats and he had spent the winter at home and that was enough to start things going. She hadn't told him about it. It would be a surprise for him when he turned up in the fall. She'd be big by then. But his mother and father would notice and say something, write to him. Maybe she'd send him a letter after she'd been to the doctor, though she didn't need any doctor to tell her what she knew perfectly well. She could feel it in her belly and her breasts, that she was changed, that a child lived inside her. It would be different being here with a baby. Jack had offered to get her a dog, in case she was lonely, but she'd turned down the offer, so far anyway. Dogs were all right, and now and then when it was very quiet on a summer night and then suddenly there was the loud call of an owl as she was lying awake, or a man coughing out on the road, footsteps, the window open with a screen in it, maybe a mosquito buzzing around the bedroom, a watchdog seemed like a good idea, but it might be one of those that yapped all the time. She couldn't stand that.

There were three bedrooms in the upstairs, one for her, with Jack in the winter, and two for children when they came. If they had more than two, the kids would have to share. In a few months she could start to get one of the rooms ready. When they were first married Jack's mother offered her a cradle that she'd used when the boys were little, and Mildred knew that her own mother had saved baby things. Her mother would be pleased to be a grandmother again. Orville had a couple of kids, but he lived up north of Kingston, and her mother didn't see them a lot.

Mildred was growing accommodated to her quiet summer life, putting in the vegetable garden and doing down beets and cucumber pickle and strawberry jam, maybe raspberry if it was a good year for them. Everybody said she must be lonely, but she didn't think she was. Jack's father used to walk down from their place a few miles away sometimes, and Mildred would make him a cup of tea, and old Joe would sit there in the kitchen, his tea on the table in front of him, hardly speaking, as if the silence locked him in, and he couldn't break through. Sometimes he looked around as if the house was strange to him, he couldn't figure out why it was there, why he sat in it. Usually, when he came to visit, he would leave her a newspaper, maybe from the week before, and at night she would look through it. On the back page she'd find a store ad, and study the drawings of the dresses that they had for sale. Her mother had a sewing machine, and Mildred used to make herself a dress or a blouse sometimes, going into Kingston for the pattern and fabric, and as she studied the drawings in the advertisements, she looked for one she might be able to sew. Skirts were getting shorter, and Mildred knew she had nice legs, but now as she imagined such a dress she realized that she would be pregnant and what she needed to make was maternity clothes, big loose things to hide her swollen belly.

After studying the ads, Mildred would start to read the stories about politics, and sometimes they made sense to her, and sometimes they didn't. They were still talking about the Great War, and borders and reparations. The war was over, but somehow it wasn't. She asked Jack questions about the war sometimes, but he didn't say much, only tried to make it all sound cheerful, as if a bunch of the men had gone off on an adventure, like a hunting trip, but there was a red scar on his leg, and she knew he'd been in hospital for a while. Once he mentioned a friend named Tim, but then he shut right up and wouldn't speak another word. They didn't talk about Herbert. He was a good man, Jack, and he tried hard. As the air grew darker, and the cottonwood fuzz fell on the still water of the swamp, Mildred listened for a bird or a cow lowing, but there was only silence, and she was strangely aware of things to come. She could see the two of them, her and Jack, in a church somewhere, maybe not here, when they were old. Everyone was coming round to congratulate them because it was their wedding anniversary, and Mildred knew how that old woman would be feeling, knew that all she could think of was a baby that died, one winter night, snowed in, and the little thing just wasn't strong enough to keep on breathing. Why did she know already that one of her babies would die? Mildred thought. It wasn't fair. Was it the one she carried inside of her now? These things that came into your mind, weren't true, they were just dreams.

As she sat on the stairs, tears were running down her face, but she wasn't quite sure what she was crying for, Herbert perhaps, or that imaginary baby, or maybe poor Jack. He was a good man, and he did his best. She knew that. He had dug up a piece of garden before he left that morning to meet up with his boat in Toronto, and she knew she should go out and plant a few rows of peas, if she wasn't so dreamy and lazy. But maybe when you were pregnant it was like that.

5

Mildred sat on the stairs, in the place she'd chosen, nineteen years old, married less than a year, waiting, wondering what the rest of her life would be like. She could hear the wind in the trees outside the house, the noise it made in the last of the leaves, the draught of air coming across the field strong enough to bring them down. Another week or so and the trees would be bare. The last apples on the trees down the hill had fallen. Jack would be returning home for the winter in the next day or so. He'd left the boat when it finished unloading ore in Hamilton. They were tying up for the winter in Hamilton harbour. Jack would catch a train to Toronto, stay for a night with his sister Eleanor, then take the streetcar from her house to Union Station to catch the Kingston train. There was a chance that he'd meet someone he knew on the train, someone who could offer a ride down to the ferry dock, and when he got to the island, there would certainly be a friend or neighbour with a horse and wagon, or maybe even a car, who would drive him to the house. It was possible to walk the distance – Mildred had done it a few times during the summer – but it was a long haul with his heavy duffle bag and maybe a new suitcase. He'd talked about buying the suitcase at one of the ports where the boat loaded or unloaded. She supposed that if he said that, he would do it, though she didn't know him so well yet that she could be sure.

Jack was returning for the winter. Mildred wasn't sure what she thought about that. They'd been married in the spring, and not too much later he'd gone off to catch his boat for a summer to be spent shipping around the lakes, and while he'd tried to keep sending letters, he didn't have much to say, and maybe she didn't either, when she answered. He said that when he got back they'd get a horse and buggy or a car, he wasn't just sure which, so they could ride down to the ferry and the general store. Walking all that way was too much like the army, he said.

The army. Their lives had taken shape because of the army and the war. Mildred had been Herbert's girl – he was Jack's younger brother – a handsome laughing boy she'd gone to school with, but Herbert didn't come back. He was killed at Vimy Ridge, and they never found his body. He was listed as dead. He'd been blown up by an artillery shell, and they never found enough of him to bury. By the time he died he'd been overseas two years, and Mildred sometimes had to look at a picture of the two brothers to remind herself what he looked like. Then he was gone. Jack was overseas too, but he was in a different regiment, and he was one of the lucky ones who survived.

Jack paid her a visit, after he'd been back from the war a few weeks. They'd met up once or twice in the general store, where she helped out on Saturdays, and he didn't say much, but then one Sunday he came round to her mother's house in the village and her mother made him a cup of tea, and afterwards he asked Mildred to walk down the shore a bit. So they did that, and he started talking about Herbert. At first she thought he was trying to make her feel better, or something like that, talking about how Herbert carried her picture with him, but gradually she realized that Jack was suggesting that he could take Herbert's place. At first she was shocked, but then she could understand how it seemed to make sense. In a way. She didn't have too many boys after her – Butch Therrien, but he was RC and a drinker, and her mother had warned her off becoming a baby machine married to a drunk.

She didn't exactly agree with what Jack was saying, but she didn't exactly disagree, and within a few months he was talking about an old place near Button Bay where he could get the land and what was left of the log house cheap, and he had enough money saved up to hire a carpenter to frame up a new section of the house and put on a second storey. Mildred went on not exactly saying yes and not exactly saying no until she found that she was married and Jack was working the lake boats for the summer, leaving her to her gardening and some canning, and now he was coming back.

As Mildred sat there on the stairs, waiting for her marriage to be real again, waiting for her husband's return, she began to hear voices, her own voice, and Herbert's, and they were standing in the long grass at the edge of the schoolyard one day in the early summer, the last day of school it was, last day forever except graduation day, and Herbert wanted her to walk with him through the woods to the back road and home that way. She knew if she did that, when they were alone in the woods he would kiss her, and she was excited about that idea. She wanted to go into the woods with him, and once in the secrecy of the woods she wanted to tell him lies, the worst awful lies she could think of, to say that her mother beat her on her naked body with a buggy whip and when her father found out he took the whip to her mother. Mildred had no idea why she wanted to say these things about her parents, who were good, church-going people, and if they got angry with her they just kept their lip buttoned, and let her figure out where she'd gone wrong.

But even though she wanted so much to go through the woods with Herbert and say the worst things she could imagine, she also wanted to argue with him and say no, she wouldn't do that. Something stubborn locked tight in her chest. She turned and started back toward the schoolyard, toward the road, and when he grabbed her hand she pulled it away and began to run. She thought he'd run after her, but then he didn't, and on the road she caught up with Edie Brimley and walked home with her. Mildred was mad and disappointed that Herbert didn't chase her, and she knew he'd spend the summer working on his uncle's farm down near the foot of the island, and she'd hardly ever see him. And then in the fall he joined up, and they just had a few weeks before he was gone.

As all that came back to her, Mildred saw a picture, clear as a movie, of Herbert running uphill in the war, and she knew he was thinking about her, and then the shell burst right where he was standing.

It didn't seem quite real even yet. She wondered, on her wedding night, what she should tell Jack about Herbert, but she didn't say anything, and neither did he. None of that seemed very real. With Jack it hardly started and it was over. She didn't know how to think about it, but she supposed it was like that sometimes. Men were different from each other. She was married to him, and she had a house, and her husband was coming back today or tomorrow, and she supposed you could have babies like that. Once she almost asked her mother, but then she didn't.

Stitches in Air

Dear N,

It is New Year's Eve as I write, and the others are all gone. The end of a decade, the beginning of another with the tip of a new millennium just visible over the horizon of years. I am invited to a party at Sam Pruitt's house. Through his family he knows the rich and influential men and women of the district, who will be in attendance, and he and his wife flatter me by this invitation since I can perhaps further his career. Jenny F. is invited for the same reason. While the celebration goes on, I am sitting at what has become my desk, that Victorian mahogany library table with an inlaid and gold-embossed leather surface, which I claimed from the original reception area. I said that the broad expanse would be useful for spreading out and examining and cataloguing materials as they are added to the collection.

There is no window here, but if I were to climb the stairs, I could look from the landing into the darkness and see flurries of snow drifting over the lawn, which descends in a gentle slope to the riverbank where a green flat-bottomed rowboat is pulled up on the grass. Old George who plants and weeds the gardens and trims the lawn has been away a few weeks recovering from surgery, a hip replacement, and no one has taken charge of the boat and carried it up to its winter shelter. This afternoon as I stared out I imagined entering the shed to find the oars, then heaving the boat across the frozen grass to the water, holding the gunwales in my two hands to climb in, rowing out into the grey river, the boat growing smaller and smaller until it was invisible.

In front of me lie three pieces of lace displayed on their storage backings, a piece of *punto in aria* sewn in Italy in the sixteenth century, a collar of bobbin lace from Ghent a century later, and a table runner of Victorian machine lace. No purpose except to please my eyes with these three bits of delicate workmanship, which I have just extracted from the storage files – I wandered there seeking a clue, chose these pieces as if they might reveal what I needed to know. Each has a tag carefully tied to a corner of the lace, and on the tag the filing code. The code consists of a sequence of letters and numbers, and each sequence has four parts, indicating date of accession, source, type of specimen, and storage location. With this system it is possible to look up in the catalogue all the accessions for a single year or all the samples of *punto in aria* to be found in the collection, etc., etc. This information is currently being catalogued in digital form as well. I take some pride in the clarity and usefulness of the system. During my months of study-leave, I made notes on the procedures used at the V&A and the other museums I visited and refined them to our purposes.

Lacemakers began their apprenticeship as early as the age of five, or so I have heard, and with years of work, the eyes suffered, and the back. Vermeer's pretty lacemaker, arched so charmingly over her bobbins, will be a bent, blind old woman, useless, her fingers locked into half-clenched fists, hunched in a corner, turning herself toward the coals of the single chunk of peat on the brick hearth, searching for heat.

White lace, and yet the three samples are all of different shades, a curious silver quality to the *punto in aria*, a grey tone to the sample from Ghent, and the Victorian machine lace the tint of thick cream. The lacemaker arrives out of the blackness each winter morning, her face mantled with blood drawn to the skin by the chilled air, and she takes her place at one of the worktables. Her needle begins its quick clever movement. Somewhere a circle of nuns stitching, one reciting prayers as they work.

Ladies and Lace. The title of one of the many catalogues on our shelves here. For most generations lace was worn over layers of heavy clothing, but a famous Yves St. Laurent cocktail dress has a scooped back of black Chantilly lace, the openwork descending almost to reveal the nether cleavage. *Why do respectable women dress like whores?* One of your *belle-mère's* questions. She stared hard at me with her queer dark eyes when she spoke. I took it as a question merely rhetorical. I was trained as an archivist, not an adept of sociology. And my clothing was, like hers, discreet. As my makeup. *Butter wouldn't melt in your mouth,* she would say, taunting me, and then she would tell me about her apartment in *Vecchia Roma*, walls so ancient that in one corner there was a shard of inscription in classical Latin. Rather than tearing down the old buildings to make new ones, they shored up ruins and built among them, what the architects now call infilling, so that her three rooms were of all the ages, going back two thousand years and more, a Roman wall, a medieval wall, a modern wall, mortared together to make her nest, her hideaway before your father discovered her and made her rich. That apartment, she liked to tell me, was the place where inspiration struck her, one evening as she looked down on the street below where the families moved about in the *passeggiata*, that slow daily progression through the neighbourhood, and toward the end of her crooked alley, she saw an old woman sitting by the door of her shop, her knitting in her hands, and as centuries unravelled, the old woman was always there, knitting the same stitches a thousand years before, all ages were one age, the age of the eternal goddess of the skilled fingers, and that vision told her what she must do, what she must create, and your father made this possible.

Butter wouldn't melt in your mouth: I was pretty little B., new to her job and eagerly at work, cool, precise. Little did she know. And what am I now? Experienced, capable, living for my profession, they say, almost priggish, rather inclined to solitude. Jenny F. and I pretend to friendship, though we are not exactly friends. There is too much unspoken between us, and true friendship is impossible on such terms. She is in touch with you, from time to time, reporting.

New Year's Eve: will I write to you until the clock's magic is accomplished? After tomorrow's day of recovery from the antic hours of festivity, the holiday season will be finished, and we will return to our habits. I spent Christmas Day with my father in his apartment in Toronto, listening to him tell his dreams. He recounted to me over our morning coffee a dream of a half-derelict building. Listening to him, the house I pictured was this one, this Victorian castle, once your family home. In some dream future it is derelict, and with all its additions, overgrown, an insoluble maze. My father had come upon its wreckage. Sometimes, he said, it appeared that my mother was lost in the distant rooms. The dream presence of his children reminded him that he was worried about G. She's not a bad girl, he said.

Driving back on dark country roads, a little snow flickering in the beam of the headlights, my beloved white Toyota humming sweetly and reliably over the road, I pondered the chimeras of the night mind. I recalled my single visit to Dr Mudge, the hour I spent on his couch. I hadn't imagined that they used couches any longer. They were brisk and practical now, I believed, staring across a desk, offering stern admonitions and selected pharmaceuticals. I lay on that old leather sofa, unable to see the man behind me whose voice solicited my secrets, enquiring about my lesbian experiences, though I continued to tell him there was no such thing. I was preoccupied by my helpless position supine on the couch, wondering whether I should lie with my ankles crossed, thus appearing resistant and tight-assed, or whether to uncross them and so indicate that I was loose and available. As I took my position on the cracked brown leather, I began to suspect you had told him he could do as he pleased with me, and I could hear his breathing there above me, behind my head, and I didn't know where he was looking, what he was thinking, if he was staring at me, as I lay there, available, helpless. Of course I never went back. I made the appointment with the thought that speaking to him would allow me to be silent with the others, but I learned instead perfect retention and security, practised them adroitly, no matter how pressing the temptation to blab.

I stare across the room at the fabric in the large glassed frame on the wall. It is a very fine coverlet, woven in Cape Breton in 1845 by a Gaelic-speaking woman, donated to us by her family. The front of the frame is hinged so that the object inside can readily be changed. Many of the nineteenth-century weavers were men, so we collect only the specimens to which a woman's name is convincingly attached. All this to honour the intention of our founder, your *belle-mère*. She was a little ahead of her time in her obsession with the applied arts as found in women's work and able to create the collection before there was much competition for the materials she desired, though the samples of early lace from Europe must have been expensive. Your father was content to subsidize her collecting. The sixteenth-century flounce that lies in front of me was one of her first purchases, bought in Rome from a textile collector who also did a little discreet dealing. She was afraid that it might be a forgery, but all the experts accepted it as authentic *punto in aria* of the period, a very small piece of course, a narrow flounce worked by a needlewoman four hundred and fifty years ago, a girl in an orphanage, I've always believed, being taught a skill like one of Vivaldi's violinists at the Ospedale della Pietà. Orphan girls, trained to needlework and music.

Punto in aria means 'stitches in air', a fabric that is defined by what is missing, a pattern fabricated around empty space. Styles change; we are fickle by nature, always demanding novelty, the new-fangled, the untried. In the next century, that great void was no longer indispensable in the designs, but even when the solid areas grew larger, more thickly stitched, the fabric was always a net with openwork, a circumscription of blankness. Openwork. Cutwork. I made the first cut myself. Since then a pattern of fabric and emptiness, a net to catch memories. *Punto in aria, gros point, point plat. Point de neige:* what I would see perhaps if I walked up the stairs and looked out, a lace of snow over the grass.

I returned from England, and you were gone. In the silence certain occasions. Pieces of clothing retained your smell. I would arrive at the door, and turn the key in the lock, hear the deadbolt shoot free of its seat deep in the door frame, and I would shiver as I entered the apartment, for I knew that you had been here once again, and before I took off my jacket, I would tiptoe down the hallway into the bedroom where the blind is always drawn down, to stand by the closet looking at the rank of blouses, the row of skirts, the jeans and trousers draped with archival care over wooden hangers, examining each one, putting out my hand, seeking your traces. Or I would turn to the chest of drawers, a handsome piece of furniture in the style of the thirties, finely grained veneer, the piece designed with an oddly mannered mix of curves and adjacent straight lines, and when I opened the drawers I sensed you there, what your elegant fingers had touched. Once I had traced you, the spice of your presence, I would return to the door, shoot the dead bolt into its sheath, hang up my coat and prepare for my evening which now contained, as a room the bitter scent of smoke long after the fire is out, you. I would shed my clothes and dress in those which held souvenirs of your touch, your fragrance, and I would feel your fingers on my skin.

I did not grow up with fine antique lace. The lace I knew was my mother's lace curtains, which were, like everything about the way she kept our house, a little behind the fashion of the times. My friend Sara had bean-bag chairs in her house and walls of barn-board in the TV room downstairs, pieces of old harness hung on them. Oh B., I wouldn't give it house room, my mother would say of such outlandish gestures. She was a little older than the parents of my friends; she and my father had met late, married late, had children late, and I was late-born, five years younger than G., so my mother belonged to an earlier generation than the mothers of my friends, who wore jeans and tie-dyed T-shirts that showed their nipples. My mother wore cotton blouses and tailored slacks. She shuddered at the sight of G. going off to high-school in tight jeans. I hadn't yet reached adolescence, and I allowed my mother to dress me as she wished. I felt a tenderness for her, almost as if I had foreseen the future and must love her while I could. My dark hair was long, and each day before I left the house for school, she would comb it and her clever fingers would plait it in two braids tied at the bottom with ribbons. When she was done with me I was, in appearance, an old-fashioned little girl, and I don't regret it, since it pleased my mother, and she had little enough time left to be pleased. As I prepared to go out the door, she would kiss me and tell me how beautiful I was.

The lace curtains: I found them wrapped around her, the daintiest of shrouds. She had been looking out the window of our small house, waiting for me to return from school perhaps, and suddenly she had felt some distress, faintness, vertigo, and she began to fall, her fingers gripping the curtains, pulling them down, and as she went to the floor, the fabric entangled her, and she died there, too young for death, but it came to her all the same, and I saw her lying there when I entered the house after my day at school, and at first I thought this was a silly trick she had played. She made jokes, hid and jumped out to startle me. She was always inventing games for us to play. My mother was full of life. How was I to recognize her death? I was a good speller, and once in a spelling bee I had successfully recited the letters e-m-b-o-l-i-s-m, but it was only a word, not something that took place in my mother's brain. The first thing I did that day was to sit on the floor beside her and begin to tell her about school, about my teacher, as if the pretence of normal life would bring her round, but the story staggered, words failed. In the silence I reached out to touch her face. It was growing cool, inert. I knew I should phone someone, but I couldn't think who to call. My father worked at jobs all over the city and the surrounding district, framing new buildings, repairing old ones. I never knew where he was on any given day, though perhaps my mother did. G. would be hanging around the school, or on the bus coming home, or hidden away doing whatever it was that left on her face that pleased, sulky, haunted look. I thought of phoning our doctor, but I decided he would be busy in his office with his patients, and I wanted someone to come quickly, to bring my mother back to life, to save me. So I called the police. It took a long time for them to arrive, and when they came in the door, what they did was to ask questions and write things down in a small notebook. They wanted to know where my father was, then they wanted to send me to a neighbour's house, but I wasn't going to do that, leave my mother alone with these two men, who were so very stupid and unsuitable. The police eventually found my father, G. arrived home, and they both wept uncontrollably, and I, since tears are catching as a cold, wept too, though it was not till the funeral, when I saw they were putting her in the earth, that I truly knew my mother had abandoned me. Abandonment. Abandon.

Lace curtains: you, hidden behind them, hidden behind everything. I should abandon this scribble, go to the party, chatter pointlessly with Sam and his wife, drink too much and find some man to take me home. That would not happen, of course. Most men are, for all their reputation as sexual monsters, cowardly. It is when they are in groups, of soldiers, teams of athletes, gaggles of bikers, that they grow courageous and commit gang rapes, excited by watching each other. The primitive horde. Respectable men at parties are all attached to wives or lovers or their sad memories. It is a human weakness, remembering.

Jenny F. will be at the party, my friend, perhaps my enemy, my doublegoer. We came here at the same time, she taking up her position only a month after I had taken up mine, and we have succeeded in working in harness – is that the right image? Are we two Clydesdales plodding side by side, two oxen in a single wooden yoke? Neither of us will acknowledge the yoke, which is, all the same, locked on our necks. We are friends; we are not friends. Neither is in charge. We are both in charge. Who was responsible for this organizational blunder? Your *belle-mère*? Her committee, of which you were a member? I think it was she, and I think it was deliberate, a refusal to give her visionary project into anyone's hands. If no single person was responsible, her influence could still be paramount, and was until her death. She might, in her will, have clarified the matter, but she chose not to. If two males had been left with this blurred definition of authority, it would have become a battle, and one would have triumphed, but Jenny and I have tolerated the muddle, and it's possible that things go better this way, that women are more subtle in their assertion of territory. Jenny is a sturdy personage, whose tread is firm. The red hair – or is that strawberry blonde? – is always clean and shining, and in a moment of abstraction, she will take a handful in her fingers and draw it across her face toward her mouth, hold it to her lips as she thinks. You remember that gesture, no doubt, from a time when the two of you sat alone together, and you poured out your heart to her. No? I am convinced of her secret knowledge, and how else would she have come to it? The Christmas present: *Something for a cold winter night*, she wrote on the card, and that too might have been interpreted in more ways than one. She is one, she tells me, of a family of five sisters, all red-haired. There is something unnatural, fey, about that. Five evil spirits gathered around the sleeping hero.

We shared an office in those early days, and we watched each other, sipping morning coffee, afternoon tea, exchanging small confidences. We would go to our separate desks, and I would think of you, as I feigned concentration on my work, my plans for the storage and cataloguing of the collection, the design of the downstairs spaces.

And this office, where I scribble these pages, after a long lingering out of days, after expectation and disappointment and strange fulfillment, would be all new to you. Or have you kept a key to the building? Do you come in the dark of night, knowing the code for the alarm?

I keep my diaries locked up. It is not just the desire to leave traces on my garments that brings you here in my absence, but also the desire to know what I might have written about you, how many of your secrets I have told. I keep the words hidden. Memory catches a hint of an event, and then I bring out the hidden diary and find details that had been lost, how you stood by the door of the building waiting for me to put myself in order, gazing out, silent.

The Victorian lace, appliqué on machine net, has in its design a cornucopia, the horn of plenty, with its spill of flowers and fruits. Plenteousness, all the things that have happened, might have happened, came and went unobserved. Part of the superfluity of history, here collected, the excess, the overflow. Put away the pieces of lace, return them to their place in the cabinets of the fabric room, temperature and humidity controlled, the air filtered to keep out moulds. Before touching them I put on gloves. I am always startled by the sight of my hands in the white cotton, blank hands, awkward unfeeling fingers. I think of undertakers handling the dead, though almost certainly they wear latex gloves. Since the cotton gloves must fit many sizes of hand, they are shapeless, generic, flattened things, like a child's crude outline of a hand, without the subtle differences in shape of the fingers, the varied length and placement of the phalanges, the slight bend perceptible past the last joint. The idiosyncrasies that G. would look for in my hands when she had decided to tell my fortune, on rainy evenings of the summer after our mother died. I would hold out my hand to her, afraid not to, and she would run her fingertips over the skin, searching out bends and hollows, and examining the lines of the palm, and then she would frighten me with her auguries, what was meant by the length of the fourth finger on my left hand, the shape of my thumb. In the white gloves, all these particularities are shrouded, indeterminate, and an awkwardness occurs in the grasp and articulation.

Years later when I went to visit a psychic in a bare room at the front of a house on Bathurst Street, she was less polished than G., less dramatic and thrilling, bored was the impression she gave, and her English wasn't very good, but once she began to speak there was a certain flat conviction to her words, as if she was reading from a text already prepared for her. She knew she had powers, but she took it for granted; it was as ordinary as the ability to do mental arithmetic. What she said was accurate about the past, my mother's death, and then she predicted you. *He come to you, this beautiful man, then he go. You happiness. You unhappiness. Always to keep secret.* A few more words then her crooked hand with its plump palm, some kind of stain in the cracked skin as if she had been soaked in tea, set down my hand and that was the end.

Careless, daring, I left these pages unguarded on the desk while I returned the lace to the cabinets. Anyone might have glanced through them. While I was in the pure filtered air of the vault (while you were reading my words), I opened another drawer, at random, and there lay a needlework picture that I had all but forgotten, a stitching of colours on a backing of coarse canvas, the kind of thing used for samplers – of which we have several exceptional examples. What I brought out with me is not a sampler – the work of a clever girl, with a name, Alice Morrow, and a date, 1879 – but is in fact a stitched portrayal of a child, in a white dress, and behind her, a landscape, evergreen trees and flower gardens, and in a top corner a white house with a green roof, the mullioned windows little rectangles of black. The needlewoman attempted to give a sense of dimension by lighter and darker shadings, but still the face of the child is flat and naive, a round face with red lips, wide eyes and dark hair, bland as milk, sweet as honey. Perhaps that was what my mother wished for me as well. She made me a dress of fine white cotton, gathers and stitches of smocking on the front, and I would wear it as we visited my great-aunt Lil, who would offer me a humbug from the dish at her chair. I tried to keep still and not cause my mother distress by my twitching and poking where the stiff fabric of the dress itched my skin. I knew, as a child, that my mother was in danger, that she was a treasure on loan which might be called back at any time. And was. They put makeup on her, the undertakers, my mother who had never in her life worn makeup, whose scrubbed skin and brushed hair were testimony to a scrubbed and brushed character, and when G. saw her there, lipsticked, rouged, she made a scene – they had turned her mother into some kind of doll. G., always the bad daughter – who refused to visit Aunt Lil, wore her sweaters too tight, her skirts too short, to our mother's dismay – now out of her bad, crazed love would have seized the body in the satin-lined box and thrown it on the floor and scrubbed the face until it looked like our mother, had she not been dragged away. Myself, I was abashed and proper, or pretended to be so. It was a role I had mastered.

Makeup: I liked you to watch me as I rubbed foundation into my skin, lightly shaded my cheeks with a brush, a smaller brush to spread lipstick on my mouth, one finger drawn over my eyelid with a hint of eye shadow. My dark, long eyelashes have no need of mascara, but once, tempted by something you had said, I coated them grotesquely, thickened the eye shadow, painted my mouth large with a dark gloss, posing so you could stare at my false face.

The needlework girl turns her expressionless eyes away from the sight of us, and she walks the lines of cross-stitching back to the garden, where the red tulips, embroidered in silk thread, catch her glance, and then she shrinks into the perspective distance, where everything is minuscule and neat, past a little patch of forget-me-nots, each no more than one tiny blue stitch, and she enters the inch-high house where life waits for her, duties, the cold rooms to be cleaned with broom and cloth, her husband to be attended in his sickness, the rigours of childbirth. She is the perfect wife.

You seldom spoke of your mother, though it was what our histories had in common, the loss of a parent. The person who spoke of her was your *belle-mère*, who had composed a list of her perfections, which she would recite in your presence, you severe, perhaps displeased, but never speaking your displeasure. It was one of her ways of attempting to take possession of you, that recitation, claiming you for her own. If she invented your mother, your mother's son came into her keeping. I averted my gaze from the dark eyes, set close together with an oddity of placement of the iris, a hint of strabismus, so that her dark gaze was fixed and narrow. It added to the force of her looks, as I sat across the table from her in the early meetings of the committee, battling to assert my independence, my professional competence, though I was her creature. Later she wished to send me to England, and I went. When I returned to find you gone, she was different, as if moved by other interests now. We were, both of us, broken by your loss. Or perhaps she saw only that I was no longer capable of defiance. She did not need to exhibit her mastery of me. She had wished to prove herself to you, but of course everyone did. I would notice how in your presence Jenny F. chose her words with especial care, held herself very upright. Proud flesh. Yet you were soft-spoken, undemanding, though with that edge of coldness, as if something in you could never be touched, the structure of bone. Osteology. He is an untouchable man, Jenny F. said to me the day she arrived. I was put on my mettle by that remark. And if I were to go to that New Year's party, to stare into her green cat's eyes? All of the five sisters have green cat's eyes.

I heard a voice in the hall upstairs, went to look. Nothing. The lights out except those that remain on all night as a deterrent to burglars and vandals. By the front door, the desk where Yvonne sits, our new receptionist – a tall, breastless, hipless girl with a long, strangely beautiful face, a slight bump at the bridge of the nose, a high brow with straight hair drawn back from it, a face from an old Flemish painting. Her husband is one of those weedy boys with an unthriving bit of whisker at the end of his chin. I wonder how they are passing this New Year's Eve. Perhaps quietly toking up with a few equally thin and silent friends. In university I spent weekends like that, smoking up and eating subs. Waiting. At work Yvonne sits at her desk with our reprint of *Le Ménagier de Paris*, the words of an aging man as he writes out advice for his young wife, moral disquisitions, recipes. Yvonne says she plans to make it into a novel. Behind her desk are postcards of medieval manuscript illuminations, scenes from ordinary life, three women baking bread in an outdoor oven. Perhaps she's thinking about her novel as she sits with her friends, a little high, listening to a Cowboy Junkies tape. Outside the windows, the earth is veiled in *point de neige*. In the darkness I can make out the hull of the rowboat, the gunwales traced in white lines, two curves that meet at the bow as the two flat seats collect the falling flakes. That voice again: I have already looked, and found no one, though the old house is a kind of maze that might hide an intruder, the narrow halls and back staircases and doors that lead to other doors. Everything prompts suspicions. You would know your way around the old rooms by touch, since you lived here as a boy. Here you lay sick with measles in one of the upstairs rooms, feverish, and in your dreams, terrible women hovered, avid as succubi, and even your kindly mother watching over you grew winged and vengeful. This was your delirium, and you walked in your sleep, to be found crouched in the attic defending a small animal that only you could see. You told me that so I would know that you recognized the succubus. Walls have been removed since your childhood, doorways opened, and in the basement the storage rooms and annexes added. I never considered until now that the old green rowboat must have been yours, when you were a boy, your hands on the oars, hours spent on the water in silent contemplation. I tried to know everything about you, spying on you when you were away from me, and yet I missed the obvious. You avoided my questions, knowing I wished to eat your heart. One night I watched the door of your apartment from darkness until dawn, but even as I watched I suspected I was on the wrong track. A ladder at the back window, and you climbed down and met her in the woods by the shore. At dawn I drove home, phoned you, pretending to have just wakened, begging you to meet me in the evening, then took a shower, hot, then cold, and made my way here to work.

I watched you with Jenny F., knowing what I knew. Now you write her letters, a spiritual intimacy. The gift she left me, here on this table, was a message. The way it was wrapped, white tissue drawn into careful pleats with a bright red ribbon, like a fine cotton dress stained with blood. When I tore open the gift wrapping, I was at first puzzled. It was only gradually I understood.

In her sturdy solidity Jenny F. reminds me of one of my high-school teachers, though Miss Tate was not a red head, but ash-blonde, her hair cut short, robust, short-legged, heavy-thighed, with plump breasts that she tried to conceal in loose sweaters and shirts. If I had wished to answer Dr M.'s impertinent questions about lesbianism I might have told him about Miss Tate. We all knew, somehow, that she loved girls, though she was perfectly discreet in her behaviour. A gifted teacher, she made the history she expounded lively and personal. Yes, a good teacher, and she thought me clever. I thought she had a little secret passion for me. She made classes a pleasure, and I went to her at the end of the year to tell her so. This was my final term, and apart from a graduation ceremony, would be the last day I walked through the halls of that school. She was alone in her classroom when I came, and I was pert and full of smiles as I thanked her. She was, as always, serious, her voice measured and grave. I stood near her desk at the front of the room, and she was leaning back, her hips against the edge of the wood. When I asked if I should kiss her goodbye, she said nothing, so I bent forward, and as I put my lips to hers, I thought I felt her trembling, and cheeky as can be, I slipped my tongue into her mouth for a second, then drew away, met the pale staring eyes and turned from her, strutted away with a little switch of the hips. Miss Tate was not at the graduation ceremony. I was unduly pleased with myself over that kiss, so very daring and clever. It was only years later, when, to my surprise, she turned up here with a class of high-school girls for the regular school tour, looking older, smiling at me but saying nothing, that I thought I had been cruel. A lesbian experience for Dr Mudge. Of course he would have had no real interest in that little story. He wished for something gross and sweaty. I might have told him how at seventeen one summer afternoon I allowed Peter Loomis to penetrate me, once I was assured that he was well-armoured in rubber. When we were done, I was embarrassed by what had occurred, how my body had gone its own way, sudden startling events, un-controllable as blushing or hiccups. I hoped that Peter hadn't noticed. To distract him, I demanded he pay me twenty dollars for the privilege of entry. He stared, wordless, unable to take it in. But you're not one of those, he said. Wasn't it worth twenty dollars? I said. I was relieved by the unsettling effect of my demand, his discomfiture, confusion. Things were back under control. I was aware that my rebellious body wanted to have him inside me again, but I only smiled and put out my hand for the money. At last he gave me two ten-dollar bills, and I tucked them into the pocket of my jeans. As I was leaving his house, I passed his mother upstairs in the kitchen baking a cake and watching a portable TV. Do you have to go? she said. You could stay for dinner. No, I said, my father's expecting me.

A week later Peter was waiting outside the store when I finished work. He told me he had another twenty dollars, but I told him the price had gone up, and when he insisted on knowing how much, I said a million dollars and walked away. I despised him a little for giving me the money when I asked for it.

The stitchery-girl smirks at the thought. She is above it all, the white child who will be the perfect wife. Doesn't the perfect wife grow cold as the years pass, bored with the bedtime routine, preoccupied with your career and sociability? The perfect wife has difficulty distinguishing between her father and her husband. Men are much the same in a perfect world. The perfect world where I'm certain you must remember me from time to time, imperative, cunning, addicted. Like the villainess at the centre of your book.

The man behind the pseudonym. The lack of an author photo, the one-line biography are hints of concealment, but for all my pride in my intuition, I didn't catch on. I found the gift, red on white, blood on the snow, here in my office, and I carried it home in my leather briefcase. When I reached my apartment, I left it on the kitchen table, and it was only when I was ready for bed that I picked it up, tore off the ribbon, and ripped away the pleated tissue. I read the title.

Gray's Anatomy. I put the book down on the table, beside the white tissue and red ribbon and stared at it. With this strange gift, I thought, Jenny had introduced irony, always a dangerous step, for irony is a powerful solvent, and once it is evoked, the safety of a bland conformity is gone forever. *Gray's Anatomy*. A joke I couldn't comprehend. I reached out one finger and idly opened the book, glanced at a few lines, let it fall closed again, stared at the cover. *Gray's Anatomy*. Giggled aloud at my obtuseness. The book was a novel, using the title of the world's best-known medical text. I laughed again, at how I had been misled. I opened the book, read the opening lines of the first page. *Long-boned, yes, the girl in his bed was long-boned and beautiful and naked, but unfortunately she appeared to be very dead. The* first chapter of the book had a title. *Osteology.* Beneath it the lines I had read. *Long-boned, yes.* I flipped pages and found that each section had a similar title. *The Articulations. The Nervous System. Male Generative Organs.*

After the trip back from my father's on Christmas night, the last part of it in thick blowing snow that made the driving difficult and exhausting, I fell into bed, but in the night I woke from a dream about you. I was among trees, watching for you, and then I crept up to a cabin and looked in the window, and you were sitting inside, at a table, concentrating, a pencil in your hand. There were birds flying around the room, but you appeared not to see them. I woke out of the dream. *N. is the one who wrote that book,* I said, speaking aloud. I turned on the light, took the book in my hand, and now, as I turned the pages, it all came clear. I remembered a friend in graduate school who had written and published a couple of short stories; they were, he told me, very closely based on real people, but the models never recognized themselves. You killed me at the book's end. Or was it me you killed? Maybe it was your perfect wife. The lady or the tiger?

You told Jenny F. to give me the book. And do you expect me to respond? Are we to begin once more? You could be found, I know, if I made a concentrated effort. Now Jenny F. has put your text on the themes of our story into my hands. You have the last word. As you follow out the necessities of your intrigue, there are little reflections of an old reality. *They might have met in any number of ways, but they would certainly meet.* You and I were destined to collide, somewhere in time and space. It was inevitable, as the falling object is certain to strike the earth.

The first and fatal interview. Your *belle-mère* met me at the bus terminal – I was to call her by her first name, she said, but I never could – and drove me here, pointed out the bathroom where I might – yes, she said it – freshen up, and the board room I was to enter when I was freshened. So I emptied my bladder, washed my hands, checked my makeup and went through the doorway I had been shown. Three people sat at the long table, and one of them was you. *That is the most beautiful thing I have ever seen,* a voice said. A voice new to me, although my own. How does it happen to us, that we look at another being and are seized, changed, imprisoned, and in the same instant set free. *Who ever loved that loved not at first sight?* I had read those words, not taken them seriously. I understood impulses, preferences, judgments. Not this. Beauty is one word for the terrible recognition, the meltdown of the personality. I was nothing but my desire for you. I was brave enough to meet your gaze, those gentle astonishing eyes. I was introduced to you and to an elderly woman, a retired professor of classics who was chief among advisors. You were a doctor, they said, and I wished you to survey, palpate, cut me open, cure me. Then I was interviewed. You asked few questions, and those you asked were framed to make it all easier, lobs so that I could snap the ball quickly back over the net. Yes, you were being kind, as if you knew that I was wounded, helpless, in terror that I might be sent back to Toronto and never see you again.

Behind your shoulder was a window, and in the open space beside the river, a boy was running, trying to get a kite in the air. If the kite flew I would get the job, I decided, and while trying to pay attention to what I was saying I watched him, and at last the delicate paper ship lifted off. I answered the next question with more confidence. If I lacked training in museology, I could be sent for further study. The kite was high in the air, I would be hired for this job, and I would have you, even if, as was inevitable, you were married. No. Married to your career, to your high standards of behaviour, to some careful future, the perfect wife.

The meeting of the man and the woman in your book: that long description of the cottage at the edge of the sea, mountains behind it, the little beach among the tall firs, and your hero escaping there from the complications of his life, dead bodies, threats, conspiracies, and he swims in the clear water, the sunlit sky above, and then as he comes to shore, he sees her drawing, the pad on her knees as she sits on a rock. She is unflustered by the naked man.

Does the perfect wife know that you have published this under an invented name? Perhaps she takes all the characters to be aspects of her varied perfection. Told her name, I have chosen to forget it.

My return from England. It is always in the present tense, the moment when the queer dark eyes stare at me and instruct me that you are gone, that you have married and moved to a new place. She will be the perfect wife, the voice says, and I stand frozen, determined to reveal nothing. She accepts my smiles and congratulations, while I hold myself upright, in defiance of the depletion in my brain that tells me I am about to faint. I walk away, lock myself in the washroom cubicle and wait for death. From that moment on, everything around me seems to be a little out of synchronization, like a dubbed movie where the lips and the words do not resemble each other. I live a life in translation.

That voice upstairs. Again, when I went to look, no one, the halls dim as I walked through them, a light here and there to repel invaders. Standing in front of Jenny F.'s office, I thought I heard a sound inside, turned the handle and slowly opened the door, half expecting to find her there, and you with her, but the room was empty, beyond the window the manic dance of the falling snow. I switched on the light. On the wall above her desk, the print of Vermeer's *Lacemaker*, and two wildflower prints, reproductions from the Catharine Parr Trail-Agnes Fitzgibbon volume. We are close to the country where the Strickland sisters endured the pioneering struggle, bearing the consequences of their husbands' worldly incompetence. On the other walls are copies of Mary Cassatt prints, a print of a painting by Gabriele Münter. Back in the hallway I listened, heard nothing but the various sounds of electricity, the buzz of a light fixture, the hum of the heating system. I recalled the night at the V&A when I had stayed working late, and on the way out of the building, got lost, blundered into a storeroom full of plaster casts. The huge copy of Michelangelo's David rose above me, the Perfect Naked Man, the figure so large it had required a fig-leaf fifteen inches long to shield his parts from the widowed queen's gaze. In the darkness of the storeroom, the offending genitals were shrouded in darkness. I could make out only the ghostly shape of the hips in *contrapposto*, the tall torso rising toward the ceiling. Ahead, a Virgin and Child blocked my way. Beneath an archway supported by heavy columns, I stopped, hoping to work out how I had come into the room, where the door must be. Turned, and I was walking beside a row of empty display cases, heavy wood frames with glass tops, my fingers just touching them now and then. A crouching figure. A head detached from its neck. Arms. Legs. In the gloom I was hemmed in by severed body parts. And I could hear voices around me, one voice at first, yours, but no matter how I listened I couldn't make out the words. The tone was severe, then coaxing, then once again severe. A second voice, a kind of duet with the first, and I knew it was my own voice. I had fled the prison of my body to meet up with you in the wreckage of a great apocalyptic battle, stumbling on it in the dead of night, when the killing was over, the souls departed. I could not find my way, until at last I heard a door open, and I called out, and the security guard – a man I had often met at the night entry – found me and guided my steps with his flashlight.

Tonight no one will discover me in this empty building. In the attic, where Sam Pruitt has his little conservation lab, the spirit of the delirious child defends the helpless furred creature. I stood by the window on the landing, and the thick flakes whirled and turned in the dim reflection that came from somewhere to illuminate their flight. Stitches in air, the boat vanished in the blowing snow, the current of the river unseen, unceasing. Out there in the winter darkness, eyes seeking my eyes, lost thoughts attentive to my need, the unremembered struggling to return. As I write this down, I observe the little scar on one finger of my left hand, the healing not quite perfect, in spite of your careful needlework. Stitches in flesh. Cutwork. Stitches in air.

Your doctor-detective will return in later books, and each will have the title of some well-known medical text. You will become pseudonymously famous, but the perfect wife will never know who is the author of these outrageous fantasies. You will encode all your secret moments in another thriller called *The Circulation of the Blood*, or *Common Diseases of the Eye*, eventually one called *The Interpretation of Dreams*. Dr Freud is out of fashion, but it would make for an excellent title. You are on to a good thing – that delicious chapter called 'The Digestive System', in which the sly, obviously criminal chef explains to Gavin Gray the function of each of the knives on his carefully organized rack, this followed by the dinner with the young woman who chatters gaily about cannibalism. Yes, I wished to eat your heart.

That was one of the drawings on the wall, my devouring of your heart. Those sketches which began to inscribe themselves when I came back home after the momentous events in your examining room, wild with triumph, unable to contain myself. I ran up the stairs from the street, closed the door behind me, noises coming from my throat, less than music, or more. On the table by my bed was a black felt marker I'd used to label a parcel, a birthday present for G., and suddenly I had it in my hand, and I was drawing on the wall, and writing, creating a kind of cartoon history of my triumph, the lips of your kissable mouth and a balloon with words, your inner thoughts, and I put myself there, the story I'd invented, oval face, dark eyes and tiny nose, poor little thing, helpless, frightened, and then my vast hungry mouth about to eat your heart. I inscribed a rectangle, and inside the rectangle I told it all, though words wouldn't contain what needed to be said. Once, when I was a student, I enrolled in a one-semester course on the history of love poetry, taught by a short, dry, acerbic man, who had no business, one would say, with such things. We began with the Song of Solomon. *His banner over me was love.* I drew a mountain and two figures, hand in hand, walking up the slope toward the sun.

I was unable to tell where your body ended and my own began. It was you who stood in my bedroom drawing in heavy black lines on the pale green wall. I laughed. It was ridiculous and wonderful. I would sit in my white wicker rocking chair and write in my diary, using the cartoon on the wall as an aid to memory, my way of inscribing the invisible forces on the world. You would see my mural, and understand what I felt.

As we stood at the glass door that first night you visited, I searched my bag for the key and noticed the dark car pass slowly by. We were being watched. My mother would say, when we were walking down the street, *Someone is keeping an eye on us, little B.,* and at first I thought she meant God, but then I came to understand that it was the voluntary network of spies, the curious, the gossips seeking fodder. Our two dark figures, bulky in winter coats, were reflected in the glass of the door, and then we were inside and going up the stairs. I double-locked and bolted the door behind us and led the way to the bedroom, switched on the lights. You were not pleased by my creation. You stared at it as if at something diseased. Funny, I said, it's really quite funny, but you didn't hear me. I turned off the light and began to tell a story about a man who had treated me with great cruelty, how he had hurt me, lies, of course, but told with passion and tears, and as I told it, I coaxed you, and in the darkness you set aside your shock and distress. When you left I remembered my mother's words, *Someone is keeping an eye on us, little B.,* and I thought of you going out into the street, eyes in a parked car a block away, notes set down. I wondered why we could not be free. The perfect wife-to-be had sent her spies. The police suspected you of something – trafficking in love potions.

Near midnight, the year about to end. A few minutes ago I picked up the phone and called my father. He said it was good of me to think of him. *I've been dreaming about your mother a lot*, he said. His search goes on. He was watching the New Year's Eve festivities on television and assumed I must be doing the same. Or at a party. No, I said, I was just thinking about the past and the future. You were always a wise girl, he said.

After you left my apartment, I looked at the wall where I had drawn and written our history, saw it with your eyes. I knew you would never come back while it was there. On my way home from work one night, I stopped at the hardware store and bought a gallon of paint. It took three coats to cover it, and when it was gone I wished that I had I had a photograph of it, a record of what I had made. For every poem there is another secret poem, my professor of love once said. Each of us has hidden stories. I painted over one of mine.

In the top drawer of my filing cabinet there is a box of chocolate creams that Sam Pruitt gave me for Christmas, and I take them out, set them on the table in front of me. I will celebrate the New Year by eating one or two.

Two identical chocolate creams, one in each hand. Jenny F. and I are paired, doublegoers. The perfect wife too is my twin. Your book is very clever in the way it blurs the two women, the wife and the mistress so that at the end, we do not know who it is that has been killed. Your doctor-detective sees a gun lying on a chair and picks it up in his shaking hand, the door opens, there is a gunshot, and as he falls, wounded, he pulls the trigger, but we never know who has murdered. A post-modern elision, with a little ironic epilogue. Because, perhaps, you don't even now understand who it is you wish to kill, whether the succubus who took you in with lies, who intoxicated you with freedoms, or the perfect wife who brings order and good sense into your life, the respected and respectable.

There is only one woman, one man. That's the kind of thing one writes after midnight while eating chocolate creams and remembering what should be forgotten. I imagine a book that continues where yours leaves off, a book where the doublegoers meet and exchange roles. I might have been the perfect wife. Marriage is abstract and governed by rules, a salvation from the perversities of our individual existence with its detailed and wayward desires. A salvation, and yet with time –

99

deprived, hopeless in the face of the routine – even the perfect wife will become once more manipulative, false, lubricious.

Once upon a time I thought I was out of harm's way. I had chosen a sensible arrangement with a musician, the handsome Lonny. I worked in the archives. He did research for his thesis: *False Relation as an Expressive Device in the Early Music of William Byrd*. We spent time together on weekends. I told myself this was sufficient, though a rebellious voice in my head sometimes called him Loony. Once or twice I let it out, and he sulked, and I swore to behave. It was what life must be, I said, until the day I attended to a small performance at the Conservatory. Apart from his studies in musicology, Loony was, he had told me, a member of an early music group, played recorder and sang. Everyone has hobbies.

In this public performance he was singing, he said, told me little else. He was, as it emerged, a countertenor, falsettist, an imitation castrato, making that strangest of sounds, girlish, outrageous, and he was here presented in a scene of erotic thrills from a seventeenth-century opera by Cavalli – Lonny was Endymion, a half-naked shepherd boy, and opposite him a soprano playing Diana, goddess of the Moon, goddess of chastity, and performing Moony and Loony's duet with many an unchaste wiggle of her perky bottom. Loony in a sort of furry bathing suit and sheepskin cloak, she in revealing pale blue, both stricken with love, goddess and shepherd, hooting like dickiebirds in heat. A deal of kissing, pretending to kiss, withdrawing from a kiss. Voices, soprano and alto, an endless orgasm. False relation indeed. By the end of the month Moony was in Loony's bed, and I was out. I became the goddess of chastity, perforce. A week later I found an advertisement describing the job I now hold. I knew it was time to move on.

I didn't tell you that, not wanting you to know I had been betrayed.

You gave me gifts sometimes but never bought me clothes, as if you wished to avoid too much domestic intimacy. You tried to set limits, to prove you were not deeply involved. There was no place in your plan of a courtly and pragmatic existence for this; you expected a simple system of tension and release, useful, uncomplicated, and what I offered you was a woman who wrote and drew on the walls a crude account of her power over you (yours over her), huge letters at the top saying EVERYONE LOVES ME. You presented a silver bracelet, a respectful and respectable kind of gift, and I ruined the gift by making it part of the mad comedy we were playing out. You gave me an expensive fountain pen to write my diary, and I used it to inscribe tattoos on your secret skin. We must be careful, you said to me. You looked haunted, and I half expected a dark messenger to come from you and murder me. Yet you came back to me, and back, until, in my absence, you escaped. Now I have the book in which you do me in. Foolish of me to pretend that the corpse in the story might be that of your seemly and upright spouse. She has a sense of limit, and in a few more years you will settle into a comfortable boredom with her. The naked bleeding corpse is mine. G. warned me about you. I sent her a letter telling her not the truth but some hint of it. Never trust a respectable man, she wrote back.

At the core of your bland, satisfied life, I will remain, however many times you murder me on paper, for I am more than words on paper. I have invaded your nerves, the primitive stink-eating monsters of the limbic brain have set free their cravings on me. At the sight of me, those lizard whims will stir once more, imagination and hunger taking hands and crying for a death. You gave me a name, and it can't be taken back.

The blank face of the stitchery child sickens me now. I want to be rid of it. Shall I lock these pages away before I go into the storage vaults?

Left them. Once in the vaults, in the cleansed air, gloved in white cotton, I began opening drawers at random, looking at needlework, hooked rugs, knitted socks, some of them old and worn but with unique patterns, an Aran sweater knitted long ago, a very beautiful stitch. Each woman's stitchery was unique, I've read, so that when the body of a drowned fisherman washed ashore, no matter how decayed, how eaten by crabs, the woman could recognize it as her own lost man. Wool outlasts the flesh it warmed. I might have knitted such a garment for you, and sent you out into the river on a winter's night, to be swept away, vanishing in the blizzard, going under, lost. I see you as a boy, a heavy anchor holding the boat steady in the current, a fishing rod in your hand, dreaming of a life to come. You looked to see if you were watched, and if not, brought yourself off by the quick work of one hand, and I was there with you, my hand on your hand.

I closed the last of the drawers and moved on to the library shelves, catalogues, reference works, and the section of cook books, regional publications from the Women's Institute, various churches, and the handwritten collections of recipes picked up here and there. I took out one bought at auction. A bright Saturday in October. Your belle-mère announced that we must go to this auction – she had seen quilts and hooked rugs in the listing of goods to be sold – that you would drive us there. I hadn't dared to get in touch with you since the afternoon in your examining room a week before. It was arranged that I would wait in front of this building. She was there in the front seat, and you avoided my eyes. I wondered if you were afraid of me or only wished to tease me by pretending to be distant, professional, the good doctor who had stanched the flow of my blood. As we drove, the older woman in the seat beside you was telling the slightly daring story about how she got to Rome, though I was to gather later on that there was another, and more disreputable version, but it was a lively tale about a woman whose bravery led her where she might not have gone, becoming secretary and driver to a senior staff officer, travelling not far behind the front as the Allied troops moved north through Italy, and in Rome meeting the man who became her husband. Not really her husband, the other story went. I suppose you heard both versions, or perhaps, in your upright way you heard only what she wished you to believe. As I listened to her talk, I stared out the window, where the maples along the road caught the sunlight, brilliant scarlet, the annual show. In the farmyard where the auction was being held, fallen leaves were trampled by the small crowd, but the branches held a thousand more. With an affectation of professional care I examined rugs and quilts, though she and I were both as excited as children by the event and wished to buy for the mere glory of it, and we agreed that she would do the bidding, and I stood back from the small crowd and looked at the stone farmhouse, its fine proportions, the mullioned windows. The old farm life had been lived in that house, days dim and sweet, and after the auction it would be bought and renovated, used as a summer home. The auctioneer's voice sang on. She bought one rug and two quilts, and I folded them carefully and took them back to the car, where you opened the trunk for me, and I placed them in it with care, and while we were away from the crowd I spoke to you. At the front of the crowd our leader was bidding on something, and at first I couldn't see what it was, but it appeared to be a box of worn pots and pans. She took possession of it and brought it back to where I was standing. She took out of it an old three-ring binder and showed me that it was full of recipes, written out with a pencil in a very small hand, explaining that we ought to begin a collection of recipe books, and this would be the first, and then suddenly she was saying that she had met a friend in the crowd, and they wished to drive back together. N. will drive you, she said.

I've brought the recipe book with me. I had to promise you, the next day before we left the motel, that I would find an excuse to go to some other doctor, to get myself off your list, but I never did. I could make my jokes about threatening you with exposure, the physician who broke his oath by having one of his patients.

The motel scene in your book: an assignation that goes wrong. He goes to the place for cheap love, but she is not there, the woman who's promised to meet him. Restless, he turns on the TV. And on the screen he sees her, playing out her role in the story, as if it were already written, performed for the camera, concluded. A knock on the door, and he finds himself in the hands of the police, accused of being part of a kidnapping plot, sent there to pick up the money. The woman vanishes, leaves him only bitterness. You grew afraid of me. A man fears the eating of his heart.

Tomato cake. I've never heard of such a thing before, a cake made with a tin of tomato soup, brown sugar and butter. I flip the page to a recipe for mustard pickles. Every year in late August Jenny F. takes a few days off to make her pickles. Once she invited me round to help her or perhaps to observe – I didn't know why I was invited – and when I arrived her thick hair was tied up in a scarf, she wore a soiled loose blouse, grey sweat pants with a yellow stain on the thigh. The air was hot, damp, thick with spice. Bottles of mustard pickle stood inverted on the counter. In the heat of the kitchen Jenny – always so perfect, immaculate, carefully dressed – was sweating, and she wiped her forehead with her sleeve. Her husband was away somewhere, avoiding this sensual disorder. It was like a dream where you find yourself in the midst of an orgy, being urged to join in, yet fearing dissolution. As I walked away down the sidewalk, I wondered if the hot, stinking atmosphere was what you found when you came to me, everything tropic, dissolute, famished.

Marge's recipe for Date Loaf. Ammonia Cookies from Bea's mother. Here and there, little drawings, labelled in a child's large printing. A round face with round eyes and mouth, and large tears falling. Printed underneath: *Dorty when she got the Smacks.* A recipe for gumdrop cake has *Good!* printed beside it in the same childish letters, a large heavy exclamation mark at the end. My fingers in their white gloves turned more pages, and I noticed that the fingertips were blackened from the dust on the old paper. Ought to be carefully cleaned by a paper conservator. I looked at the coded tag, which in its numbers and letters made precise reference to that October afternoon in that farmyard with its log barns.

On another page, a recipe for beef stew. About to flip further on when my eye caught a phrase at the end of the instructions, written in the same hand as the recipe, the pencil perhaps pressing a bit harder. Or did I imagine that? *He hit me again. Said I spilled the whole d____ salt box in it.* I pushed aside the book. *Dorty when she got the Smacks.* My face was hot as if a strong hand had clipped me across the cheek. We had stood together under that tall maple and I had imagined the calm and stability of the old life, but this was one of those isolated farms where there was a lot of hitting. G.'s third husband once punched her in the head. She picked up a tin of peas and broke his nose with it, then she had to drive him to the hospital.

I opened the recipe book again: *Stuffed Pork. Mary's recipe (Jim's favourite).* On another page: *Raisin Cake (from Jim's mother).* At the foot of the page two round, schematic children's faces, *Dorty and Me* printed beside them, then scribbled out. Beside all this a long shape with a shoe at the bottom, labelled *Uncle Jim's Wooden Leg.* So she married the wrong man, the one who hit her, instead of Jim, who married Mary, and then they all pretended to be friends. Her husband had a better house, a bigger farm lot, and with the wooden leg, she figured Jim was a poor bet. By the time she figured out that she was wrong Dorty and Me had been born, and she was stuck out there.

In England, there was a nice man – older than I am, happily divorced, as he put it – who said he'd never known anyone like me, so beautiful, he said, so different from the run of girls. When I told him I couldn't stay in England he said he'd move to Canada; he was an experienced draughtsman, he could get work anywhere.

There has to be a perfect husband in the story. The demon lover and the perfect husband, and who does she choose? The lady or the tiger? The life I missed, the woman with her recipe book in the isolation of a cold farmhouse in winter, waiting for her husband to come back, knock her around. Maybe she married him for his passion, but after you've been slapped a few times, sex isn't much of a consolation any more. I turned more pages. *Strawberry Pie, heard on the radio*, and the next page, *Fish Soup, good for Pike or Pickerel*. And at the foot of the recipe a note. *Got this from Jim's mother. Made it for after his funeral.* So Jim was gone by then, and maybe Dorty and Me grown up and left, and did she still get hit? To fill her evenings, she was making those quilts we bought, and the rug, or maybe that was the generation before. Something her husband's mother had sewn in the silent hours when the snow piled up around the house and barn.

It wasn't easy, to shed my own blood. I'd hatched the plan a week before, and made sure that the knife was close at hand, downstairs in the still unrenovated space where we did cataloguing in those days. I had some cardboard that was my excuse for using the sharp hobby knife. I waited until you were in the building, one of our monthly meetings just over. I had concentrated on drawing your eyes toward me, testing the power of thought, and once or twice I knew you glanced my way, and I looked up, as if by accident, and met your look, but if there was a message in your eyes I could not read it. Before you had a chance to leave the building, I walked down the stairs, set out the cardboard, sliced it and then slashed the scalpel blade across the ring finger of my left hand, a deep cut, and it made me cry out, and I seized a tissue from the box to soak up the blood and rushed up the stairs. Alice, our receptionist in those days, was the first to see me, and perfectly following the script, she screamed, and then there you were, took hold of my hand, asked me sternly how I'd done it, and I said the knife had slipped, and in a second, you had taken out a clean white handkerchief, wrapped it round the finger, told me to hold it tightly in my other fist, and we were in your car on the way to the hospital. The finger was throbbing, but I could have cried out, not with pain but with joy. I was in your control, and you were in mine. You had touched me. You would look after me. Another few steps in my arrangements, and you would be mine. *I have plans for you*, the villainess says in your thriller. *The plot is carefully constructed.* Yes, you were right, I had a future in mind for you, and at the hospital, as you cleansed the wound, closed it with sutures, your skin touching mine, your careful stitches closing the gaping hole in my flesh, I was in the first stages of my ecstasy. You were too polite to tell me how stupid I was to cut myself.

As I reach out to turn another page of the cookbook, my finger is throbbing with the pain of that old wound. I can feel your sutures in the healed flesh, almost perfect, with only a tiny scar at one end. You did a good job. You always did a good job. Turn a page. Loose clippings, mostly recipes, fragments of advertisements on the back, Coming Events, a card party. One of the fragments of newsprint, unfolded, proves not to be a recipe, but a short account of the execution of a woman in Louisiana who was convicted of killing her husband and hiding his body in an old well. *Faits divers*, they call such things, the subject matter of the great Russian novels. Her fantasy of escape.

One of my *faits divers*, the short news items of my life: Professor C., who flirted with me after class, and once took me out for a drink, driving us miles away where he thought no one could recognize us. He never touched me, but flattered me on the subject of my beautiful eyes, my intelligence, stared at me with plaintive devotion, then later gave me a very low mark on my second essay, left it in a box outside his door at the end of the term, when I couldn't find him to complain. That's his little pathetic kind of fuck, G. said when I phoned and told her. I could have murdered him and stuffed him down a well. Hidden bodies – where we stood in the farmyard, perhaps there was a grave beneath our feet. He had found the clipping. I didn't hear her ghost crying out. I could think only of you.

If there are other riddles in the recipe book, I'll leave them there. I suppose it was her only privacy, the only place he wouldn't find what she had concealed, and what's there is elliptical enough, though any husband would see the point of that newspaper story. I could come back to this in daylight, write an essay about the recipe book as an abortive, secret diary. As context, I could discuss the other recipe books in our collection, the way they express a sense of community, ways of cooking passed from hand to hand, the books as a locus of both community and solitude. We have talked about publishing a series of essays on various aspects of the collection, this could be one of them. A little book of such explorations: it will be my secret answer to your secret novel. Your *belle-mère*'s collection has become my playground, my prison. I visited her in hospital, near the end, hoping to find words to express how she had altered my life, drawing me out of my pleasant, unremarkable job in the university archive and bringing me here to this eccentric, factitious assembly of junk, which perhaps made sense only to her. She brought me here, and that afternoon I stared at her pale face in the hospital bed to see whether, on the margin of oblivion, she would tell me the secret, why she had chosen me. *N. has been here to see me*, she said to me, *and I feel the better for it.* Your name was the first word out of her mouth, and there was adoration in her lips' caress of that familiar sound. You had come and gone, avoiding me, afraid perhaps that I had some new trick to take you in. I was your last appointment in the afternoon, just a few moments to have the stitches you had put in my finger removed, but I insisted on telling you my sad story, so well researched and prepared – the sad tale of my sad tail – my eyes holding yours, pleading for your help, refusing to let you send me to someone else, then pulling the johnnie-shirt all the way up to my waist, feet in the stirrups, your eyes wide, your lips parted. I was unfair.

Dutiful, you had come to the deathbed of your *belle-mère*, some kind of farewell. She had arranged your perfect marriage. She let you go. No sign of her in your novel. You set her free. It comes to me to think that she was the only one you truly loved. I didn't expect love, though I thought I might achieve recognition in your eyes – the osprey at a height, knowing its prey. I told you that only you could release the stricture, ease the pain – lies, but a metaphor for truth. You were the incubus meant to descend on my sleep. Meaning: Oh cutie, I had the hots for you like nobody else.

Was it the wooden leg that kept her from marrying Uncle Jim? She couldn't imagine him taking it off and hopping one-legged into her bed. A one-legged man with an erection would be a rum sight. If I am to write my essay I must avoid such ridiculous speculations.

I will mail this, and you will read it. Or not. Morning will come, and I will walk along the snow-covered streets, leaving the tracks of my shapely little boots in the new snow. I will turn the key in the door of my apartment, and the deadbolt will slide out of its hole. It will be no surprise to find you there, standing naked at the window where you have been watching the street, waiting for my approach. You will turn toward me, and I will be unprepared for a man with no face.

A few weeks ago I arrived home late one dark evening, aware that a car was parked near the door that leads to my apartment, and as I was about to enter, the door of the car opened. I stopped breathing, closed my eyes, my heart beat faster. You had come back.

No.

It was Jenny F.'s husband. She was out of town for a day or so, a family matter she had said to me, carefully not explaining. Perhaps you had summoned her. So here he was, waiting in the dark. As he dressed he asked if he might come back, and I said no. He wrote me a letter which I have saved. It was a day or so later that I came home to my apartment and knew you had been there, your secret visits beginning once more.

Out there in the winter darkness, your little boat is waiting. It waits for one who will make her escape over the blackness of the frigid water, ice just beginning to form in the shallows. The flight of the imprisoned queen – Mary, Queen of Scots, her nineteen years in captivity, and the busy work of her needle. I once had a plan for a book, to be called *The Queen's Needle* and to contain illustrations of all her embroidery panels, signed MS for Mary Stuart, the products of the patient hours of those lost years, her fingers busied while the mind, as quick and tenacious, planned for her escape. Then the assassination of her cold scheming cousin, and at last, the throne of England. This time she would not be distracted by a tall pretty boy, *the lustiest and best-proportioned long man* she had ever set her eyes on. Long, yes, she thought, he would be long, long, long, but in the event, one can guess, what length there was gave little pleasure, and besides that he was a sot, so she took to her bed the Earl of Bothwell. Between the fanatic Covenanters and her chilly cousin, she was trapped. Thus the imprisoned years of needlework and letters and plots, demanding to see the cousin queen she would never meet, and at last, on a cold February morning her head, in its auburn wig, was hacked off. The snow, and the darkness and the waiting boat, the flight she never made, the needlewoman queen, with her habit of ordering the murder of those who inconvenienced her. Fitting the world to the ancient and abstract pattern of her stitchery misled her into the belief that any action she performed would be blessed. It was her cousin, who knew how cautiously a woman must proceed, who kept her throne and died in her bed. Whether by luck or tactic Elizabeth was cold, and her virginity was negotiable. When it became necessary, she signed the death warrants.

Who set the trap? Who sprang it? It's possible that my plotting was like that of Mary Stuart, busy and futile. The obfuscating, delaying, indecisive cousin won out. I sit here in the first hours of the new year, telling my story to you, who already know it as another and different story, yours. Perhaps I am not the spider spinning but the web being spun, the creation, not the creator, and I have a sudden vertiginous moment of helplessness, unable to breathe, as if all the complex inner occupations of the body, the soft systems of flow and return, declared their power, their triumph over me. The events of the committee meeting, when I was for the first time interviewed; I wore a suit with a small black and grey check, and a pale grey sweater, tight enough to outline the lovely shape of my breasts, but not tight enough to appear cheap – women must be so careful – and you sat on the far side of the table, affecting to be reticent, untouchable, all the while planning the enticement, a second's glance stripping me naked as you were plotting to have me – meek, helpless. You read on my face my willingness. Had the *belle-mère* brought me to you as a rat is thrown to a caged eagle? The cup of coffee she put in my hand contained the love-potion. She had lost you, but she could continue the enthrallment through me. It was my heart that was to be eaten.

Prisoners. We are all held captive, Mary Stuart in an English castle, her cousin in her masque of royalty. The detective solves only the crime that has been presented for him to solve. That is what books and movies and TV shows are all about, the illusion of meaning. In truth there are many answers to any good question. Who killed Cock Robin? The whole of creation.

Not my words: there is no such category in this archive. I am taking the dictation of some night voice invading from the past or the future. And something in the dark brain insists it is my mother's voice, even though I have no memory of any such dark sayings from her. Of course I was a child, and understood as a child, and she would never have told me her most serious thoughts. If she spoke about the universe, she would not have directed the words to the understanding of little B. Our parents fail us in this way, by keeping us safe from the vertiginous complexity of their most wonderful thoughts. My job is not to enlarge the range of speculation, but to create order, to place what has gone before in clear and consistent categories so that access to all we've saved is easy. I am an archivist. I clear the path to the desired information.

Morning is coming toward us across the world, the bland sanity of daylight into which you will vanish like all my memories. On top of my filing cabinet in a wooden tray is a letter from a large textile museum asking about material they are seeking for a planned exhibition. I might turn my chair to the computer keyboard and draft an answer. I have already sorted through the catalogue and made a list of possibilities.

Though it is early and still dark, the lacemaker is already at work, and her time is not the time of a clock but is measured out by her quick needle as it draws the thread over and over again, ten stitches, a hundred, a thousand, an inch of work accomplished, an eternity of wasted life to produce the flounce of a wide collar. As worn by Voltaire, Pompadour, the King himself. She bends toward the candle to see that each detail is perfect. Back and forth, her needle makes patterns in the air. In the previous century she mastered embroidery. In a future century she will learn knitting. When I go home I will attend to my household duties, sleep, perhaps phone G. later in the day. I won't talk for long. I sense that the newest husband resents my calls, especially if we fall into old joking ways and start to giggle. He is younger than she is, and very handsome, G. says. I have never seen him.

I might put on the white gloves, turn more pages of the recipe book, searching out the clues, but you would not care to hear them. You have your own stories to tell, the adventures of your doctor-detective, the villainess who appears, unexpectedly, wherever he goes, a figure in the hospital corridor, or at the health club where he works out, a woman in grey sweats lifting weights and then appearing at the pool, a naked figure blurred by the plastic goggles he wears. He wonders what it is she wants from him. To lead him to destruction, an assignation at a cheap motel where the police arrest him, and later, when he seeks her apartment, he is struck on the head, knocked unconscious. 'The Nervous System', that chapter is called. She is the embodiment of arcane knowledge, what must not be revealed. It was clever of you to have Jenny F. give me that book, to taunt me with your triumph.

I returned the recipe book to its place on the shelf. To write about it, I would need to search all the other handwritten collections to see if they have stories to tell, a few mysteries, clippings about whales beaching themselves on a distant island, a soldier appearing out of the jungle, a woman who left her fortune to a bird. 'The Nervous System'. I looked about me as I stood in front of the bookshelves, cases of stored material on all sides, and it no longer cried out to be seen. We are going through the woods, and it is spring, and you lay me down on the wet ground with the mud and roots, open me slowly like one of the buds on the tree above us, everything damp and swollen with the annual germination. I can no more resist you than the earth can resist the lengthening light. I have invented you for this moment. I will go away, and when I return your absence will be all I know. I can write no more of this. Time to fold it up and put it in its envelope. Soon it will be daylight, and I will set the alarms for the building, slip on my dark overcoat, wrap the white cashmere scarf around my neck and set out to walk to my apartment, the prints of my little boots in the snow behind me, a trail easy to follow for anyone who might wish to track me. The January sunlight, reflected from the white crystalline surface of the snow, will be bright. As I walk through it I am scandalously beautiful.

Housebound, 1969

Arrived back out of chill and bitter dreams, he lay in the upstairs bedroom of an old house on an island in winter. Cold. Cold. Cold. Like some terrible Arctic myth, a man alone and helpless. Wind coming off the frozen river half a mile to the south, the Seaway shut down for the season. The man tugged the covers over his head and pulled up his knees, his body a tight ball, conserving its heat. If he uncovered his head, he thought ice might form around his mouth, breath hardening to frost. Who is he? Let's call him Wicker. Nicknames appear and stick. Wicker knew he should go down and light a fire in the kitchen stove but it was too much for him. It was all, every bit of it, too much for him. Looked toward the back window. Why was he awake? It was still almost dark. Light a fire, feed the three-legged dog, attend to the blind pony; the little cast of characters that shared his life here. There was a story his kindergarten teacher once told him about a bunch of old and crippled animals who decided to become musicians. He couldn't remember much of it. That was when he first started school, when they still liked him, before they found out that he was a criminal. Maybe, Wicker thought, he'd be as well off to sleep out in the shed, cover himself with hay, get the dog to lie down with him. He would have taken the dog into the bed to help keep him warm, but the creature was afraid to come into the house. Each day he called and petted it, even tried to drag it in, but he never could. Albie or somebody had terrorized it. Wicker hadn't figured out where the dog slept, in the shed or out in the woods with the coyotes, but when he went to the door in the morning it was waiting by the back stairs and it gobbled the dog food he put in the bowl. Priss and Albie hadn't told him the dog's name, just told him to feed it once a day, it and the pony, and to shovel the manure out of the pony's stall into a heap beside the spot where Priss planned to grow potatoes in the summer.

So the dog he called Three Legs and the pony he called Pony. What they'd left him with as they set off for Florida. Priss was a volunteer with the E. Fry in Kingston, helping out some girl Albie once knew in Toronto, and Albie had just made parole, and somehow he and Priss met up, and Albie convinced her to buy this old house on the island and fix it up, but first they decided to go someplace warm for a couple of months. When Priss and Albie made an offer of the house, rent-free, Wicker thought it was a pretty good deal, but now he wasn't so sure. He forgot to ask them before they left about the oil space heater that sat downstairs near the front window, and he figured if he tried to start a fire in it, it might explode – he'd heard they were dangerous things – and anyway he couldn't figure out how to turn it on. There wasn't any switch, just a little spigot. He figured it was better to freeze than burn. The pile of wood for the stove in the kitchen was mostly crooked-looking chunks, too big to burn, and every time he swung the axe to split one, the blade bounced off a knot, or he missed altogether and slashed the earth close to his toes. At night he dreamed about bleeding to death out there in the yard, a toe lying raw on the surface of the snow, surrounded by frozen balls of horse manure. Faced with all this he remembered how warm it was in his prison cell, three meals a day, and he wondered if he should get himself arrested and sent back. Wouldn't take much to convince his parole officer. He was free now, could do what he wanted, but he was miles from the store, and he didn't have money anyway, and the doors and windows of the old house let in the bitter wind, and it would be winter for a long time yet.

A man should try to think of ways to get out of the cold. Join the American army, if they'd take him, and get sent to Vietnam. The Vietcong hid out in the jungle; if they had jungles it must be warm. He wore a steel helmet and slowly put one foot in front of the other, his rifle pointed ahead into the green canopy of leaves. Snakes. In jungles they had snakes. And the Marines shaved off all your hair. Since he got out of prison he'd been letting his hair grow, he liked it long. The Marines made you run and climb and plough through ditches.

Wicker lay curled up and shivering for a while and then, in a kind of desperation, threw back the covers and jumped out of bed. The cold air burnt his skin, and he was shaking almost too hard to get his clothes on. His last clean pair of underpants, a T-shirt, then his shirt, two pairs of pants, one on top of the other, socks pulled up over the inside pair to keep the air out, another T-shirt over the shirt, fitted too big but good for this, Albie's probably, found in a closet, and then a heavy knitted sweater he'd found in a drawer, and his coat on top of that, gloves, a hole in the right thumb. On the bedroom wall was a long-out-of-date calendar with a drawing of one of those pin-up girls, wearing high heels and tiny shorts and leaning forward to put gas in a big old-fashioned car that was sitting at the pumps. Old gravity-feed pump. She wore a tight blouse that showed the shape of her titties. What they put on girly calendars before women started showing everything for *Playboy* and *Penthouse*.

Wicker headed downstairs. When he got to the kitchen the sun had just begun to appear over the horizon. He looked at the pile of wood by the stove, no kindling chopped, so he shoved in some news-paper and lit it, knowing it wouldn't make enough heat to warm anything. He'd split kindling. Cut off his toe. He was hungry, picked up a piece of stale bread out of the package and bit off a piece.

This was the mess he was in. He had a couple of slices of bread left, nothing to put on them. He took another look in the cupboard by the kitchen window and saw a plastic container of ketchup. Probably frozen, but he unscrewed the top and stuck a knife into it, got a dollop on the knife and spread it on his piece of stale bread. He was hungry enough that it tasted pretty good.

He grabbed one of the bags of dog food they'd left him and dragged it to the kitchen door. The sky was getting light, and Three Legs was curled up on the snow at the foot of the stairs. When he heard the door opening, he jumped up and started to wag his tail. He was an unmatched sort of dog, the front end with more fur than the back, his remaining legs – one missing in front – too short for the length of the body, a wild look in the eyes as if some coyote ancestor lurked there, ready to snarl and attack, but the beast cowered as it waited to be fed. Wicker filled the dish with the dry lumps of food, and the dog scoffed it down.

Wicker shoved the bag of dog food back in the house and crossed the yard to the shed with its one stall. The pony had just dropped a load, and the turds were still steaming in the cold. He shovelled them up and threw them on the manure pile, then set the shovel by the door, and lifted up one of the bales of hay, cut the strings and grabbed some of it in his gloved hands, took it into the stall and set it in the manger at the front of the stall. The pony pushed its side against him. He wasn't sure whether the creature was being friendly or trying to push him away from the hay. It snuffed, took a mouthful and shook its head as it began to chew. He was supposed to give the thing oats twice a week, but he could never remember when he'd done it last; he took a coffee tin and filled it from the oat sack and put the oats in the tin trough at the end of the manger. The pony smelled them and began to suck them up with his wide lips. Have to bring out some water.

Wicker wondered whether the pony noticed the cold. It seemed to have a thick growth of hair, as if Nature had got it ready for the winter. Better than Nature did for men and woman, left them naked in every season, scrabbling for something thick and warm to cover themselves. As he was about to close the shed door, he noticed the broken chair lying beside it, an old wooden chair painted blue. Wicker picked it up as he went out, latching the door behind him and carried it over to the woodpile, beside it the stump he used for a chopping block. He set the broken chair on the block. There was a chip out of the blade of the axe. Wicker took the axe in his two hands and gave a swing at the chair. The blow glanced off the seat but didn't break it. The axe never did what he expected. Maybe it was the chipped blade. The chair would make good kindling if he could get it smashed small enough. He'd noticed it in the shed before, lying in a corner, but it was only this morning he realized that it would be pretty easy to break up and burn. If he could chop it to bits without killing himself. He'd never swung an axe before he came to the island. There wasn't a lot of wood-chopping around the east end of Toronto. He put down the axe, took the legs of the chair in both hands and smashed it down on the chopping block. The top of the chair back came loose and slithered across the snow. He picked it up and snapped off the two rungs that were attached. He held one of them across the block with his left hand and took the axe in his right to chop it in half. Half of it broke off and flew into his face, caught him across the cheek. It stung, and he put his fingers against it to see if he was bleeding. The other chair-rung; he laid it across the block and stood well back as he swung. The two ends flew into the air, but neither of them got him. He kept smashing and chopping at the chair until he had it reduced to a pile of kindling, enough for two days if he was lucky. Then he searched the pile of wood for a chunk that looked as if it might split and set it on the block. He stood still, gathering his forces. Then he gave the axe a mighty wheel over his head. Missed the piece of wood and it stuck into the chopping block. Cursed while he tried to pry it out, but the next time he swung the axe, it hit the target, and the length of wood flew apart into two halves. Before long he'd have enough wood to get the fire going, and once it was started he might be able to burn some of the blocks that wouldn't split.

Wicker was almost warm after swinging the axe. He could hear the blind pony crunching his oats. People ate oats too. Porridge was made out of oats, he remembered that. He'd boil up some of those oats on the little two-burner hotplate. Only one burner worked, but it might keep them hot enough. He thought there was molasses in the cupboard. Boil them with water and molasses until they were soft and mushy and he could probably get them down. It was starting to snow.

2

Morning again. Cold again. The kindling made from the bits of the broken chair was gone. Chop up the shed. Dry enough to burn. Move the pony into the house. Wicker jumped out of bed and started putting on clothes. Outside the clouds were low and dark, as if it might start to snow any minute. Just like every other day, he took food out to the dog, and walked through the new snow to the shed. Before he fed the pony, he clipped leather reins on the bridle and led the animal outdoors. There was no enclosed paddock for the creature, so once or twice a week Wicker would walk it a hundred feet up the road and then back. The dog followed them, keeping a bit of distance from the pony's hooves, as if it might have been kicked once or twice. On the way back Wicker started to run and the pony trotted happily along at his side. Back in the shed, he stroked its neck, which quivered under his touch, and led it back into the stall. It seemed able to find its way without stumbling into walls, though Albie had sworn it couldn't see a thing.

'Later on,' he said to the pony, 'maybe I'll get on your back, and we'll go for a ride.' There was no saddle, but the pony was pretty low to the ground, and he thought he could probably stay on. There was a dirty old blanket hanging on a nail. He tossed the pony some hay and filled its water pail. Outside the shed, the dog waited for him, sitting on its haunches, its front end supported by its one leg. It walked with a rackety bounce, but still it moved at a pretty good speed. He bent down to pat the dog, which cowered a little, but stayed in its place and moved its head to rub against the hand petting it. He ruffled the fur on its neck. If it wasn't so damn cold, and if he had a bit of money, Wicker would have liked it here with his little zoo of cripples. A blind pony and a three-legged dog. All he needed now was a one-eyed chicken, but if he had that chicken he'd have eaten it by now. He went to the door and tried to get the dog to come in the house with him, but it was still unwilling.

'It's gonna snow like a bugger out there,' he told the dog. 'You'd be better to come in the house.' For the first time Wicker noticed a loose board on the side of the shed. Maybe the dog slid in under that and spent the night in the shed with the pony. Out of the snow and wind. He hoped so. Maybe he should pull the board off farther. He hated to think of the dog out there in the blizzard. Too stupid to know who to trust.

Back in the house he turned on the radio. They were playing some song by Joni Mitchell. He didn't like Joni Mitchell. Not his kind of girl. Then they talked about the bad weather coming and put on Gordon Lightfoot. Better. Wicker searched for something to eat. The last of the oat porridge was beginning to harden in the bottom of a pan. He found a wooden spoon and pried off a couple of lumps and chewed at them. Like rubber. It took a long time to cook oats down into this mush. He could do it again, but without the molasses he wasn't sure he could eat it.

He looked out the window. Something he remembered his grand-mother saying when the snow was falling. *Look at the white walkers comin' to get us. Just like the old days in the country.* Then after she said that she'd give a little chuckle and light up a cigarette, sit staring out the window, smoke pouring out of her nostrils, the cigarette held in nicotine-stained fingers. That was when his mother was working, and he hadn't yet started school, so his grandmother took care of him. It was OK until afternoon when the sherry began to get the better of her and sometimes she'd fall down. Wicker stared into the white pattern of the snow and thought of the white walkers coming across the flat land, maybe to do him damage. You could never be sure. Wicker knew what he was going to do today. He didn't let on, even to himself, but he knew. Even as he started to get ready, he pretended that he wasn't sure, that he was just thinking about it. He didn't have snow boots, but he got out the old rubber boots he'd found. First he put on another pair of socks, and then he wrapped his feet in two layers of newspaper, and tied string around the top, and carefully, not to tear the paper, he put on the high rubber boots. Better than street shoes. Garbage bags under the sink, and he took one out and with a little serrated knife, he cut holes for his arms and head and put it on, then tied string around the middle to hold it tight and put his coat back on over top. The coat wasn't actually his, but he found it in a cupboard, and even though it was stained and ripped, it was warmer than his jacket. In the drawer in the kitchen he found the big screwdriver and a pair of Vise-Grips and put them in the pocket of his coat. Then he tied more string around his waist, to try to keep the wind from blowing up under the coat. From under the sink he took two more garbage bags, put them into the pocket with the string.

It was always the same. He never let himself know. It was a kind of superstition. If you let yourself think about the crime, the thought would get out into the universe, and someone would pick it up. Words and thoughts flew around like that. From mind to mind, invisible but powerful. If you didn't want anyone to know, you didn't dare tell yourself.

He didn't have a scarf, but he found a towel and tied that around his neck and buttoned the coat over top of it. The only hat he owned was a baseball cap, so that would have to do. Freeze his damn ears. He turned off the radio, but then he turned it back on again, louder, a kind of beacon to guide him.

No matter what he brought back with him, he was going to need kindling or he'd die of the cold. By one of the chairs was an old wooden apple box full of magazines. He dumped them out onto the floor. One of them was an old Playboy, open at the centrefold, big buttery knobs. He had no time for that. He left the apple box beside the stove, and before he left brought the axe into the house. It was snowing harder now. Better to do it on a day like this, invisible, so long as he didn't die in the storm. When he got back he could chop the box into kindling right there beside the stove.

Outside the back door, the wind was driving snow across the yard. The dog stood by the edge of the shed, watching him, as if he was puzzled about what this crazy human was going to do now. Dogs had more sense. But dogs got a plate of food set out for them every day. Wicker brought the pony out of the shed, laid the blanket over its back and tried to get on. The first time the blanket started to slide and he fell off the other side, as the pony, spooked by this strange behaviour, pulled away, but he still had hold of the reins, and he drew the animal back, tied it to the hook on the shed and went to the woodpile and got the stump he used for chopping. He led the pony close by, and the poor blind beast nearly walked headlong into the stump. The dog had skittered away when Wicker fell, and now it stood observing again, its front quarters lowered as if about to run. Wicker got the pony settled beside the stump, spread the blanket and put string twice around the pony's gut to hold it in place. Then he climbed on the stump and lowered his right leg over the pony's back, set himself slowly in place and tightened his legs to take hold of the round barrel of the ribs. He sat there, and the snow blew in his face. With one hand he pulled his cap down.

It might be smarter just to walk, but coming back, or so he hoped, his bags would be full, and it was a long way to go, carrying his bags of loot. He pulled the reins around to the left, away from the stump, and he made a clicking sound with his mouth, like he'd seen in a movie somewhere, and bounced a little to encourage the pony to go, and it began to walk north up the road. He held the reins straight and tried to keep his legs tight so he didn't slide off again, then he gave a shake of the reins and the pony began to walk placidly forward into the blowing snow. To keep track of the road Wicker watched the ditches on each side as they pony carried him along. The dog was bouncing beside them with its awkward but efficient three-legged gait. Quite a little circus, riding off into the blizzard. Just like the story his kindergarten teacher told him.

3

The porch door at the back of the house was padlocked. The wind-driven snow was sweeping past so he was almost blinded by it; he reached into his pocket and found the screwdriver, attempted to force it down behind the hasp. Gloves made his hands awkward, and he couldn't get the steel point behind the plate, which was tight to the wood of the door. The cold was painful where it penetrated the hole in his right glove. His ears were stinging. He remembered a glass pane in the front door. Smash it and reach through, but anyone driving by would see it. He believed that this house was empty, used only in the summer, and that his break-in wouldn't be discovered until the good weather, and by then he'd be long gone.

The pony was tied to a tree a few feet behind him, the dog curled in the shelter of a bush nearby. Stupid dog should have stayed home, but it trotted behind him all the way even though the snow was so thick Wicker could hardly see the dumb bugger bouncing along. He took the Vise-Grips out of his pocket and pounded the handle of the screwdriver with them, and he got the point in maybe a quarter of an inch. He tried to pry, but it pulled loose. He needed a hammer. Desperately he pounded with the Vise-Grips, once banging his finger against the wood of the door. The screwdriver was penetrating, but not far enough. The screws in the padlock hasp had been well driven in. If he stood out here much longer he would start to freeze. His face was stinging, and he was afraid of frostbite. He'd heard a story in school once, about a trapper freezing to death in the Arctic. As he stopped for a minute to get his breath, looked down, panting, he saw that the earth on one side of the door had blown clear, the snow drifted up against the corner of the house just beyond. There was a little circle of rocks. Some kind of garden. He grabbed one of the rocks, but they were frozen into the ground. He tried the screwdriver, first driving it with the edge of the Vise-Grips, which were ready to come apart, the rivets loose from all his battering, then kicking the handle with the bottom of his boot. He got the steel point a little way into the soil and pried, and the rock came loose. The wonky Vise-Grips back in his coat pocket, he went at the door with the screwdriver and the rock. Mashed his finger, cursed. But he began to get the tool behind the hasp. He bashed it until he had it through to the bottom. The handle of the screwdriver was pressed tight against the wood of the door, but he used the Vise-Grips to help get his fingers behind and around it, and he pulled back, using both hands and the weight of his body. When it finally gave, he pitched backward and fell into the snow. He dragged the hasp out of his way and pulled the door open, got inside. Waited, silent, just in case someone was there. No sound. The house was dim, the light of day veiled by the blizzard outside, but he could see the kitchen ahead of him, cupboards and a refrigerator. He hoped they'd left something. The refrigerator door was propped open, and the shelves were bare. He tried a light switch. Nothing. The power was off.

He opened a cupboard door. If it was empty he would scream and smash and burn the place down.

Cans of stuff. He took out his plastic bag and began to load them in. Packages of cereal. Some Kraft dinner. Envelopes of soup. It made him feel good just thinking about a pot of soup warming on the hotplate. Candies. He put one in his mouth. So good. A bag of flour, but he left that. Didn't know how to bake anything. Tinned meat. They were all set for an emergency here. Well, this was an emergency all right. Wicker was close to starved. Matches, candles. Took those too.

When he'd emptied everything he wanted out of the cupboard, he took a look around the rest of the house. He wondered if he might find money, but he didn't think there was much chance. In the front room there was a little dish, like an ash tray, with two quarters in it, and he took those. Better than nothing. There was a television, a couple of radios, stuff he could sell if he could get it to town, but he couldn't see any way to do that, so he left them. He didn't break anything. Guys he'd worked with liked to break things, leave the house a mess, but Wicker couldn't see the point. He wasn't mad at these people. In fact he felt good about them since he found all that food, as if he might leave them a note, Thanks, I was damn near starved.

In a kitchen drawer he found a hammer. Too late now. Poking around in the drawer, underneath some packages of screws and a couple of maps, he found a small plastic bag. He held it up and looked at the material inside. Maybe he'd struck it lucky again. He opened and took a sniff.

'Very nice,' he said. 'A little dope for Wicker.'

Wicker considered himself pretty damn lucky to find the marijuana. He pushed the little plastic bag to the bottom of the left pocket of the jacket. There was a rip in the lining, and he slid it inside, make sure it didn't fall out. He thought of lying down on the couch for a few minutes, get rested up for the trip back, but he figured if he left the pony much longer it might vanish into a drift. He distributed his loot between the two plastic bags and tied them together at the top and hung them over his shoulders. They got in the way of his arms. He'd hang them over the pony.

He could hear the wind screaming through the trees near the house. It was getting stronger all the time. When he went out the back door he couldn't see more than six feet, but he pulled the door shut behind him and walked in the direction of the fence where he'd tied the pony. One of his boots felt uncomfortable, something he'd done when he was trying to kick the screwdriver under the rock. The pony had turned its back to the wind. The dog got up from the snow and gave itself a shake – not easy on three legs. The blanket had slid to one side, so he pulled it back into place, put his two bags over the pony, and led it along the side of the house to where he knew the road must be. They floundered in the deep snow that had drifted into the ditch, but got up to a flat surface that must be the road.

One advantage of this weather, no one was likely going to come along and find him. Remembering the earlier struggle to get on the pony's back, he regretted that he didn't have anything like the chopping block here to help him. When he'd patted the little horse's neck to reassure the animal that everything was OK, he lifted his leg as high as he could and slid himself over the rump and into place. He didn't think he'd fall off, if he kept his legs tightly locked against the sides. They were pointed in what he thought was the right direction. You heard stories about how horses would find their way back home. He wasn't sure if that went for blind horses, but he hoped so.

'All right, Pony,' he said, 'giddyup.'

He shook the reins and the horse walked forward. Wicker tried to watch to each side, see if he could make out a fence or ditch so he could tell they were still on the road, but he couldn't see much. They had a mile and a half to go. Maybe he should have waited at that house until the storm eased, but it could be hours yet. The dog trotted awkwardly along, closer to the horse now so as not to lose sight of them. The wind seemed to be coming from straight head, and Wicker turned his cap backward so the wind didn't catch the brim and blow it away. It was harder on his face, but better than losing the cap altogether. He bent forward to shelter his face from the storm. Wished to hell he had earmuffs. Put up his hands to cover his frozen ears, and almost fell off the pony.

He wondered if the pony was taking them back or just walking at random. It must be too smart for that. Who ever said a pony was smart? If Wicker got off he could lead the way, but he had to confess that in the swirling snow he didn't know where to lead. He patted the pony's thick neck and made friendly sounds. Maybe if the pony got lost

122

the dog would lead them back to the house. Dogs were smart. They had instinct. Wicker tried to think of something cheerful, to keep him going, to take his mind off the cold. The laundromat. That's what he used to think about in prison, how maybe one day he'd own a little laundromat, a warm and friendly place where people would drop in and talk while their laundry was in the machines. They'd call him Winston, which was his real name, and he'd hand out the change and make sure all the machines worked properly. He'd never save up the money for that, but it was a nice thought.

You could die in a storm like this. Read in the newspaper about a man who set out to walk three blocks home and never made it. His head was aching from the cold wind. He put his glove over his face to shelter it. Thought he was so lucky, finding all those groceries, but now he figured his luck was getting thin. Wished he had another of those candies in his mouth. The wind was loud and crazy, wailing. Voices. Other people. They were out there in the storm, the voices. He put both hands over his face and closed his eyes. He could see a little girl lying in a cot, her face so white he knew that she must be dead, and he was afraid that she was in the attic of the house waiting for him to come back so she could haunt him. She had died in the blizzard, and he would have to bury her in the frozen ground. The voices wouldn't stop. He could hear her, almost see her, a woman crying, and a man, he was crying too. A winter night, and they were cut off by the storm, and their baby had died, no way to get help. Wicker couldn't help them. And he couldn't stand listening to the crying, so loud all around him.

'Stop it,' he said. 'Stop crying. Please stop crying.'

4

Wicker stumbled in through the kitchen door and dropped his two plastic bags. Snow blew in behind him, and as he was about to close the door he noticed the dog standing in the blizzard, watching him. Wicker stood back and opened the door wide, said something encouraging, and the dog slunk in, then went to a corner of the room and curled himself up on the floor. After following the pony through the wind and snow, he was more scared of the storm than of being in here.

'You're right, old Three Legs, we don't want to be anywhere near that snow for a while.'

Wicker took off the rubber boots, tore open one of the plastic bags, found the candies and shoved a couple in his mouth. His face burned, and he thought his ears were frozen solid and was afraid to touch them. There was something you were supposed to do for frostbite, but he couldn't remember what it was. Rub it with snow or something. He put his hands on his ears, to try to warm them up a bit. The house was cold, but at least there was no wind and snow. Five minutes ago he thought he was on his way out, couldn't see a thing, and the pony stopped dead, wouldn't go another step. Wicker figured it was time to say his prayers, if he could think of any, then the wind changed direction for a few seconds, and he realized that the blind pony had stopped because they were back, ten feet from the shed. He'd found his way through the storm. Animals were so smart. Wicker let out a whoop of joy, then slid off the little horse's back, parked his bags of loot and led the pony over to the shed. Snow was drifted high against the door, and at first he couldn't get it open, but he kicked the snow away, then scooped it with his hands, stiff and frozen as they were, and he got the door open far enough to lead the pony inside, and into the stall. It was pretty dim, but he could see just enough to wipe the snow off the animal with an old rag he found hanging there, and he gave it some hay and a can of oats.

'You saved my life, Pony,' he said. Then he closed the door, picked up his bags out of the snow, and tried to calculate the direction to the house. The blizzard and drifting made it almost impossible to walk the few feet to the door. He fell once, thought he'd never get up, but staggered to his feet and finally came to the wall of the house, felt his way along it until he found the back door.

He was alive, and the sweetness of the candies seemed to be warming him a little. Took the axe to the wooden box. He smashed it and smashed it until it was fragments of kindling, then put them in the stove. He was getting better at starting fires, and this one caught, though the wood he had chopped was still thick chunks. He swung the axe at one of them, and it split. The axe left a dent in the floor. Once he'd burned what was lying by the stove he'd be in trouble. He wasn't sure he could find his way to the woodpile in the blizzard, and he sure as hell couldn't chop wood out there.

The radio was playing the Doors, 'Light My Fire.' That made him laugh as he listened to the crackling of the kindling in the stove. He looked around the room to see if there was anything else he could burn. A twisted piece of driftwood on top of the coffee table shiny with shellac. He didn't know why he hadn't thought of that before.

He dragged his bags over to the kitchen counter and took out all the stuff he'd stolen, setting the tins in rows, the cardboard boxes beside them. Time for a big meal, chicken soup from one of the envelopes, a tin of spaghetti with some sliced corn beef from one of the other cans. He turned on the tap by the sink, and the water ran. He kept expecting it to freeze, but so far it hadn't. He left it dripping all night long; heard somewhere that was what you were supposed to do. He mixed up water and the soup mix and put the pan on the burner of the hotplate, so starved that it was hard to wait for it to get warm, but if he drank it good and hot it would take some of the chill out of his body. He wasn't going to die, not today anyway.

While he waited for it to heat, he went and got the piece of driftwood and broke it in half against the edge of the kitchen counter. When he put it in the stove, the flames licked hungrily around it.

Heat, food, life.

From his pocket he took the little plastic baggie of marijuana. Not for now, he thought. He'd drink the soup and then wrap himself up and see if he could get an armful of wood from the pile before the snow got any deeper. After that he'd heat the spaghetti and corned beef, then maybe roll up a spliff.

Then Wicker had a brilliant idea. Yeah, right, a good one. He'd have that one little smoke, or maybe half of it, and when the weather broke he'd get himself down to the ferry. Over in the city he could sell the rest of the dope and get a few dollars to keep him going. He'd like to smoke it all, but he needed the money more than the high.

The dog was watching him from the corner. He took out one of the candies and tossed it to the animal.

'You like sweet things?' he said.

The dog didn't look too sure, but he sniffed the candy and then crunched it between his teeth, his head bent up at a funny angle to get a good grip on it.

'We're doing OK, fella,' Wicker said to the dog. 'We're doing right OK.'

Wicker woke in the night hearing noises from downstairs. It was pitch dark in the bedroom. He reached out his arm and felt the fur of the dog lying beside him. The creature's skin quivered when it felt his touch. Dim light appeared beyond the bedroom door. Someone had switched on a bulb downstairs. Wicker figured it must be the cops come for him. Better get up and stand on his feet to be arrested. He reminded himself that it was warm in prison – break and enter, one count – theft under five hundred, one count. He'd be slapped back in for parole violation, maybe pick up eighteen months or two years. He climbed from bed, pulled on a pair of trousers, a shirt, a pair of shoes. It wasn't as cold the last couple of days. Cold enough in here, but not so deathly bad. Maybe it was having regular meals since he stole that food. Soup, tinned meat, a can of spaghetti. The thought of it made him hungry.

The dog climbed off the bed, a dim shape in the little bit of illumination from below. Stood beside him. Waiting.

'OK,' he mumbled. 'Let's go.' He wondered who would look after the dog and the pony after the cops took him in. Tell them that the animals belonged to Priss. She was a straight-arrow. The cops couldn't just ignore them. Though that was one of their specialties, in Wicker's experience, saying it's none of our business and leaving someone else to clean up the mess.

He was three steps down the stairs, the dog standing at the top waiting, when he heard the back door, then a voice mumbling. Cops didn't mumble like that when they came to arrest you. Cops shouted and gave orders. He came down the rest of the stairs and looked toward the mumbling.

'Priss?'

'Yes, it's me.'

'Where's Albie?'

'In jail where he belongs.'

Expecting to be banged up for burglary, then finding Priss here on her own, Wicker was stumped. Didn't have a word to say.

'What in hell is this axe doing in the middle of the kitchen floor?'

'I was chopping kindling.'

'On the kitchen floor?'

'There was a blizzard. You don't know how cold it was here.'

'What's that dog doing in the house?'

'I told you there was a big snowstorm. I was half frozen. The goddam wind comes right through the walls here. Helped me to keep warm.'

'How?'

'In bed mostly.'

'You been sleeping with the dog?'

'Sort of.'

'So now the house is full of fleas.'

'It's too cold for fleas.'

Small as she was, Priss scared hell out of him.

'You said Albie's in jail.'

'Florida. Getting his butt fucked by a dozen big bad dudes I hope.'

'Why's he in jail?'

'Because he's a criminal.'

'They have to charge you with something.'

'Conning the old retired people in the trailer park. Told them about some investment scheme. You probably know all about it.'

'No.' Wicker knew it was the safest thing to say. He remembered Albie in the joint talking about how easy it was, when you found a beaver, to get them to part with their money.

'I don't know what kind of idiot he thought I was. It took me about a week to figure it out.'

'I guess he needed money.'

'I guess he did. Some people get jobs.'

'I think he really liked you, Priss.'

'He liked me as long as I had money.'

'He thought you were pretty. I heard him say so.'

'There was only one good thing about Albie, and that wasn't enough.'

Wicker couldn't think of anything to say.

'So you drove all the way back.'

'I drove all the way back, hardly stopped to sleep, and I dropped off the trailer at the rental and caught the last ferry over.'

'I didn't hear the car.'

'Left it further up the road, where they'd ploughed it wide enough to turn around.'

Wicker looked at her. Her eyes were darkly shadowed, the lashes clumped with mascara, and she looked exhausted.

'Why's it so cold in here?' she said.

'Because it's winter. The wind comes in the windows.'

'Yeah. Albie was going to renovate it. That's why I bought it. She paused and thought about it. 'Wicker, when it comes right down to it, I'm no smarter than you are.'

'That's too bad.'

'Why don't you have the space heater on?'

'I didn't know how. I couldn't figure it out. I thought maybe it was broken. And I couldn't find the oil.'

'Maybe I'm a little smarter after all. The oil's in a tank right outside. You just open the valve and light it up. You got anything to eat here?'

'A few tins.'

She opened the cupboard door.

'I don't want any of that. What about coffee?'

'I ran out.'

'Of course you ran out.'

'Well, I don't have a car, and it was too cold to walk to the store, and I don't have any money.'

'How in hell did Albie think you were going to look after this place? Oh, I know. He didn't care. I had the money to rent the trailer and take him to Florida, and I was too stupid to ask questions.'

'Everything's OK here. The dog and the horse are just fine.'

'Albie's three-legged dog and his blind pony. I thought it was kind of cute the way he kept bringing home these crippled animals. Big-hearted, I thought. What a joke.'

She was shivering.

'Oh hell,' she said. 'I'm too tired to light the space heater. Let's just all get in the bed, you and me and the dog. Maybe I'll get warm enough to sleep. But don't you put a finger on me or I'll break it.'

So they tramped up the stairs, took off their shoes and got under the covers, and the dog curled up on top.

'So what are you going to do next?' Priss said.

'I thought I might join up with the American army. Go to Vietnam.'

'No, don't do that, Wicker. That wouldn't be cool.'

So they talked a little longer, and then they slept. When Wicker woke sometime in the night he found that Priss was cuddled up against him for warmth, the dog on the other side, and he thought this was not bad at all, though he knew it would never last.

An Act of Oblivion

So there was Leah, my second wife, in bed with me and snoring. Since we had been divorced for years, the noise might have been regarded as an imposition. The next day she was to fly back to California. Ours was a short marriage, not exactly unhappy, an attempt to turn an old friendship into something more, an attempt which didn't take. My fault mostly. When she arrived at my door, Leah brought California wine and Greek olives, and no sooner was she in my apartment than she began, as is her way, to flay the world with the verve of Thersites. I think we began with her students, for she had tired of being a feminist saint, of finding girls-as-fresh-as-dew-on-the-grass waiting on her front steps, eager to climb into her bed. Wasn't a lesbian and no longer thought she had a feminist duty to be, and while she was happy to put up with the young for a required number of hours a week, that was about enough. On the other hand. Men. Even apart from me as a bad example. I had never been told before the extent of her grudge against Ben, that she was one of his cast-offs. In his travels, she was a minor destination. Ben was the same with Philip Leigh in the early days, she says, allowing himself to be adored and served, or so Leah would have it, herself expressing some mixture of guilt and affection for Philip who could never decide who or what he was, a worrier, an occasional and incompetent lover when they were in their London days, given to drunken tears over Ben, guilty trips to gay clubs, and she unsatisfied and always cruel, hard on him, frustrated and angry. As for my own stupidity, it was beyond all bearing. Our marriage had no chance because I was still mooning over dear dead Brenda. From the beginning, of course, all my friends recognized Brenda's destructive nature, the way she dramatized herself because she was empty, made scenes because she could make nothing else, but it was clear that I, the dimwit, found it exciting, and there was nothing for them to do but watch me make my mistakes. *She was really a very stupid woman, you know. She didn't even pretend not to be. Stupid, really, stupid, stupid. An actress, vapid, and a bad actress at that.* From there we went on to excoriate other friends and acquaintances, some of them unknown to me. After that she trashed herself, she like all the rest of us scoured with the lye of harsh words until my turn came again and I thought I must know how the skin felt after a sauna, whipping with twigs and immersion in ice water.

The sight of her at the door: we are, of course, no longer young, and the face loses all easy softness. The long jaw and buckteeth, especially when she smiled, and she was smiling. Wrinkles of course. I was gladdened by the sight of her, and she pushed her way in. She didn't have that many old friends left, and she'd take no crap from them. That bloody fool Philip who had neither the wit nor the courage to come out of the closet and minged around with his tail between his legs when he should have had it between someone else's. And now he was dead. By now she was in the kitchen opening the wine and pouring it into tumblers, giving me one and taking a good swig from her own, as I tried to explain that I hadn't been drinking. *Is this another belated tribute to dear dead Brenda? That stupid cunt. I don't really care, old pal. Guilt sucks. I want company. Just drink the wine.* She took another gulp of the wine and so did I, and it was dark and tannic and rich in the mouth, and I was about to put out my glass to toast our meeting when I noticed a tear running down her face, and there was nothing to do but take her in my arms and hold her, and soon enough we were kissing, her face wet and hot. *We used to be young, and there were worlds and worlds. Why didn't you hang on to me? Just because I wasn't pretty? Oy, men drive me crazy*, and then we were in bed.

We talked halfway through the night. She has a good life, success, enough money, a pension on the way. She is invited to give papers at the best places. A colleague with an invalid wife serves her turn. The worship offered by the lovely girls isn't all bad. But Philip's death last fall drove her to get on a plane to Toronto after her last class of the term, offering herself the excuse that she needed to study some pictures at the AGO, when what she really wanted was to walk through the cloisters at University College, to look at the trees just coming into leaf in our late cold northern spring, and perhaps to come and see me. A tribute to the inevitability of the past, a pained assertion that it could have been different. Couldn't. We talked about the teachers who had stood in front of our classes, most of them gone now. Standing in the cloisters, she had remembered the night I had kissed her at a party almost better than our brief marriage. Say that we were young. That we were young. That we were young.

As it grew light outside, I saw the traces of morning on the flat brick wall beyond the window, the sound of Leah's snoring close beside me. I was to wake her at seven, and she was planning to force me to clean up the apartment then I would perhaps to go to the airport with her, and she would climb into one of the silver spaceships and return to paradise.

Leah stayed longer than she had meant. I told her she snored, and she said I did too, and we bickered and behaved, in a general way, like the old couple we perhaps should have been. She asked a lot of questions about my son James. The two of them were great friends during the year of our marriage, and she probably understood him better than I ever did. Her visit here came prompt to the hour. Only a month ago, Sweet Lucy Lumpkin (that's what I had taken to calling her, a way of achieving detachment, I suppose) decided that my vasectomy disqualified me as a long-term investment. So she packed up the elegant photos of herself that she had given me and said so long. The vasectomy was an excuse, of course, but what the hell. Sweet Lucy is younger than I am and prettier than I am so I watched her go with some regret, though I was recovering by now. Put simply, I was beginning to be of a mind to have company and warmth, and here was Leah arriving out of the past. She took me to the AGO with her, and I failed to understand the importance of what I was looking at, and she got to lecture me about my blindness.

When Leah flew away, she left behind a nicely printed and illustrated library newsletter which she'd picked up; it's from one of our medium-sized universities and has a photograph of Philip Leigh on the first page, and an article about a recent donation made to the university under the terms of his will. A notable collection of incunabula, especially works printed by Aldus Manutius, as well as a number of early works from the Hogarth Press including all the ones handset by Leonard and Virginia Woolf, a privately printed bibliographical work about the Hogarth Press, and a manuscript of memoirs called (just imagine!) *The Life of the Mind*. Leah underlined the last item and in the margin placed a large question mark. *What did Philip have to tell? They only accepted it so they could get the damn books. Imagine, Philip writing about what it meant to be Philip. The life of the mind indeed. But he was born to suffer, I suppose and needed to tell us all.* She went on to tell me that among my virtues was the fact that I never pretended to be too smart. Leah's idea of a compliment.

A few months ago, I was at Philip's funeral. Marion Leigh called me, and I felt it my duty to turn up. He was the first of my college friends to go. The funeral was at a small Anglican church in one of the towns north of Toronto, and it was conducted by a bishop, accoutred with mitre and crozier, and I was sure that Philip, who had grown more and more formal as the years went on, very much Mr Justice Philip Leigh, would have been gratified by this. Marion was there with their two pale daughters, and it was a stiff and seemly occasion. Marion invited me to come to their house afterward, but I made my excuses. It had always seemed an unhappy house, and I didn't want to go there. I gather that Ben, dutiful, did go round.

I have saved things, and somewhere in a drawer there is a postcard of Kew Gardens, bought from a newsagent near the station. It was the early sixties; Brenda and I were married, in fact she may have been pregnant with James, but I was in London on my own, and I had been with Philip walking in Kew Gardens in the rain. Two dark figures under black umbrellas moved over the green lawns. Philip was talking to me about his book purchases and his unhappiness. I was in London for only a week, lucky enough to catch an assignment that made it necessary, and I didn't want my week spoiled by either his bibliophilia or his articulate agonies. We had met in a pub for lunch, and now this. Lacking the moral poise to do other, I made bad jokes. *Dum spiro, spero*, I said, remembering that Philip had liked Latin tags. At last he grew silent, and we walked on through the rain until we saw the muddy banks of the river, the tide out. When he finished his doctorate he came back to Canada and in later years he married, a beautiful woman younger than he was. He was a lawyer and then a judge, living in a grand house in the country, with wide lawns and great trees. I made occasional visits. He had grown formal, as if always on the bench and speaking for the record, the sentences unrolling, precise, a little ponderous. In his later days, when not on the bench, more and more a hermit. A strong hint of hostility the few times I saw him.

A small white stone. I saved that as well. The sun was hot on my back as I sat on the dock and watched a figure on waterskis moving smoothly along behind a powerful motorboat against a background of rock islands and dark evergreens. It was Philip's younger sister Libby whose tanned legs and arms and perfect body stirred me up, made me breathless. I had been invited to their island on Stoney Lake for the Labour Day weekend. Then I was going home for a short visit to my parents before I went back to the university. I'd spent the summer in Toronto, working in a factory that manufactured cardboard boxes. It was a boring job, which I'd got because the owner was a cousin of my mother's, but it had put the necessary amount of money in my pocket. Philip had called and invited me for Labour Day weekend. I was supposed to be going home, but I postponed the visit.

Late at night, after Philip's parents had gone to bed, we sat in the living room of the big cottage, and I tried not to stare at Libby, who lay in a chair with one of her eloquent long legs thrown over the side. She was about to go back to Havergal for her last year. She didn't say much as Philip and I discussed campus politics, and the great world, but I imagined that late in the night she would meet me on the dock and we'd swim naked in the moonlight. Philip had a cousin at Harvard, and he'd been hearing about the bright young Senator from Massachusetts who might be the next American president if the fact that he was Roman Catholic didn't prevent it.

'Do they really care?' Libby said, as she got out of the chair and started to walk away. 'About his religion?' I wondered if she knew how intently I was watching her. I could taste her.

'There's never been a Roman Catholic president,' Philip said in his deep careful voice. 'That's what stymied Al Smith when he ran in 1928. He was an acceptable governor of New York, but when it comes to the office of president, they're always afraid of the political influence of the church and the Pope. *Tempora mutantur?* Well, perhaps, but just consider the issue of birth control.'

Libby made a face and walked away, mumbled goodnight and went to her room. I imagined her taking off her clothes and sleeping naked in her honey-gold skin. Philip was talking quietly, as if to himself.

'I couldn't invite him,' Philip was saying.

'Who?'

'Ben.'

'Why not?'

'My parents wouldn't have a Jew here, not to stay.'

There was no answer, not that I could think of.

Now on Sunday afternoon, I sat in the sun and watched Philip rubbing lotion on his chest while the boat brought Libby past the dock. She dropped one ski and went on another circuit of the channel, her body leaning back, one leg in front of the other, the water curving away from the single ski in a low white-topped wave. It was comfortable here, the sun glittering on the blue water at the edge of a beautiful lake, where Ben, a hairy, heavy-breathing semite, couldn't come. I dived into the water and swam out to retrieve the ski that Libby had dropped. Before we left the next afternoon, I picked up a small white stone and put it in my pocket. In the winter, I would look at the white stone, and I would imagine what I would do to Libby if I had her. Later, during one of the times Brenda and I were apart, I had my chance – she deceived her husband to be with me – but in spite of the long honey legs and the luxuriant growth of hair at the top of them, I was always waiting for the phone to ring, Brenda calling me, or I would rush home in case she was at the door. Evidence – the old vulgarity to the contrary – that they are not all the same in the dark.

Sulky. That was how Brenda looked when I met her backstage at Hart House Theatre late in the winter of 1958. It was an age of cheerfulness in women, and her grim face, pout, moody darkened eyes suggested strong feelings of an encouraging sort. We looked at each other and recognized a possible fate. I'd just had a little chat with the theatre's director, getting a few remarks for an advance story on his next production. He spoke in rapid sentences, nervous and red faced, looking a little as if he might fly apart at any moment, but he gave me what I needed. I was on my way out, turned from the narrow entrance to the box-office and bumped into a sulky blonde girl with grey haunted eyes. And there one part of my life began and ended. Now I lie in the bathtub and look across my thickening belly to the bony events that are my toes, and think how easy it is to summarize a life, after the event. Sadly so. I bumped into her, and her face caught my attention and made me think I could have her and must, and a few years later, I was pursuing her with a gun.

Ben warned me against Brenda. It was a rainy fall day, and the two of us were huddled in a corner of the cloisters of University College.

Victorian Gothic, but not without charm on a grey November morning, to look across the quadrangle to the yellow brick walls on the other side. Why were we huddled there? We had met crossing the quadrangle from the men's residence, I on my way to the office of the *Varsity*, he on his way to the Junior Common Room to play bridge, and we sheltered from the rain in that corner of the cloisters, since he said he must talk to me before I ruined myself over that woman. As we stood there, the lanky figure of Professor Bartley loped toward us, pale balding head out in front, long legs running to keep up. A tattered academic gown blew in the wind – they still wore them to lecture in those days, imitation Oxford everywhere – and the long figure nodded to me and ran off into the college to explicate *Hamlet*. The November rain fell and my friend Ben, now Senator Benjamin Augenberg, soft in his sinecure, appointed to comfort and responsible for offering the country sober second thought, stood in silence to watch him go and then turned to me again to warn me against that sulky blonde who would ruin my life. I am compelled to wonder, on behalf of the ghosts, the unlikelihoods, if it was inevitable on the rainy afternoon that Ben would end up with a seat in the Senate, a widely respected public figure? Perhaps the auguries were there when he stood up in the JCR at the mock parliament and debated both sides of an issue, defending the resolution, then crossing the floor and offering a passionate rebuttal of his own speech. Such clever boys we were.

It was Philip Leigh who organized that debate. Ben's disciple and admirer. You saw them crossing the campus together, side by side, Philip the taller and thinner, bending to listen while Ben explained things to him. After graduation Ben went directly to Osgoode Hall, getting himself underway, putting his career together. We would meet for lunch now and then. His lunch, my breakfast, usually. I was doing my first stint on one of the dailies, and I worked late and rose late. He was already deeply involved in the fortunes of the Liberal Party and provided a certain amount of backroom gossip, some of which I was able to use or trade to other reporters. When I asked about Philip, he was vague. Philip was far off at the London School of Economics.

As far as I can tell, Ben and his wife, still together unlike so many, are a happy couple, and he is a contented man. There was always something substantial, solid about Ben; complacency would be an unkind word, perhaps an unfair one, but if he is riddled with anxieties and insecurities, I have never seen them. A rich voice, and he always spoke with the certainty that he was right. Probably he was. He was substantial. He and his wife Anita live in a substantial house on a substantial street in Rockcliffe. Once, years ago, just after they moved to Ottawa, we paid them a visit there. Ben and I were in touch regularly in those days and he hired me as a speech writer for two or three of the senior Liberal candidates. I had to write the speeches in hours stolen from my magazine job, staying up half the night primed with scotch, but the candidates liked the work, so a lot of it came in. Ben would hand me a set of policy notes, and I would turn them into a speech. Sometimes I had met the candidate, but in other cases I took my chances. What is he like? I would ask Ben or one of his assistants, and I would put words into this stranger's mouth. In most cases, it worked out, though I once heard part of a speech on television, and realized that I'd given some pretty ornamental rhetoric to a man who spoke in units of four words. By the time we went to Ottawa, Brenda had begun to refer to Ben as Sir T. Bone Steak. The visit degenerated. They always did. After I had passed out, Brenda tried to get into bed with Ben's fourteen-year-old nephew, or so she claimed as we were driving back to Toronto.

I have a box full of photographs, James's childhood, a lover from the chaotic years, my first wedding. (Leah and I avoided photos at the second.) In the wedding photographs there are several dead people. There is my father, deep in conversation with Brenda's father, who has his hand on my father's arm, taking control, taking possession, his eyes fixed with the salesman's concentration, all this in the background, and there too is Leah, old pal, in conversation with a tall man who stoops to speak to her, Malcolm Ingalls, managing editor of the magazine where I was working, a sweet man and an editorial genius who drank himself to death. A few years later on, he and Brenda sought oblivion together, or so the gossips would have it. Brenda and I are laughing in that picture, heedless, ready to take on the world, while Ben, in his fine three-piece lawyer's suit, watching us, is standing beside a couple of other young journalists and in front of Brenda's smiling brother, and you can tell that Ben is one who will survive. Will I survive? The picture doesn't make that clear. Brenda is wearing a dark suit, ready to depart, and I imagine her flesh burning beneath the dark cloth, and if I look closely I think I see my trousers flagged with a premonitory erection. In the farthest corner of the picture is my mother, and she is looking down her long nose, watching something happen. I sit at my kitchen table with a cup of instant coffee mixed with an edible oil product that turns it white, and I study the photograph. There are dirty dishes piled by the sink, and once I return the photograph to its drawer, I will wash them. Or so I intend, but it is easy to do nothing, to think instead, or dream, remember, fail to understand.

At the bottom of a box, an undergraduate paper on Tennyson's 'Maud'. A Saturday night in 1958, my narrow room in the men's residence. No party to go to, nothing to do, and I was reading in fits and starts, working toward that essay. A knock on the door, and when I opened it, I found myself staring at an odd figure in a topcoat and fedora, and it took me a foolishly long time to recognize that it was Brenda, dressed up, however unconvincingly, as a man. Or boy. Well, something approximately male. In order to sneak into the men's residence. The rules that kept us pure were enforced in those days, and if we were caught we might both be tossed out of the college. I dragged her into the room, and we fell upon each other, whispering and giggling. Quiet, quiet, I said. The man in the room next door was a tall, clever West Indian economist, no prude, but fussy about noise when he was working and capable of inadvertently putting the cat among the pigeons by coming to my door to complain. I hoped he was out somewhere. On the other side was a Latvian immigrant of mature years, not without malice since he thought I was soft on communism. So we had to keep it quiet. While I undressed her – I never had before, but it seemed to be what she had in mind – she explained how she had picked up her more or less masculine attire in the theatre of the Women's Union where she was appearing in a play. She had to get herself back to the women's residence by midnight. Those were the rules. Truly. By the time our son got to university it seems to me that men and women were using the same showers. *Tempora mutantur*, as Philip liked to say. Philip is dead. Brenda is dead. Had I been a braver boy that night – as brave as Brenda, though I never was – our son might have been conceived four years earlier, but I had no rubber goods available and was terrified of impregnating her, so we lay on my narrow bed and stared, and we kissed and fondled each other until we were gasping and enervated, and as we slipped her out of the residence to meet her midnight curfew, I vowed that come summer, we would find a way to be together without all this fuss. And did: I spent more on safes than on food. In the meantime when we spoke it was to fight. Moods. I was to learn about moods. When I phoned her after that Saturday night, she had nothing to say. Was closeted with her friend Arlene in their sorority of secrecy and resentment. Brenda had moods. I was being punished. Though she didn't say it at first, she would not forgive me for my carefulness that night, for not being man enough to screw her and take my chances. Brenda never forgave anything.

A cursory reading of 'Maud' reveals hysteria. Though further readings make clear Tennyson's attempts to create some ironic distance from this state of mind, it is impossible not to reflect, at least momentarily, on the possible contribution made to the hero's state of mind by the extent of the author's suffering from his recently acquired and ill-fitting false teeth.

Such juvenile bravado. It is impossible not to reflect on the possible contribution made to the critic's confident state of mind by the memory of Brenda naked on my narrow bed. The essay is full of smart-alec jokes while at the same time showing off the kind of structural analysis and sensitivity to tone that would assure me of a decent mark. Contained rebellion. My cheap cracks at the expense of the laureate (who grew the beard and moustache to conceal the way the false teeth changed the shape of his mouth) were weapons in my own battle to escape from my all-too-Victorian childhood, the yellow brick house with stained glass windows beside the door, a place that aspired to be a Victorian parsonage. My mother had once been in love with an Anglican cleric, a man along the lines of Tennyson's 'snowy-banded, dilettante, delicate-handed priest.' She was no more than a girl, and he went away, and after business college she married my father, who was then a clerk with the railway. After the war in which he served in the Quartermaster Corps, though he was almost too old to enlist, and in which he earned a commission, he went into the insurance business, bought out the small agency, and they created a respectable life. My mother collected Victorian baubles – cameos, jet, ornamental screens – when they were least fashionable. My father was not out of place among the plants and gewgaws. It was in his nature to move quietly; his own hobby, fishing, was a contemplative one, and they gave every appearance of being happy together. My mother was a little bit of a snob but she was not a prude. She had been raised on a farm; the hen's fluster and the rooster's pride were no surprise to her. My own priggish annoyance with carelessness about language is no doubt an inheritance from her old-fashioned standards, but at university, I was in love with the modern, Eliot and Pound and Picasso and Schoenberg, and when I set out to write about Tennyson, it was an act of aggression. I remembered my mother's recording of Victorian songs, and to amuse Brenda I would render a melodramatic 'Come into the Garden, Maud.' I liked to scoff at Ruskin, who had apparently panicked and run at the sight of his young bride's bush.

In the summers, my father and I would sit silent in his small green boat anchored on the wide slow river, waiting for a fish to bite, saying nothing. I had always wished that he had done something romantic in the war, been a pilot perhaps. He had done his duty, and that should have been enough for me. On Sunday mornings I went to St. Mark's with my mother and memorized the Book of Common Prayer. At night in the privacy of my room, I read Hemingway.

The telephone rang, and it was Leah, calling to see if my curiosity had yet driven me out to that country college to read Philip's manuscript. *My* curiosity? I said that obviously hers was consuming her, and I asked if they had done such spectacularly naughty things in London that she was afraid of seeing them recorded and perhaps one day published.

'We did the usual,' she said, 'though not often and not well.'

Until Leah's call, I had been planning to go to that university library at some future moment when I was too bored for anything else, but for the sake of her curiosity and mine, I decided to get on with it. It was a strange thing all in all, and I wondered if I might regret it.

Every life has its own world of important places, features of climate, notable sights, its own reading of a particular geography and history. Old jokes: I used to divide my life into *ante Brendam* and *post Brendam*. She was high noon. This is before, and we were drunk. To begin with – early in the evening – we had gone to the King Cole Room in the basement of the Park Plaza hotel. It was where students went, if they had the money and the proof of age and a girl or two with them. In those days a beverage room – which served only beer – had two parts, the Ladies and Escorts and the Gentlemen, and the room where men were sent to drink alone was, in almost every case, small, depressing, foul. Often called 'the other side', as if across the Styx. As a result none of us wished to drink there, and when you walked in, you always hoped to find, in the Ladies and Escorts, a table with not too many escorts and at least a couple of ladies. Each bar had a rule of thumb about how many escorts a given lady might have. Otherwise you were sent to the narrow and sordid little space on the other side of the wall and if you couldn't bear that you went home.

Ben had phoned several girls to see if one would come with us. No one was willing, but Philip in particular was determined to drink beer so we headed for the men's room and found a table and by some miracle of good temper on the waiter's part – we were all underage – we were served. At the table next to us a pale-faced man, drunk, stared at us with damp lost eyes, and then made a couple of attempts at friendship. Recognizing us as students, he let us know that he had never got to the university himself, though sure as hell he had the brains for it. He was restless. He was a rover. Itchy feet. Philip agreed that he looked like a man with itchy feet, and I'm afraid we giggled heartlessly. After our second round of beer, he suggested that he come and sit with us, but Ben took charge and said that we were on our way. The man, who had ignored or not noticed Philip's sly little jokes, took offence and mumbled something about Jews being busy making money, and we drank up and fled into the night.

'Queer as a three-dollar bill,' Philip was saying.

'Who?'

'That drunk.'

'He was just a drunk.'

'No, he was a queer. I hate queers.'

'Yes, we all know that,' Ben said.

'Oh fuck off,' Philip said.

A group of undergraduate girls was coming toward us, and Philip made a deep and graceful bow toward them. One or two laughed.

'The ladies of the corridor,' he said.

After midnight, we found ourselves in a dark noisy basement where a piano, sax and drums were playing contemporary jazz, loud in the small space where men and women crowded together in every corner, listened with conscious intensity and applauded at the end of every solo. The pianist played after the manner of Thelonius Monk, grabbing odd handfuls of notes. Across the room, a woman dressed in black with pale makeup and big eyes nodded in time with the beat. I watched her and hoped she'd look toward me, and once I thought she did. Ben and Philip were talking intently, but I couldn't hear them. I watched how the woman in black moved her shoulders with the music. Would I ever have a woman like that? I can remember that night, hardly out of childhood, I felt as old as the universe. I left Ben and Philip and went out into the streets, walked a long way, stopped to piss in a back lane and saw the distant light of a police car. I couldn't imagine what future was waiting for me. Brenda, but I couldn't imagine Brenda. Our meeting was hidden in the mind of God, like all the time that was to come. Fate, and we must seize it and hold it for our own.

Philip in London, and the indirection of his words when he tried to talk: I helped not at all, left him behind and went off for a drink with Leah. Everybody's pal. She had always been in love with Ben, back as far as high school, she said on that street corner in Bloomsbury. Philip and I, we both are, she said, that's what we have in common. After we all graduated, she had gone off to the Courtauld Institute, and she and Philip, who was at LSE, had become a couple, of a sort. They did things together, there in the endless maze of old streets and dim byways that was London; both lived in the shadow of the British Museum. She asked for news of Ben and then said no, she didn't want to know. I remember standing with her in the National Gallery, looking at the Leonardo cartoon in the dim light, all that was allowed lest the delicate thing be damaged. At university, because Leah was everyone's friend, we didn't expect her to have feelings. I had kissed her once at a party, a deep slippery kiss in a dark corner on one of those nights when nothing made perfect sense and whatever happened was right, but now, in London, I saw her for the first time as an incomprehensible, passionate woman, prey to murderous regrets, too sharp-witted, capable of hate. A moment that made our marriage possible, and perhaps also made it impossible. We sat in a Lyons' Corner House and drank milky coffee, and after a while there was nothing to say. Nothing happened, one would say, though we mentioned that perhaps we would see a play together. Didn't. Years later, not long after Brenda's death, she turned up. She had an appointment at Queen's, but she preferred to live in Toronto, commuting, paying for a *pied-à-terre* in the limestone city. Brenda was gone, and I was falling apart, and suddenly we were married. Then we weren't.

Leah has a successful career. She showed me her book on the minor followers of Caravaggio and the more recent, shorter book on the women painters of the time, Artemisia Gentileschi and that lot. No doubt she has done many other things. I failed her, but it wasn't my only failure. She and Philip were Ben's castoffs. Surely he was not to blame for being strong and loveable, kindly and heartless.

Go and find Philip's manuscript, by way of alimony to Leah, if nothing else.

It wasn't a long drive to get to the university that held Philip's bequest, and anyone who has spent a lifetime in southern Ontario has driven most of its major roads at least once. I knew that I had come this way years before to interview a university professor, though at the moment I couldn't remember what it was that he had done that justified the interview. Invented something. Won a prize. It was one of hundreds of interviews over what sometimes felt like hundreds of years.

Once at the campus, I parked and looked at a map that was posted at the entrance, but it gave me little help, so I stopped one of the pretty children who are students now, a girl, Eurasian I would have said, an extraordinary face, and asked directions to the library. When I did as she told me, I came to a large brick building with wide steps and a porch with small columns. Once inside I asked again, this time an irritable man with straight grey hair and glasses, and he sent me up some stairs and along corridors until I came to a door with a large glass pane, one of those old pebbled glass panes which show you only light and darkness, vague shapes, and the door announced that inside were Special Collections and Archives.

Enter, smiling, a journalist. Behind the counter was a tall stately woman, longish hair, probably dark with assistance, a long nose, and as she turned her head to me, I caught the glint of contacts. Large breasted, upright, formidable, she was studying me as if I were keeping a secret and she determined to ferret it out.

I asked to see Philip's manuscript of memoirs, feeling as if I might be asking to look at their collection of eighteenth-century pornography. I was there out of the merest vile curiosity, wanting to be the first to know Philip's secrets, claiming to be a journalist, which appeared to be an obvious lie. The woman at the counter called me by name, and when I stared stupidly introduced herself as Eva Peltzer, an old roommate of Brenda's.

It's been a long time since I've seen you, Eva, I said, and she explained that she had been at the funeral, and I explained that I had been drunk and noticed no one. We mentioned James, and I told her that he was a wandering scholar. As I spoke, I watched her, I could almost see the young self, and the return of time past was like a sickness coming on. Not her fault. We got back to Philip's memoir, short, just jottings I was told, but I persisted. I thought there might be something in it. Of interest. Mr Justice Philip Leigh. Magazine, whatever. I was babbling. And now that I knew who she was, I was remembering things and noticing her breasts, big and apparently still firm.

You have to get permission, Eva was saying. It's in the will. Permission from Senator Augenberg, and I was laughing but unable to explain the joke. In fact I needed permission in writing from Ben Augenberg before I could see a word.

Eva and I stared at each other, and I reflected on the way the young face I remembered had gradually altered into the face that looked at me, skin losing its elasticity, darkening around the eyes, cheeks reddened, perhaps a little too much makeup to conceal these things, the things that were happening to all of us, but there was still a challenge in the features, a glitter in the grey eyes. I'd be back with my letter, I said, not sure whether I would or not. I was about to turn away when Eva said, *If she'd married someone else she might be alive.* Brenda, never to be forgotten. I am left to imagine what Eva was told or what she imagined. The story of my life. Probably her remark was true. Of course it was true. One thing leads to another. List in alphabetical order the causes of the war with an assessment of the importance of each.

It was an idea from books and movies. Newspapers, the voice of the modern world. Cut and paste, reporters talking tough in the city room. Ernest Hemingway at the *Toronto Star*. Already, television was winning all the marbles, and a couple of years later Hemingway would put a shotgun to his head. The world I wanted to join was gone. Writers were making nests in the universities and IBM was scattering its spores, but late at night at the *Varsity*, when the last copy went off to the printers who were working at their linotypes which poured poisonous hot lead into the slugs, somebody grabbing a cab to go and read proofs, the rest of us wandering into the night, we could feel a sense of drama, that the stuff we'd done tonight would be out in print on the campus in the morning. There were still two evening news-papers in Toronto; reporters still ran from the political conventions to the nearest pay phone to dictate their copy. The world was perhaps no longer shaped by the schedule of the daily papers, but I had learned to write a good lead and get the facts straight, and I had the sense that I was a craftsman whose trade would see him through.

I suppose it has. I learned quickly enough that I wasn't the kind of reporter who was happy asking rude questions or going through the garbage cans of celebrities, I never got a column, and my thin voice never tempted me away to the microphone world, but through hard work and native wit, I became one of the best deskmen in town. I think that was widely believed, though Malcolm Ingalls was the first person to say it, and he was perhaps less than objective. I could sense where a story was going and send someone to get the missing bits.

You spend all those years calling them stories, and gradually you've written so many that you realize that's what they are. Fairy tales. Writing a good lead meant finding the appropriate slot, fitting the world to the process, but making it sound just a little bit new. I've sometimes thought that deconstruction and postmodernism (such ugly words, but I suppose they stand for something, if only a kind of defeat and despair) are defensive reactions against the sheer multi-plicity of words. If there are so many stories, it's obvious that none of them can make sense. So we develop a code of senselessness. Incoherence is the rule. Everything is other than it is. *Le discours*. Words, words, words. Even when I was still a young man, McLuhan was turning the modern against itself. I'd heard Marshall McLuhan give a kind of informal tutorial when I was an undergraduate, speaking rapidly and abruptly in that crisp voice, and afterwards I found myself irritable, though I couldn't have said why.

It was one evening in my last year, and I was living in a furnished room near the campus, in a tall narrow house owned by a daft old woman who kept rabbits – and late that night, I met Brenda at the apartment on Spadina, opposite a funeral home, an apartment which she shared with her friend Eva, and the two of us went back to my room and all the way I vented my irritation. The bias of communication gives me the shits, I said. As I pulled down her black satin panties, Brenda, often snappish in heat, said it was all because McLuhan was so much smarter than I was. Of course I raged and sulked and she provoked me further, and I was rough with her. In the middle of the act, as we mumbled breathlessly against each other's faces and hair, I heard her whispering, asking if I'd like to do this to Eva. When I didn't answer, she asked again. Anybody, I said. Everybody. When we were, for the moment, satisfied, she lay on her side and watched me, asked again. I looked at her face, the blond hair rumpled, the shadowed eyes. I reached out and touched one of her breasts.

She talked about Eva and what I wanted to do to her until I was aroused again. Probably that's what she intended. So we recited the things I would do to Eva while I did them to Brenda. It was wonderfully exciting and tempting, and I wondered whether she would tell Eva all these things when she went back to the apartment. I could never imagine what they talked about when they were together. I had heard them say cruel things about Arlene, who used to be their friend but wasn't any more, about her ugly underwear and the stupid things she said about the family she was going to have and how scared she was of sex. I knew Brenda tyrannized over both her friends by being experienced and outspoken. I could imagine her telling Eva things she'd invented about me. Bragging about my cruelty and appetite.

I'm such a good whore, she said as we lay there. That's what they tell me.

Who? Who told her that? Her secrets, the burning edge they gave to her presence. It was in her nature always to hint at something held back.

She would never stay overnight with me, didn't want the other men who had rooms in the house to see her leaving in the morning. Again, late that night, I walked her home.

She wanted me to write an essay for her, on Hemingway, since it was something I could do in my sleep, and I agreed. When we parted, she told me that she'd tell Eva what I was planning to do to her.

Perhaps she did. As I walked home through the empty streets, I was thinking about McLuhan, the cleverness with which he turned everything on its head or inside out. Did I, even then, recognize something easy, something brilliant and slippery, too true and yet false, one step on a downward road to relativism and nihilism? Fact had vanished, and there was only gesture. Pound and Eliot had opened a door, and McLuhan was saying that we had to walk through it. I could claim now that I understood all that, but perhaps Brenda was right and I only resented his cleverness. He was right, or was at least the voice of the future, I know now. There are no facts, most would say, only ways of speaking. History is fiction. (And fiction is history – I can't read Hemingway now.) The things I have saved have meaning only for me, and only for now. Perhaps the meaning of it is in what I've forgotten, what I didn't see.

I did write the essay for her, and she mentioned it loudly at the reception after our graduation to the professor for whom it had been written. I denied it all, of course, and made a joke about the time we'd spent discussing Hemingway, then dragged her away before she went on to something else.

It is not a god who sends us to hell, but our own selves, wishing it. It was Brenda's deepest wish, to burn. No one could ever hurt her enough. *Mea culpa, mea culpa.* Philip Leigh liked to say that when he'd made some small blunder. I believed, had always believed that it was my culpability that caused Brenda to be in pieces, drenched in blood, to be as she was. It was said of us that we were alcoholics, helping each other to perdition, but when I wasn't with her, I drank temperately. It was no effort.

I am trying not to remember. James was five and had just started kindergarten. She arranged for me to meet him at school one day. I stood by the car and watched the children who spilled out the door, so tiny and entire, carrying scraps of paper, dropping things, coats buttoned wrong, faces full of their day's business. I tried to remember myself at five, to remind myself that James was already a person with thoughts and opinions. At that moment Brenda was having a baby scraped out of her. It wasn't mine, she told me, when I guessed, as I was meant to guess, where she had been. I sat on the side of the bed and wept until I choked. I didn't believe her. I believed that the child was mine. I can remember the look on her face as she told me what she had done. *There is no health in us*, I said to her, aware even as I wept that it would have been more difficult to raise two children, that I had not especially wanted another child, that her decision was convenient. Then I got drunk, and I don't remember.

This evening I went back to the bar where I met Ben last week – I had called to discuss Philip's manuscript, and since Ben was planning to be in Toronto, I met him for a drink at the place where we always get together. He had a letter ready for me, though he thought it unwise of me to read the manuscript. Philip was a liar, he said more than once, and in fact he had never consulted Ben about making him the memoir's guardian. He could probably go to court and get that part of the will set aside but won't bother. Ben looked the same as ever to me, and it was hard to remember that we are getting old, that the past is longer than the future can ever be. It was something about that thought that took me back to that bar tonight, as if, sitting alone, remembering, I could catch a glimpse of myself, but all I saw, as I nursed a gin and tonic, was what we call life going on, a young woman who went out into the hallway where things were quiet, to talk on her cell phone, busy about her business. When I looked in the mirror behind the bar, I saw a lighted window in a building behind me, the furnishings of an office, a man walking to a desk, picking something up to read. A man alone there working late, one moment of his affairs caught in a magic mirror that made what was behind me appear to be in front of me. The young woman finished her call and came back in to join friends at a table behind me. The man in the office, tall, balding, walked past the window again. The seat beside me, where Ben had been a few days before, was empty. I finished my drink and left the bar.

James has been in Vancouver and visited his uncle. I suppose James wants to be part of a family and has forgotten or will ignore the past, sit down for a beer with his uncle Paul. Surely James must remember how Brenda used to go and visit her brother during his years in prison. No one, I think, knew that I had helped to put him there, as I would again, believe me, any day of the week, my anonymous call putting the fuzz on his tail. In those days, I would have said I disliked the police, jolly, thick fellows asking for my licence and the car registration. A childish rebelliousness whenever I saw one coming. Men were expected to hold their drink and get behind the wheel. So you tried to avoid them; it was the way of things, but the bank inspector gaff was beneath contempt, robbing nervous pensioners of their savings. My wife's brother. She was loyal to him, even afterward.

Good-looking, Paul was, well-dressed, sincere in a phony kind of way, the lively bonhomie of the sociopath. Nothing behind the eyes. Always shaking my hand. I wonder whether Brenda suspected that I was the one who shopped him. She always said she didn't suspect what big brother was up to until he was arrested, but I didn't believe her. She must have known those men for what they were. Paul had no obvious job but he had money, and he was often on the road. Work, he said. Making deals. Well, that was what the family did. Her father – also well-dressed, sincere and dishonest – made his living that way, as he'd explained to me from the first, though I didn't altogether understand how it all happened. Making deals. I had always suspected Paul of the worst, evil and crass he must be behind that blowhard friendliness, but when I turned him in, I knew nothing for sure. Saw a newspaper from London, Ontario, just after he'd come back from there – I knew because he'd called Brenda from a pay phone near London the week before to say he had a chance of a good deal on a fur coat and he wondered if she'd want it. He was always getting her things like that, and of course I resented it, that my wife was being dressed in fur by her handsome older brother. He held the coat as she slid her arms into the sleeves, and he stroked her shoulders as she made appreciative sounds. Stolen fur, I suppose. Then I found myself looking at the London *Free Press*, and there was a headline about a crew of phony bank inspectors who'd been working the city. Pensioners had lost thousands of dollars. So I called the cops. From a pay phone and then walked away. It was three months later he was arrested in eastern Ontario.

Paul did his time in Kingston, Brenda and her mother making regular trips up to hold his hand. Janey, his girlfriend – a brittle miniature with hair out of a bottle and eyelashes out of a box and a lot of makeup, the whole outfit prettily assembled – dropped him the minute she heard the charges and Brenda denounced her for her disloyalty, but myself I thought it showed a lot of good sense. I thought now and then about having to meet Paul when he got out, but when he made parole, Brenda and I were living apart, and by the time we got back together, he'd moved to Vancouver. Now and then I've dreamed that Paul is looking for me, to get his revenge, a bulky figure with weapons. In the dream, I struggle vainly to fight him off, then I wake and listen for footsteps approaching the door.

That family: the first summer – unmarried, officially pure – I went to see Brenda at home in the big white frame house on a corner lot in a small city, and her mother set me up a cot in the basement. After dinner we went for a walk and made love, tormented by mosquitoes, behind some bushes in a public park. At the dinner table her father boasted with a casual brutality about a truckload of washing machines he'd bought out of a bankruptcy, driven to a suburb of Toronto and sold at a good price.

Paul, who was back living at home for a few months waiting for his criminal career to take shape, did the proud son. The wife, small, nervous, put-upon, made agreeable noises. Daddy told me I should write a story for the papers about his refrigerators. When he got up from the table and went to lie down, Brenda stuck out her tongue at his broad back, like a recalcitrant six-year-old. We left a day earlier than we had planned and, at Brenda's insistence, managed a quick and awkward coition in the back seat of the darkened bus taking us to Toronto. Another moment: the first night, when I had gone down to the basement to go to bed, her father ran down the cellar stairs behind me. I thought I was in for some questions about whether my intentions were honourable, but instead got an incoherent sermonette about Brenda having ways about her. But she was a good girl, smart as can be. He knew I appreciated that. I said I did. Was he trying to warn me about what the future would be like? A stupid cunning man. We were apart when he died. I asked her if she wanted me to go to the funeral with her. No. Brenda hated her father, but she hated me more, at least at that moment.

Hatred, oh yes, sometimes there was that between Brenda and me, but we were connected, attached, two one-legged beings clinging together to walk. There was the intimacy of those who have shared the same bed, the same bathroom, an endless series of days. I just remembered the soft furry white cover on the toilet of her parents' home when we first went to visit there, and how when I stood in front of that toilet, I could imagine a small naked child in that bathtub, her fingers soft with soap exploring herself, while the noise of family life went on outside the door, her father shouting in his loud voice for attention, and I could smell the kind of soap she still used. For years, I kept the small plastic container that once contained the first diaphragm she used. The diaphragm was long gone, but the plastic container was here. I found it when I moved out of the house, and I kept it as evidence. Last night I remembered a time when she came home late from a rehearsal with a black eye and refused to explain. In the morning she told James that she had fallen and hit her head. I hadn't realized she had a lover, when they'd already reached the point where he beat her up.

Life is like the sequence of tenses: one thing precludes another. This rather than that. In his later years, my father decided to take up gardening. He said there was nothing good on television any more, there were no more fish in the river, and he wanted to be out in the fresh air. Every time I went to visit, he told me that. He liked to take James out into the yard with him. It wasn't a big garden, and I was never sure how he managed to spend the time out there. I would admire his tulips or lilies or chrysanthemums, depending on the time of year, would carry a lettuce or a few beans into the house. There was a wooden lawn chair nearby, and much of the time spent gardening was spent in the chair, studying the garden, planning the future.

By then he had retired, taken his long sad face out of the daily world, sold the agency. Sadness came from somewhere within to haunt that face, the hollow cheeks, the damp eyes. Perhaps he thought that the garden would bring him health. He'd been brought up in the days when fresh air was a synonym for vigour. In fact I remember when I was young, he always donated money to the Toronto Star Fresh Air Fund, which was one of those good works pursued by that newspaper of Methodist rectitude, a collection of money to send poor city children away to summer camp. That and the Scott Mission for down-and-outs were my father's charities. My mother gave money to St. Mark's Anglican Church and got me confirmed there, but my father was not much interested in St. Mark's.

He was buried from that church though. One day he didn't come in from the garden, and my mother found him lying among the green beans, looking as if he might have fallen asleep there. A stroke, and silence fell on the long melancholy face. It was inevitable, of course, that, having spent his life selling insurance, he had none himself, and the house, which had once been paid off, had been remortgaged. Bad investments, my mother said, when I asked her how that could have happened.

Though we had long been apart, Brenda came to the funeral with me and James, invited herself when she heard the news. Why not? It was during one of the spells when she was on the booze, but though there was a smell of whisky on her breath, she behaved well, even in the face of my mother's hostility. Mother, son, daughter-in-law, that infamous constellation of grief and anger, or so I thought. I was always very stupid. Brenda took James back to Toronto with her while I stayed to help my mother sort things out. A week or so later, Brenda delivered James to the house on Major where he was living with me most of the time, drank what she could find, and offered to take me to bed. I could never resist her, and the softening belly, the now bigger, heavier breasts, all new to me, were intoxicating, but I was relieved when she left. In the night, she had spoken my name, as if she was about to tell me something, but no words followed. I remember still watching her go down the walk in the morning, in a red leather miniskirt, the fashion of the time, going off to a meeting of a group which was assisting draft dodgers and deserters in flight from the war in Vietnam. She was a passionate opponent of the war and the USA.

As I skate about the apartment in my slippery wool socks, there appears out of the rubble a theatre program for an evening of one-act plays at the Women's Union theatre, one featuring Brenda and Alan Hutcheson. Last year I was sent a book for editing which dealt with certain matters theatrical and I discovered that Alan is now a kind of elder statesman of the stage, his years of giddy fame apparently gone past. He was a short determined boy of unclean habits who lived in a grubby basement under a lot of pipes and ductwork. A thin silent girl was sometimes there with him, looking no cleaner than he was. We went to parties there. Once Brenda, overexcited after a play in which she and Alan had appeared, insisted on making love in the grubby bathroom down the hall, her panties around her ankles, while someone knocked on the door wanting to use the toilet. Then she spent the rest of the evening in a corner telling secrets with Eva and Arlene. At his parties Alan would recite parts we all thought he had little hope of getting. He was not the best actor on the campus, I would have said, but resolute, and that, along with a powerful gritty voice, did the trick, and there he was, on Broadway, a star. Came back to appear at Stratford – *noblesse oblige* – and we met him there after a performance. He had gone out of his way to get in touch. Otherwise we wouldn't have. I wouldn't have. Late that night in the little house not far from the river, we drank to old times, to the plays he and Brenda had done together, the incomprehensible one-act thing written by an undergraduate with a strange name, never heard of since. Sometime in the night, I dozed off or passed out, and when I woke the grey light of dawn was haunting the air, and I was alone. Brenda and Alan, I assumed, were in a bed upstairs.

We were being civilized in those days, toying with dangerous freedoms, and I got myself up and walked down to the river and sat on a damp bench watching the white vile-tempered swans pass by on the soft mirror of the Avon. When we saw Alan in the movies later on, I was prey to dark imaginings. Once or twice I reviewed his film performances and went out of my way to be generous. When I taxed Brenda with her infidelities, she denied them all, and swore that on that occasion she and Alan had slept in separate beds and met in the kitchen for breakfast, cooking the eggs and bacon that we ate when I returned to the house. She said it with a boldness that was intended to be provoking, and after the words were spoken, the grey eyes with their bruised hollows watched me to see what I would do, if this time, finally, I would kill her. What she wanted, I have thought sometimes. I never knew what she wanted.

We were sitting in a small courtroom in the old city hall. Ben was there and I was, and a number of others, and Brenda, who was on trial for theft over two hundred dollars. Another of those days when I looked around me and felt a quiet terror of what had been and what could be.

Brenda had quit acting, or it had quit her. It was what I most admired about her – I thought she was wonderful on stage, shining and stylish, all that wild energy focused – but she let it go. Months and years had gone by, we had some good times, we drank and fought. We met our friends in the bars or invited them round for dinner. I changed jobs now and then. After James was born Brenda stayed home for a while, being a housewife. It was what other women did. She talked about writing a play, but that never happened. I never heard what the subject of the play was to be, wondered. She went to work as somebody's assistant. Johnny Hustle: he sold advertising for a number of smaller magazines and radio stations. There was a short-lived government job, then a long period when she was around the house, but not by choice. We were apart and together and apart.

During one of our separations, she began to clean houses. At first I heard nothing about it, and when at last I did hear, not from Brenda, I was sure it wasn't true. She was a proud, touchy woman who wore rubber gloves to do the dishes – when she did them – and couldn't believe that she was out there scrubbing the toilets of the rich. I called and asked her, and she said of course it was true.

What kind of perversity was that? I kept asking her, and her answer was that it was work she could find and keep, and she was determined to work

A way of getting at me, making me feel guilty; that was what I accused her of. I was doing all right – at a small trade magazine now, able to keep us afloat – but I wasn't setting the world on fire. I was doing all right, but no better than that. So we were going down in the world, was that it? What was she going to do next, I screamed at her, apply for welfare? We shouted a little and hung up. I tried to imagine her on her knees in Forest Hill, scrubbing. She'd surprised me one more time, I'd have to admit that. I was a snob like my mother, and ashamed. She'd said that and was right. As always when she was angry, she attacked me for the stodginess of my family.

One afternoon a few weeks after that conversation, Ben called me at work to ask if I'd heard. Heard what? as we say in those cases, knowing that a blow to the head is coming. Brenda had been arrested for stealing from the houses where she was cleaning, and when they took her in, she'd got the police to phone Ben. Maybe it was a way of making sure I was involved. Motives. Who's to know? Ben got her out, and since he didn't do criminal law, he found her someone who did, and now we all sat in the courtroom, Ben and the small, polished, soft-spoken man who represented her, and Brenda, with me there to show that she had the support of her sometime hubby who would take on the task of making restitution. The lawyer had talked to the prosecutor and offered to plead her guilty and accept a suspended sentence on the understanding that she and I would get back together and pay back her customers. Apparently she'd flogged what she'd stolen to various pawn-brokers who were prepared to give evidence. They remembered her face. So, always, at all hours of the day and night, did I.

We waited nervously at the front of the small courtroom until His Honour came in, a slender, good-looking man who was too young to be a judge, and in a few minutes of soft-spoken conversation, it was all settled, and we were sent on our way to be happy. On the way out of court Ben gave me a look that meant, I thought, he had foreseen all this long before, and that he knew it would all come to a bad end, but there was nothing he could do. That's what I thought it meant; who knows with a look? Brenda and I picked up James from the sitter and took him out to a drive-in for kid food. We didn't tell him where we'd spent the day, and I don't think he ever knew. We went home and put him to bed and drank temperately and made love – just what the judge must have had in mind – though all this happened in a kind of blankness. All the words echoed and then vanished.

The two of us lay in bed in the dark, and I tried to think of something to say that would show my forgiveness or acceptance, or whatever it was that was required, but in fact I felt nothing but a deep weariness. Then, out of nowhere, Brenda started to quote poetry.

How sweet the moonlight sleeps upon this bank.
Here will we sit, and let the sounds of music
Creep in our ears: soft stillness and the night
Become the touches of sweet harmony.

Shakespeare! She was, most beautifully, quoting Shakespeare on trance and ecstasy. My cock in her hand all the while. You see why I had to love her.

She chose to phone Ben from the police station. Why? In the early days, she certainly disliked him. I remember how just after we were married, he came to dinner, and it ended badly. She got drunk and called him names then left the table and slammed the bedroom door behind her. In those days, she liked to claim that Ben, like all my friends, was queer, that he was in love with me and jealous of her. After Ben left, I sat in the living room of the apartment with a book until Brenda appeared at the bedroom doorway, pale and naked, her face wet with tears. Of course I went to her. I could describe a particular curve or wrinkle of the flesh, a smell, little blond hairs, things we did, but it was not what words can say. It was just this. This. This. It was a putting away, of time, of meaning, of language. This and this. A world under the sea, a paroxysm among the drowned. Life is not comedy or tragedy but archaeology, a poking about in middens for fragments, what's left. Anecdotes to please the broken will. My mother and I are standing on a bridge, and we see a child get into deep water and go down, and she screams, and a man races down the bank, dives in, and the child is saved. I was four years old.

Deathbed confessions. It was not in fact my mother's deathbed, not yet, but her cancer had been diagnosed, and the end that is always sure was a little more than sure; its timing was predictable not to the day or week, but to the season perhaps. She'll never see another summer, one said. She had moved herself to a facility for old people where she had some independence, but would have increasing care as she needed it. Initially I was surprised by her pragmatism and firmness of purpose, but only surprised, I came to think, because I had never known her well. I had decided early on to accept my parents at the conventional estimate. They were parents, and one knew what parents were like. Everyone does this in their youth, and after my first youth, Brenda had exhausted my capacity for imagination and love. That puts too good a face on it. I was selfish and unconcerned and didn't want to know.

I was visiting my mother in her room at the facility. That was her word for it, cold and clinical and deliberate, and it was the word we used. Outside the window was a green lawn, with yellow leaves fallen in a pattern under a clump of white birches. We were talking about money, how she had sold the house and was using the little capital left after the mortgage was paid off to keep her through her final days. She didn't speak of her death, give it a date, but she had calculated, carefully enough, what the cost of her care would be and how long her money would last. She was sorry, she said to me that day, that there wouldn't be much for me. My father always hoped to leave me something. And I answered that I always managed, that I always had work. My mother had wanted me to enter a respectable profession, medicine, law, pharmacy, not the hit and miss half-bohemian world of journalism, but over the years, she had got used to things as they were. It was a pity, she had so often said, that there was no money left. I

156

asked, as I hadn't before, about the bad investments. She looked at me, the long acute face with its prominent nose, pointed directly at me, assessing, accusing.

You still don't know, she said and that was where I should have stopped, and I knew that, wanted to terminate the conversation, get up and walk away, but there was curiosity as well. Tell me a story. No don't. Tell me. Why did I feel helpless? It started right at your wedding, she said. They used Brenda for bait. The father and the brother. They were both up to it. They latched onto him at the wedding. He wasn't a strong man, decent and intelligent, but not very strong, and he couldn't ever resist them, when they came to him with their schemes. They got money from him, and if he tried to refuse, they'd threaten to do something bad to the marriage. Where did the money go? I asked. Schemes. Investments. He thought they'd help to make us rich, but the money never came. After a while, he just gave them more to make them go away. Brenda knew, my mother insisted.

Out on the lawn, an old man in a straw hat stood among the leaves under the white birches, looking around him, confused, as if he couldn't remember where he had come from or why he was there. A woman in a white uniform came and took him by the arm and led him away. A leaf fell into the silence.

Start the conversation again. Unsay the words. On this October afternoon, while old men get lost under the trees, Brenda is back in Toronto, where she has an apartment near Pape and Danforth. I don't know what she does there.

Yes, my mother says. She was the bait. They knew what she was.

I don't recognize this old woman. She was firm, proper, now and then looked down her long nose, but I have never before heard hatred in her voice, though perhaps I saw it in her eyes when she saw Brenda at my father's funeral.

I was at the door of the room, looking back at the way the sunlight outlined the profile of her long face, thinner now. I said I'd be back soon. A week later she was dead, and all through her funeral I imagined myself going after Brenda with a gun in my hand. You can find a gun if you need it badly enough and have money, and if you have spent a lifetime as a journalist and know your way around the city. You go to Tony Marinelli, and he sends you to someone else. You can do that, but once you have the gun, do you know what to do with it? Pull the trigger and kill someone, that's the conventional approach. You learn it from TV. But I suspected that the process of shooting someone was very noisy and messy. Would Brenda believe that I knew what to do with a gun and was prepared to fire it?

I can only partly remember now or imagine, the state I was in. Craziness. I was off my rocker, but there was, I think a determination to be nuts, an insistent delight in every crazy thought. As if it was my duty to life to be insane. I did buy the gun, a few days later, and I started toward Brenda's apartment. Did I intend to kill her or was my intention merely to terrify her and learn the truth, what she did or didn't know? If there was a lover there with her, I would kill both of them. It was traditional. These things happen. You read about them in the newspapers.

Fate had its own ideas. As I drove along the Danforth, an old man pulled carelessly out of his parking place at the edge of the street, and before I could brake and as I was turning the wheel in a futile instinctive gesture, there was a noise of rending metal and my head cracked against the steering wheel. He had driven into the front fender of my car. I put my hand carefully to my forehead, and there was blood. The old man was still in his car, sitting behind the wheel, talking to me, gesturing, but I couldn't hear a word, and as I was about to get out to confront him, I looked at two boys who were watching from the other side of the street, and a thin woman in a red dress, and I realized that the police would be called, and that I had a gun in my pocket, a gun which would get me into no end of shit if it was discovered. I slipped it out of my coat pocket and as I pushed it under the seat, I discovered a bag that had held Chinese food, and I put the gun inside it and pushed it well back into the mess there. The old man was short and burly, someone who'd earned his way with his muscles. He had a moustache and thick greying hair, and he was out of his car, shouting across the sidewalk to a waiter who stood in the door of a restaurant. I found some Kleenex and wiped my forehead. There was more blood. I held Kleenex against the cut as I got out of the car.

Everyone was watching us. Maybe they thought we were going to fight. That would have been as likely as anything else that was happening to me. I'm sorry, old man, I wanted to say, I don't have time for car accidents, I have to go and kill someone. I could have got the gun and shot the old man. People did that.

I looked at the crumpled fender. The engine was still running. Why was that? Didn't I turn it off? The waiter from the restaurant was coming toward us. He talked quietly to the old man who listened and then turned to me. The old man didn't want to call the cops. He was afraid of them. With that gun under the seat, I had reason to be afraid too. The waiter, maybe it was his son or nephew, some kind of relative, said if I brought the repair bill to the restaurant, they'd see it was paid. So I agreed. The waiter took the old man's keys and in a few seconds, he had the car back in its parking place. I got in mine. I took the Kleenex away from my forehead and studied it. Maybe the bleeding was stopping. A guy in a car behind me honked. I cursed at him, but he couldn't hear me. He pulled round. The engine of my car was still running. I put it in gear and drove on, uncertain what I was going to do, but more or less automatically driving on to my original destination. I'd never been to Brenda's apartment, but I knew the street it was on. I would get there, get out my Chinese food bag with the gun in it and carry it to her door, then pull it out and murder her. I tried to get a look at myself in the rear view mirror, to see how much blood was on my face, but when I did, I lurched toward the other lane of traffic. My head was aching now, and I felt dizzy, but I was sure it wasn't from the blow. It was the craziness that had accumulated there over the years. I thought of my mother, ashes, her bitter memories calcined, gone in smoke.

I drove on to Brenda's apartment, but after I'd found the street and parked the car, and before I went to the door, I locked the bag containing my gun in the trunk. I wouldn't kill her, not today.

She stood back from the door to let me in. We went down the stairs to her apartment, which was in the basement. There wasn't much furniture, two canvas director's chairs, and a futon folded against the wall which featured a large blowup of a black-and-white photograph of Brenda playing Gwendolyn in *The Importance of Being Earnest* and looking beautiful. One night during the run of that show she threw a butcher knife at me, missed, and I picked it up and threw it back, missed. She sat on the futon in front of the picture. On a table beside her was a forty-ounce bottle of gin. I sat in the other chair, wondering what she saw in my face.

The door to the bedroom opened. Dirty jeans on long legs, a black T-shirt silk-screened with a red image of a screaming face, leather jacket, a narrow almost elegant face: twenty or twenty-one he was. She could always find someone unlikely. He looked past me to Brenda. Asked to borrow money, was refused. Gone.

I told Brenda I had come there to kill her, and she spread her arms, a gesture that meant go right ahead, and I could see the shape of her breasts under her sweatshirt. She stared at me, and the darkness around her eyes was like a circle of bruising, and the flesh was loose and wrinkled with tiny folds. My wife, and beautiful.

Your father, I said. My father's dead, she said. He was a jerk, so what? I know he didn't live up to the wonderful middle-class dignity of your family. So what? He's dead.

Did she know about the money they took from my father? She was the bait. They knew what she was like, the both of them. The words of an embittered dying woman. I thought about that photograph of the wedding, all the things that were happening, or might be happening around me while all I could think of was my cock and where I'd stick it as soon as we were alone. I looked at Brenda in her chair, and I wanted her.

We said a few bitter words. If I'd had the gun in my hand, it would have been easy enough to pull the trigger. I explained that I had a gun, but I'd left it in the car, and we stared at each other and I left, wondering if I might come back some time with the gun in my hand. In fact Brenda saved me the trouble. Two months later, she got enough barbiturates to do herself in. When I heard the news I threw up, then I cried, and then I pounded my fist against the wall until it bled.

Is it our duty to remember, or our duty to forget? There is a good argument either way. We are, in some ways, only what we remember, the person no more than the accumulation of past actions, the sum of earlier intentions and abilities; thus the failure to remember is a failure to know who we were and so who we are. We are creatures of time, and time is enriched by the ringing of old harmonies, old discords. It is my duty to remember what happened between Brenda and me. We can choose to make life intricate when it might be seen as only muddled.

As I stared at Eva Peltzer on my way out of the library to which I'd returned to read Philip's bitter, false, not-very-enlightening memoir, her face scarcely masking her righteous anger on behalf of my former wife, I looked at her sumptuous breasts. Brenda was always jealous of your big tits, I might have said, and she used to make me tell her what I would do if I had them in my hands. What did she tell you?

On the other hand, we might maintain that the past is a drag on our movement forward into what life is left to us, like a man walking uphill with a corpse tied to him to be pulled along over the stones and ruts. Driving away from the university, as I looked out of the car window over the landscape of farms and woodlots, a small creek in the valley below, I saw a dark figure struggling forward with that load behind him, a man in silhouette against the sky and the geometry of a rail fence, myself dragging Brenda's dead body, naked and pathetic, bits of grass and rock catching in the hair. The car reached a hilltop, and I turned away and looked across miles of landscape to the silver glitter of the lake. The future, if I cut the rope. Instead of picking at the wound, let it heal and vanish, without a scar, on the perfect surface of the skin. She is gone, and I have the last word. Philip had treasured resentments, and I had spent the afternoon in the company of his ill-wishing power of recall. One kind of truth. An unpleasant way to spend the time, all in all, and as I read I was aware of Philip's intention that his rancour should come among us and leave wounds. Are we the better for it? Isn't it time for an act of oblivion as after a civil war? History is no more than a rummaging for excuses, a template for revenge.

Choose to remember, choose to forget. Time goes by, and we grind our noses on the wheel of the world, and perhaps we come to suspect that all choices are arbitrary and often ridiculous. Or illusory. Leah left behind a biography of Glenn Gould that she had been reading on her flight to Toronto. *In counterpoint all voices should be equal*, it says somewhere, but that is a counsel of perfection. I can't make all voices equal and since I can't, the thing to do is to put my foot down on the accelerator and move more quickly on to tomorrow, though I suspect that Brenda will continue to come back in dreams, tempting me to reach for what cannot be touched.

Who would have guessed that a field of artichokes is a beautiful thing? Here in California I learn much that is new. The pages that I cut so neatly out of Philip's manuscript, using the sharp Swiss army knife that my son James gave me one Christmas, have sailed out into the Pacific. What is the use of years of training as an editor if you are not free to excise the superfluous? Tomorrow Leah and I will drive to south through Carmel and Monterey and there will be much to discover.

3.

Late Hours

Where Is He Now?

'Hello.'
'So is he there?'
'Who is it you want?'
'Don't kid around. I'm in a hurry.'
'I'm sorry, but ...'
'Oh for Christ's sake. I'll call later.'

'Hello.'
'Is that the doctor?'
'What?'
'Is that the doctor?'
'I think you've got the wrong number.'
'I'm sorry. It's late, isn't it. I'm really sorry.'

'Hello.'
'Is he there?'
'Who is it you want?'
'Oh for Christ's sake. Emmanuel. Would you just put him on?'
'I'm afraid you've got the wrong number.'
'Is that 721-8543?'
'Yes.'
'Then where is he?'
'This is my number. I just moved in here, and it's the number they gave me. Your friend must have moved or changed his number.'
'So what's his new number?'
'I don't know. I don't know anything about him. This is my number, and that's all I can tell you.'
'You don't have his new number.'
'No.'
'Well, has he moved?'

'I don't have any idea. I don't know the man, and I don't know his number, and I'm going to hang up now.'

'Yes, hello, could I speak to Mr Emmanuel please.'
'I'm sorry but there's no such person at this number.'
'Excuse me?'
'He's not here.'
'Please when will he be available.'
'You have the wrong number.'
'But I was told ...'
'I'm sorry, but he's not here.'
'He will be back?'
'No.'
'He will not be back.'
'He doesn't live here.'
'He is living where?'
'I don't know.'
'It is important for me to speak with Mr Emmanuel.'
'Look. This is my number. I just had a new telephone put in, and this is the number they gave me. I don't know anything about the man you're looking for. He must have changed his number or gone away.'
'Mr Emmanuel has gone away?'
'I don't know.'
'Where has he gone?'
'I don't know.'
'You don't know where he has gone?'
'Right.'
'It is important.'
'I'm sure it is. But I can't help you.'

'I shouldn't have called at this hour. I'm really sorry. I'll call again.'
'Who is that?'
'I'll call another time. It's all right.'
'Who is that speaking?'

* * *

How are you making out, James, being all alone there?'

'Getting used to it.'

'Don't you find you're lonely?'

'Sometimes.'

'I never understood why you suddenly took leave of absence and went away. All your friends are here.'

'Well, things happen.'

'James, why did you leave?'

'I had my reasons.'

'It was all so sudden. There was someone, wasn't there? There must have been.'

'I just needed to get away.'

'You know you're welcome to come back and stay with us any time.'

'Yes.'

'And you're doing OK.'

'I'm making notes for something, an article, maybe a book.'

'Good. I envy you the free time.'

'It might turn into something.'

'You keep in touch then. When you feel lonely just pick up the phone.'

'I will.'

'Hello.'

'Is that you again?'

'Who?'

'Oh for Christ's sake, it is. I recognize your voice.'

'And I recognize yours.'

'He's still not there.'

'I don't think so.'

'You mean you don't know?'

'I don't have the slightest idea who it is you're looking for.'

'I already told you. Emmanuel.'

'Look, I moved to the city. I got in touch with the phone company, and they gave me a phone number, and I plugged in my phone, and now I keep getting calls for this Emmanuel person. But I don't know who he is.'

'So where do you live?'

'What's that got to do with anything?'

'Are you at his place?'

'Why would I be at his place?'

'You got his phone number.'

'You sound like a very old-fashioned person.'

'What's that supposed to mean?'

'Never mind. I can't help you. Maybe you should call the phone company.'

'Is that the doctor?

'No.'

'Is he there?'

'I'm afraid you've got the wrong number.'

'Sorry.'

'Is the doctor there?'

'No. I think you've got the wrong number again.'

'But I dialled so carefully.'

'What number did you dial?'

'721-8543.'

'That's my number.'

'Then are you the doctor?'

'No. That's not who I am.'

'They gave me the wrong number.'

'I don't know. I've had a lot of calls for someone named Emmanuel.'

'That's him, Doctor Emmanuel. That's who I'm trying to get hold of.'

'Is he someone you've seen before?'

'No. I just got his name.'

'I've had some other calls. Nobody seems to know if he's changed his number or gone away or whatever he's done.'

'Do you think he's gone away?'

'I don't know. If he has, surely you could find another doctor.'

'But he's really special. That's what they say about him. He can help when the other doctors can't. There are people like that, you know.'

'I've always thought all doctors were pretty much the same.'

'There are some who are special.'

'And that's what you're looking for.'

'Everyone is.'

'What is it that he does that's so unusual.'

'You're sure you don't know where he's gone?'

'You could try the phone company.'

'Yes.'

'Do you need to see a doctor soon?'

'In a way.'

'I didn't mean to pry.'

'That's all right. You have a nice voice. And you've tried to help. I'm sure you're a really nice person.'

'Well, thank you.'

'You think the telephone company might know where to find him?'

'They should know if he has a new number. He wouldn't just go away without telling people, would he? I don't think he would. He'd tell people.'

'I'll call them, the phone company. I guess there's nothing else I can do. I'm sorry I bothered you.'

'It was no bother. You have a nice voice too.'

'Hello.'

'I was talking to you a few minutes ago.'

'Yes, I recognize your voice.'

'After you hung up, I felt concerned. You sounded worried. Unhappy.'

'How did you get my number?'

'You can do that. Get the last number that called yours.'

'I guess so.'

'After you hung up, I was thinking about you, so I got the number and called. To see if you were OK.'

'That was nice of you. Actually I'm kind of tired now.'

'I didn't mean to intrude. I was interested in what you said about

Doctor Emmanuel. He sounds like a wonderful man. And you seem to need someone.'

'It will be all right.'

'There must be another doctor. If you really need one.'

'Yes, there's always another.'

'Would it be all right if I called you again? Later on. Just to see that you're OK. I know I'm going to be wondering about you.'

'If that's what you want to do.'

'Yes, I will. I'll call sometime.'

'Hello.'

'Yes. Good morning. Is that Mr Manual?'

'Who?'

'Mr Manual. Mr E. Manual. I'm calling from ...'

'The name is Emmanuel. Doctor Emmanuel.'

'Good morning, doctor. Sorry to have got that wrong.'

'It's not me.'

'What's that?'

'I'm not the person you want.'

'But you said.'

'No. Emmanuel has gone away. To South America to study natural healing techniques. In a spiritual community in the Andes mountains.'

'I see.'

'Hello.'

'Hello, I talked to you a few days ago. You were looking for the doctor.'

'I remember. And you were very nice.'

'Did you find him?'

'Who?'

'The doctor. Doctor Emmanuel.'

'No. He wasn't there.'

'But were you able to get a new number for him?'

'No. You see, he wasn't there. He's gone away.'

'But did you try the phone company? To get another number?'

'You told me he'd gone away.'

'I don't know if he's gone away. I just know that he doesn't have my number any more.'

'But that means he's gone, doesn't it?'

'Maybe he's just changed his number.'

'Why would he do that?'

'He just got tired of the old one. In a moment of whimsy, he decided it was time for a change. So he bought a new jacket and a new pair of shoes and changed his phone number.'

'You seem to know a lot about him.'

'I don't know anything about him.'

'You know that he bought a new jacket and a new pair of shoes.'

'No, I don't.'

'Then why did you tell me that.'

'I made it up. It was just an idea.'

'You have ideas about him.'

'Yes, I do. It's not surprising. People keep phoning me and asking for him. Someone phoned in the middle of the night last night.'

'Who was that?'

'I thought it might have been you.'

'Why would I phone you in the middle of the night?'

'You might have been lonely or upset.'

'No, that's not why.'

'You mean it was you?'

'No. I don't mean that.'

'Then what did you mean?'

'I meant if I phoned you in the middle of the night, that's not why I'd do it.'

'Why would you do it?'

'I'm not sure.'

'Was it you that phoned?'

'No.'

'That's too bad. I hoped it was.'

'I was asleep in the middle of the night.'

'Do you mind if I ask your name?'

'My name is Amber.'

'That's a nice name.'

'They're right, you know.'

'About what?'

'You are a good doctor.'

'What do you mean?'

'I've figured it out now. That's part of what you do. You say you're someone else.'

'What if I am someone else?'

'You're Doctor Emmanuel.'

'What makes you think that, Amber?'

'They told me he wasn't like any other doctor. And you're not, but you made me feel a lot better. Just talking to you. The first time I talked to you, and when you phoned me back after that, I realized that I was feeling different. I wasn't as worried, and I couldn't figure out why, but just now when you told me about your new jacket and shoes, I figured it out.'

'But I'm not really the doctor, Amber. My name is James. That's who I am.'

'It will be all right. I know it will.'

'Mr Emmanuel?'

'No.'

'Mr Emmanuel has gone away?'

'Yes, Mr Emmanuel has gone away. He's gone to Zurich for a long course of analysis.'

'When he returns please will you tell him that Marwan is calling him.'

'He isn't going to return, Marwan. He is going to achieve perfect emotional balance and move to another level of being.'

'It is important for me to talk to him. Please.'

'I'll give him your message.'

'Hello Doctor, it's Amber. I'm sorry to wake you up, but I need to talk to you.'

'Amber …?'

'You remember me, don't you?'

'I think I was having a dream, and you were in it.'

'Oh, I'm glad you dreamed about me. I'm sure that's part of it.'

'Part of what?'

'You know I can't explain, Doctor Emmanuel. But I can feel the difference. It's just something inside me.'

'That's good. That's wonderful. But I'm not really the doctor, am I?'

'Are you trying to tell me I cure myself? I know that's true, in a way, but it's not just that. There's the sound of your voice, and that I know how many others you've helped, and how you try to keep it a secret.'

'No, Amber, it's not like that.'

'Well, explain it to me.'

'What if you met me?'

'Oh, I couldn't meet you.'

'Why not?'

'It just wouldn't be right, not now.'

'You mean later?'

'No, I don't mean that. I don't think I'm brave enough to meet you. What happens on the phone is just perfect, the way you make me struggle to understand. It would be too much to meet you, doctor.'

'Why not? Really, why not?'

'I know that you always know the right thing to say, but it frightens me when you sound impatient like that.'

'I'm sorry to frighten you, Amber. I didn't mean to.'

'You've made such a difference to me, Doctor Emmanuel.'

'I'm glad, Amber. I really am glad.'

'You see right into my soul.'

'Then why don't you want to meet me?'

'Don't you think it would be too much?'

'I don't know.'

'I couldn't bear to really meet you and see you and have to shake your hand. It would be too much. To see you. And I don't usually see people.'

'Why not?'

'They get too close.'

'I'm not sure I understand.'

'You say that, but I know you do, doctor.'

'Oh, Amber...'

'What?'

'You've made a difference too.'

'Have I?'

'Yes, you have. Things are not the same. But I don't know quite what to do next.'

'You'll help someone else. That's what you do.'

'Is it?'

'You're funny sometimes, Doctor Emmanuel. Of course it's what you do. You know what everybody says about you.'

'Amber...'

'What?'

'Do you think you're going to go on feeling better?'

'Yes, I think so.'

'What will you do if you start to feel bad again?'

'I'll just remember the talks we had.'

'Will you call me?'

'You wouldn't want me to become dependent, would you? That's one of the good things about you. How you make me feel as if I've done it myself.'

'So you won't be calling me?'

'You need to have time for the others.'

'Amber, can I tell you something. A kind of story?'

'Is it something I want to hear?'

'Well, maybe not. I don't know. No, never mind.'

'I'm going to sleep now, and I know if I have dreams they'll all be happy ones.'

'Hello.'

'Amber?'

'Who?'

'Amber. Is she there?'

'No, there's no Amber here.'

'What number is that?'

'725-8093.'

'But that's her number. Where has she gone?'

'I'm sorry, but I don't know anybody by that name.'

'You don't know where she's gone?'

'No idea.'

* * *

'Could I speak to Amber, please?'

'I told you before, there's no Amber here.'

'Are you sure? It's Doctor Emmanuel calling.'

'Of course I'm sure, and I don't care what kind of a doctor you are. Don't call again.'

'Hello ... who's there? Who is that? Who's there? Is it you?'

Flight

The choir again, its baffled, looming sound, the soft rumbling of the basses, the entanglement of the harmonies, quiet drums. Why could he not make out the words? As if they were singing in one of the vanished languages, the last speaker severed. Often it seemed to him that his own words were no longer current, that those he addressed couldn't comprehend him.

The seat next to him was empty, and he was tempted to lean across it and ask the white-haired woman on the other side of the aisle if she knew the composer's name; her face, calm, lightly made up, created the impression of an educated sensibility, a likelihood of knowledge. He felt an impulse to speak to her, but he had nothing to say. Everything blew away in the stream of air from the impelling jets. They sailed through space, the wild blue yonder of the old song, toward some place on the planet where they were awaited, Brisbane or Venice or Tierra del Fuego, Polaris, that frozen city. The tops of high mountains could pierce the clouds. In New York he had seen the Empire State Building rising above the low overcast, the calm stateliness of its tower, where men and women looked out the office window and saw, not the earth, but this barrier of cloud. He could remember such things, but others were evasive, slippery as wet soap.

Past retirement age but unwilling to conclude, he was in his own charge on all his expeditions, had despatched himself. Foolishly, he had nothing to read. He took his little briefcase from the floor at his feet and looked inside, as if it might contain a forgotten magazine. He found a boarding pass, his old address book. He removed the elastic that held the old thing together and turned the loose pages. In the office, Thomas, his secretary, had everything digitally recorded and entered in his laptop. No, Thomas, he says regularly, I do not need a Raspberry or a Palm Puppet. I have you.

The tiny ancient book threatened to fall to pieces in his hand. The alphabet, obedient, began with A. Allward, Jerome. Beneath that a single name, Anneke, and a phone number, from long ago when the

Toronto exchanges had names. Walnut 5-2496. How long ago was that? Fifty years?

In the back of the address book, just past Zezulka, Brian, and pasted inside the back cover is a tiny photograph of a dark-haired young woman in a white muslin dress. Something about the cut of the dress makes it difficult to guess when the photograph might have been taken. She wouldn't wear such a dress now. Even on the day when he clicked the shutter the dress was like something her mother or grandmother might have worn.

On her face that moody half-pout: Lucy-Corinne so many years before, when she was Lucy, in the days of their marriage, the days when they would wake side by side. The photograph holds its secrets. He pasted it in the book many years after it was taken. He likes to have it close at hand.

Allward, Jerome: a round, pale face, double chin, weak eyes behind spectacles with dark, heavy rims. If he is still alive he will have changed the style of eyeglasses, perhaps been fitted for contacts. Jerome was personnel director for a company that manufactured small metal parts for everything from skis to bicycles to kitchen cupboards. The proverbial widgets. A closely held enterprise, they were regular clients – annual meeting and company banquet – until they sold out and vanished into the complex book-keeping of a larger enterprise. Jerome, pale and pudgy, was married to a woman of striking beauty, a small elegant red-head with the contours of a Barbie doll. The president of the company appeared, each year, in the alcoholic disorder of the company banquet, to have designs on that perfect body, but the woman showed no sign of being tempted. Drunken salesmen liked to speculate salaciously about her reasons. She was herself a teetotaller. Twenty years now since that company vanished.

When Lucy-Corinne meets him, she will be smiling, the smile that wholly alters the thin, fine-featured face, with its slightly pointed nose, the narrow but shapely lips, the sulky look vanishing. How they laughed together. They were amused by the same things, like brother and sister. She is older now, of course; there are wrinkles and dark patches beneath the eyes, grey in the hair. The slender figure has altered. He has kept in touch; he always helped her out in moments when she lost her footing on the spinning world. Her voice on the phone, long distance from some dark corner, words at first metallic, hard, and then, especially late at night, she might lose control and begin to weep, and her voice would thicken, grow clotted and sodden, and if he was alone in his apartment, he might find himself weeping with her. Her children, grandchildren, are fond of him, he has felt their affection.

Anneke. An acquaintance from university, married to a graduate student, a quietly beautiful girl with a slight accent. She called to ask for a job. Her marriage had broken up, and she needed work, knew he was running the hotel, but it was just after his pretty cousin Lucy had arrived to handle bookings, and while Lucy still kept a certain distance between them, she was jealous if she found him being attentive to any other woman. The dark eyebrows came down, the mouth grew thin. He knew how she would react if he hired Anneke. He had decided to marry Lucy and thought her jealousy boded well for his suit. No, he dare not hire Anneke, lovely as she was. He found that now he could hardly imagine her face. He remembered that it was beautiful.

More names under A, then under B, Buy-Ware, the enterprise whose convention was the first he put together, when the hotel was sold and he joined the company that bought it, setting up the department that organized meetings and conventions and which later became an independent enterprise. Where he spent the rest of his working life. B for Buy-Ware and B (doubly) for Bolger, Barbara, the call-girl he used to contact if senior management at one of the conventions grew frisky and demanding. Not without embarrassment he had, by means of an outlandishly large tip, got her name from a bartender at a downtown hotel. Took her to dinner at a good restaurant – La Chaumière it was, Toronto's first little French restaurant – and after dinner he explained his interest. He offered a respectful amount by way of retainer, and she looked him in the eye and asked if he wished to sample the goods. The blood had rushed to his face. She apologized for making him uncomfortable.

His work involved him with such things, men and women overexcited by the occasion of a meeting, battles for power, warriors drenched in blood but still unsated, or having arrived in the city from smaller places, tumid with expectation, willing to toss good judgment aside. Himself he strolled about, sober, careful, astute, checking off items on his clipboard, answering questions with a neutral politeness. He was not implicated in the only-just-legal corporate decisions, the libertine transgressions. He hired the janitors who would clean up afterward, while he went back to his office and prepared the invoice.

Turn the pages, and you come on C and then D, and the rest, as the little address book told the story of his life. Plunkett, Frederick. A telephone number he had never called. Many years ago now, he had run into Frederick at a university reception that his department had been hired to organize – the public announcement of a new research foundation, funded by a successful investment company. In fact he hadn't recognized the man among the crowd, but Frederick, far-sighted, had spotted the name on his lapel and come to shake his hand. A professor of classics: what Frederick had become. Once they were not-especially-friendly schoolboys; on one occasion he had been invited to spend a week visiting at the Plunkett family cottage.

The picture of Lucy in her white dress, its secrets. She will change her name when she leaves him. She will become Corinne. In the photograph – he works it out later on – she is already pregnant, so perhaps in her own mind she is no longer his Lucy. Is already becoming Corinne, French and sophisticated, brutally conjoined to a wicked man, tearing his skin with the fingernails she kept so perfectly shaped and polished. Things she will tell him when she explains why she is leaving, that he, her cousin-husband, is a good man and what she needs is a very bad one. He offers to accept the other man's child, the product of such excellent brutality, but that is not good enough for her.

In his mind's eye he sees an almost monochrome image, heavily shadowed, what appears to be a snowy field with a woodlot at its edge. Though nothing moves, there is a slight shift in the point of view that suggests the lens being accidentally shifted to one side. Careful observation will show the tips of the branches moving in the wind, and there is a slight, ominous sound of cold breeze over the snowy field. A sharp eye might notice the form of a deer, delicate, beautiful, perfectly still at the edge of the woods. A metallic click, then the explosive crack of a rifle shot, and the deer falls, its legs moving a little in some hopeless, belated attempt to escape.

The sunlight was bright on the tops of the clouds. A stewardess moved past, up the aisle. She had seen all this before. The complex interweaving of voices in the choir was gone. There was only the noise of the jet engines. You could buy earphones that would shut out the

179

noise and leave you with the illusion of silence. His eyes closed.

The dream is muddled, unaccountable, but it has its own truth. He is on a plane so crowded that many of the passengers have to stand, and his legs are growing weary. If he can get through the crowd toward the front of the plane he will find her. He is fighting with the other passengers, trying to push them aside, though it is hard for him to keep standing, his legs paralyzed. He must find her, discover a corner where they can talk. Unless she is with some other man.

His eyes opened, and he knew, waking, what he could not know sleeping, who the woman was in his dream. Always the same, Lucy-Corinne, his gift, his punishment. He thought how much he would like to light up his pipe; such a comforting habit, but it is forbidden to him now for reasons of health.

The choir was back, in full contrapuntal rage, and now there was a man in the seat beside him, and on the chair back in front shimmered a tiny spot of light, a reflection from some bright surface, and he watched it dance, the silvery golden circle. To the left it went, and up, then up again, then far back down, and a little right. It will lead him out to walk among the clouds, to fall to earth, colder and colder, faster and faster. Once he heard of a poem describing a man plunging to earth, fallen out of an air machine.

Excuse me, he might say to the man beside him, but where did you come from? Don't you know that the seat is reserved for my companion. She is here somewhere. It's where she will sit. The man would stare at him as if he were mad. Perhaps a stewardess will pass by and he can purchase a miniature bottle of whisky. Or two. Two whiskies would reveal something. It was what he had allowed himself during certain times of his life, at the end of the day. Two whiskies, and if truth be told, there was a period when he poured with a heavy hand. She would phone him from Ottawa, where, after her misadventures, she had fetched up, and he was glad to receive the calls. It's Corinne, she would say, though she was still Lucy to him. Lucy-Corinne. In his mind they were still married in spite of the divorce, and the two children were his. Was it remotely possible that Derwent, the older, the boy, was actually his son?

If he were to impregnate her, she decided in the days before their wedding, she would bear monsters. They were cousins, and it was perilous. She would bear dwarves and two-headed freaks. They were cousins. Half cousins, in fact, but he accepted her fear of the dangerous biological closeness. He made her laugh, and the true beauty of her face emerged, as he knew it would. The dark metal of her eyes burned with a glitter of happiness. He kept her as safe as a princess in a castle. They were still living together when Derwent was conceived; she swore it was the result of her first coarse, infinitely satisfying penetration by that other man. There might ... well, he didn't know, couldn't remember. He had thought they were happy. The deceived husband always does. That other man was long gone. She no longer ended her phone calls in tears. They had dinner when they found themselves in the same city. She had been married again, widowed. She would be there to meet him at the end of his flight. When he encountered her at the airport a familiar light would shine around her. Derwent was married now, and had a son of his own, called Matt. They lived in California. The pieces moved to their new places on the board. The young became the old. In his luggage, stowed in a compartment under the plane, was an album of photos which he carried everywhere with him, the personae of his life, including Derwent and his family, Lucy-Corinne's daughter Eve in her garden in Australia. In one old sepia photo his grandfather wears tennis whites, shirt and long white trousers, under his arm a racket. Back from the First World War, his hair still thick and dark, and he has just opened a hotel in a town on the lakeshore a little distance outside Toronto, capital provided by a couple of senior officers, friends from the war; it did well in the good times and survived the bad ones. Those with money always had money, or so he had been told by his mother. She didn't like the man, her father-in-law, the way he treated his son, kept him under was the phrase she used, and in the picture in the album which represents that generation, posed on a summer day, awaiting the future, she is not to be found. It was taken behind the hotel and shows the handsome man in his tennis whites, his pretty second wife, her daughter Emily in a wide-brimmed straw hat, the tall son from his first marriage, too tall for his bones somehow, putting a good face on it, and nowhere to be seen the elegant, sharp-eyed wife of that tall son. There is a picture of her in the album, later, looking posed and careful. Long, lean and lovely, his father called her. Himself, he was not kept under but pushed forward, by both his parents, but his mother especially, starting him to work in the hotel when he was fifteen. The grandfather died just after his grandson's university graduation – a three-year degree, in and out as fast as he could manage. His only real pleasure in it was singing in the glee club, and he would have aspired to a career in music but knew he hadn't the talent. The album he keeps with him has a picture of the glee club performing. The selection of pictures, episodic like the selections made by memory from life, presents a shaped and defined arrangement of the events. He goes nowhere without it.

It shows less than everything. No snapshot of his father with a tennis racket, though he played the game eagerly and well. Days after the grandfather's funeral, after all the family had left, his father invited him out to the court behind the hotel. He had never seen the man play with such ferocity. His height and long arms always made him a dangerous opponent, but on that day his serves and overhead returns were sharper, the balls at the edge of the court had an intolerable deceptive spin. He said nothing except for a soft mumbling of the score now and then, deuce, game point, and then the long arm would reach out and drive the ball fiercely at his son. Afterward he disappeared, came back from his shower calm and soft-spoken as always.

The spot of reflected light glimmered, slipped, leapt up and came back. He was puzzled to know the source of this reflection, moving with the motion of the plane, a reflection from something hanging in the sun, swayed by gravity.

Somewhere below, the fated, falling man is descending toward the earth, his skin cold and colder as the rush of air draws heat from the surface of his swift doomed body. The heavier-than-air craft is engineered to expend its fuel in long reaches of sky to achieve great distances. Its little community of strangers waits obediently as the journey through space finds its way to a named location. Anonymous here in the sky, as abstracted from continuity as the logic of a philosopher's academic paper delivered to an audience of other, similarly abstracted minds. The passengers who sit in their upright seats have names, but they mean nothing here. Names are a convenience of quotidian life, and they can be changed. Lucy becomes Corinne.

His cousin Lucy was twelve years old the first time he met her. Her mother, during the early years of her marriage, moved about a lot, and when, after the Hitler war, the husband returned from service as a staff officer overseas, they located in Montreal – not that far away, but she seldom came to visit, and always alone. His father's half-sister and his long lean and lovely mother avoided each other when they could. On the occasion of his grandfather's death, his aunt Emily brought her husband and Lucy with her to the funeral, but the husband, an upright, still-military-looking man with a dark moustache and eyebrows and hooded eyes, one eyelid hanging so far the eye was almost closed, left immediately after the burial, too busy, too much in demand to remain longer, but Emily and Lucy stayed a few days at the hotel. His aunt asserting her territorial rights perhaps. He found his father's half-sister brittle, hard to know – her daughter Lucy was a silent, sulking girl, though now and then she broke out in sudden laughter – but you could tell she would one day be beautiful. Someone, his father or his aunt, decided he could be made dispensable at the hotel, where he was now a full-time employee, and he found himself put in charge of the mother and daughter's entertainment, Lucy's mainly; much of the time her mother sat in the lounge reading magazines. Or in her room listening to the radio. He showed Lucy the secret passages of the old building, the mysteries he had discovered while snooping about when he was her age. One day he drove her into the city to see a matinee. He took his father's big Mercury, and they drove in a silence punctuated by blunt questions on her part. What were his jobs? Was he well paid? Did he plan to keep working at the hotel? He would have said she only half-listened to his answers, but during the car ride back in the evening, she asked questions that indicated she had been thinking about his words.

'Who's going to inherit the hotel?' she said. 'Will you still have your job?'

'I guess it would be my father and your mother. Nobody said.'

'So my mother will be your boss.'

'Maybe.'

'She'll be a bitch.'

'Language,' he said, 'watch your language, little girl.'

'Bitch,' she said. 'Bitch, bitch, bitch. Female dog. But I guess she could make you accompany me to the movies any time I wanted.'

He turned his eyes from the road to look at her, just for a moment. He thought she would be smiling, but she wasn't. She didn't turn to meet his look, and he concentrated on guiding the big Mercury along the dark road.

The next day after breakfast, his aunt came to him where he was working at the front desk. On the drive to Toronto he had mentioned to Lucy a pioneer log house off the dirt road behind the hotel, and the two of them, mother and daughter, wanted him to take them there. The carefully made-up face – dark lips, painted eyebrows – was impassive as she made her request. Or was it a demand? That afternoon, when he got his break, he guided them to the derelict cabin.

They walked downhill on a footpath through the woods which was the shortest way, but it had been a rainy spring, and the water in the little creek bed at the bottom of the hill was deeper than he expected, the cold water splashing over stones and fallen branches. He led them to a narrow section where there was a stepping stone in the middle. His aunt surveyed the stretch of water.

'Your big strong country cousin will have to carry us across, won't he, Lucy? We're city girls.'

Lucy said nothing, but defiantly put one foot on the stone and leapt to the far bank. Waited there, silent, watching, evaluating. His aunt Emily stood at the edge of the water. She had put on slacks for the walk, but rather than reaching her foot out to the dry stone, she stared at him now, giving him a look. Request or demand. He crossed the stream.

'Don't leave me here,' she said. He bent and took off his socks and shoes, rolled up his trousers and stepped back into the icy flow, stood by the rock in the middle and put out his hand to her.

'Your cousin is quite a gentleman, Lucy,' she said.

She took his hand. Hers was small, the skin warm and soft. She gripped hard as she took a step to the rock, rebalanced and then gave a little hop to the far bank. The toe of one shoe had dipped in the water and she scuffed it against some leaves to dry it. Then she turned and looked at him as he stepped out of the cold water, his damp feet bare and pale. She gave him a narrow smile. Lucy had already begun to climb up the hill to the log cabin.

'We'll go back another way,' he said.

His aunt shrugged, waited beside him while he put on his socks and shoes and then she walked up the path ahead of him. The next day the two of them returned to Montreal where the dark man with hooded eyes waited for them. It was nearly ten years later that Lucy came to work at the hotel; her father was dead by then, gone suddenly one afternoon at his club.

The man in the seat beside him had vanished. He looked out the window, bent forward to gaze across the wing and out over the sunlit clouds. Time did not exist in this airy universe. One might float away upward as easily as come back to earth.

The stewardess offered him a tiny snack, a glass of something. On the tray in front of him the plastic tumbler and the little cellophane packet glittered, but he had no appetite for them. Perhaps he should have ordered whisky, but he had hesitated and then it was too late. Contained, isolated, he did not wish to enter negotiation with the outside world.

Sunlight on clouds. The plane soared, like a god, untouchable, above the world. He had chosen to live in an apartment on the nearly topmost floor of a building at the crest of the escarpment on Avenue Road. On a clear day he could look past the islands to the lake. Near that window was the antique chest of drawers where he kept Lucy's things. When she was leaving he helped her pack, folding blouses, skirts, jeans and putting them in suitcases, and after he carried the first two bags to the waiting car, she began to cry and refused to pack anything else. Fled.

Over the next week he threw out the worn and useless and folded everything else carefully and placed it all in the drawers of the small antique pine chest. It was always possible that she would return, and if so, there would be clothes prepared for her. They lay in their places, sacred objects, a few stalks of lavender, renewed annually in season, to keep them fresh, though the styles were now out of date, and nothing would fit her. Yes, he would say to himself, it is a reliquary, but if I have chosen this incorrigible fidelity, it is my choice and mine to maintain.

His mother wished him to marry again after Lucy was gone, and he couldn't adequately explain to her that he remained married, to Lucy, the legal decree of divorce having no effect on the reality of it all. He had married her, and though she had chosen to abandon her place with him, he was as much allied with her as the day they spoke their vows. He couldn't help it. He had given himself and could not recant.

He didn't try to explain this to his mother, who thought he had been badly treated and wished him to find comfort with some other, more loving woman. There was no such comfort to be found. Persons were not interchangeable.

An image, darkness at the edges, as if there are trees all around, and among them, visible but dim, an old log house, some of the windows broken. In the distance the sound of frogs, which breed copiously in a nearby swamp or pond. Endless croaking of the amphibian throats. Nothing moves. In the far distance, it may be, a sound of a car or perhaps a truck. A figure appears from behind the log house, a girl in a straw hat who looks to be searching for something. Moves out of sight. Crows caw, fall silent.

Lucy believed there were must be ghosts in the log cabin. She mentioned them – not on the day he showed her and his aunt the way, for she knew her mother would mock the idea – but years later, when she came back to the hotel to work. They chattered like monkeys in those days. The two only children found there was much to say as they worked side by side. When Lucy had time free she would make her way through the woods to the increasingly derelict log cabin, seeing birds and rabbits among the trees, standing inside the ruined house seeking ghosts. The ghosts are imaginary, he told her. And are the rabbits imaginary? she said. Of course, he said, teasing her. You are the victim of imaginary rabbits. What she said when she left: I'm finished with imaginary rabbits.

Perhaps she was. Imaginary rabbits and much else, kindness, protection. His own situation was taken out of his hands, and he was left bare and shaking. When the hotel was sold she received her share of the funds, a substantial amount, but he believed it was soon gone, tossed away on ill-conceived projects by the incorrigible man she had chosen. They lived on whim, the oxygen-rich breathing of impulsive moments, great plans, foolishness, failure, anger. Himself he was, by nature and profession, provident, sensible, well-organized always. Within him, one might say, there must be blood-letting rage, unseemly hunger, but it remained buried. Disorder was, for him, a picayune annoyance, a bug in the ear.

Yet now he was finding himself confused and uncertain, unsure of the time of arrival, haunted too by the fear that his luggage had been left behind. The increase of bullying by airport security staff, the constant demand for documentation made him more uneasy, not less. Anything could happen. He might arrive at his destination and find that Lucy-Corinne was not there waiting for him. I'm finished with imaginary rabbits.

The address book lay on the tray beside his plastic glass of water. He opened it to the pages that told the story of her life, her new name, changing locations, phone numbers, a scribble in the corner, *10 a.m.* As he stared at the addresses, crossed out, replaced, he was aware, as suddenly as if he had been punched by a passing stranger, that he could no longer remember her face. He recited her features to himself. It began to return, though in a fragmentary way. At the bottom of the page were recent addresses for Derwent and Eve.

He was convinced that his bag was on another flight, gone the wrong way, a momentary clerical error by the woman who was checking in the luggage. Somewhere in Europe a baggage clerk would open the case and find within it the book of photographs. In his ear tinnitus imitated the sound of laughter. He closed his eyes to concentrate, to make it vanish.

Then suddenly he is standing, staring, lost in an airport, all the names and numbers forgotten: he can't remember the procedures for a change of flight. Down steps to a locked door, shook it but it would not open, so he went back up. The wide glass windows revealed a length of bare field, with two asphalt strips of runway. A small plane passed along the runway and out of sight beyond a corner of the building. The bright space that contained him was begabbled with the processed sound of hidden speakers, but he couldn't understand the language, couldn't in fact even make out what language it might be. Or perhaps he had suffered some kind of cerebral accident and was unable to process human speech, sound collapsing into random noise, all speech metamorphosed into glossolalia, mere music. Is speaking in tongues a primitive form of communication or a sophisticated one, like abstract art, a deliberate and cultivated withdrawal from convention into the pure principle of expression? He had no answer to that, though he was pleased at being able to articulate the question. Words had not deserted him. He walked the length of the high, luminous gallery where he was imprisoned. There were small cafés, but none had an empty chair where he might sit down, and his legs were weary, his feet heavy as bags of sand.

It's possible that this airport was the final stop, and that he had made a wrong turn, should be picking up his bag and passing through a door to find Lucy waiting for him, shut off from him by a glass wall, wondering why he did not appear to her out of the crowd, though as he pictured her, she was not what she had become but the young woman he married. She would not be waiting for him, not here where they spoke an incomprehensible tongue. It was his duty to find a screen and learn where his connecting flight could be boarded. Corinne. He reminded himself to think of her that way. You can never find anyone if you search for her by the wrong name. Corinne. She used that name still, though the second husband, the bad man she required, was long gone. She had found other bad men.

He passed a newspaper kiosk. A face on the front of one of the tabloids. Half-familiar. Some movie star perhaps. The headline was in French, and his French was too feeble to comprehend it. Hanging from the roof of the long gallery was a shape constructed out of coloured glass, something like a kite or an old biplane, a sculpture, he decided, though suspended as it was, on thin wires, it frightened him, that it might plunge, the shards of glass severing whatever they struck on the way down.

A queue of men. Waiting for a washroom, it appeared. One or two men appeared from the doorway, tidying themselves. That picture on the tabloid. He should know who it was. Attempting to go back and take another look, he found that he was lost again, unable to find his way.

As he passed by one of the cafés someone stood up from a chair, and the woman in the chair opposite looked at him and made a gesture with her hand, indicating that he might sit with her. Though he wished to rest his legs, he believed there would be perplexity and danger in the woman's silent offer, and he turned away. Once again he grew convinced that Lucy-Corinne waited for him somewhere in this glass maze. Or was it one of the airports where you must take a shuttle bus to a different terminal? He stood perfectly still, closed his eyes, to sleep for a moment on his feet. He and Lucy scuffed through the fallen leaves in the woodlot, listened to the chuckling of the little creek, quiet together, searching for her imaginary rabbits.

A voice called to him, but when he opened his eyes she was gone. He walked on, uncertain what to do next. He searched for an official who might be in charge, and finally he joined one of the lineups. At the front would be an airline employee who would set him straight.

Once more in the air, he realized that while he was on foot in the airport he should have bought something to read. He recalled the photograph on the cover of the tabloid newspaper. He knew why it was familiar. The woman resembled Frederick Plunkett's older sister, Maddy. In his apartment was to be found an old photograph of him and Frederick, at the cottage, Maddy standing beside them. A quiet, humid evening in August, no sound from beyond the screen windows except once a rustling among the leaves that might have been a bird or small animal. Frederick's sister sat on his bed, and her eyes, shining darkly, fringed with lashes, penetrated his disguises. She was so close he could make out the tiny pale hairs on her curving upper lip. Her brown tresses combed carefully, a few fine hairs falling in front of her ear. A cat-like smile.

'Would you like me to listen while you say your prayers?' she said.

'No, thank you.'

He no longer said prayers. When he was little his mother demanded it, God bless mummy and daddy and my dog Flip, and if I die before I wake. He hated to be reminded that he might die in his sleep. Soon his mother no longer cared if he prayed. She had given up churches.

'You're a handsome boy,' Maddy said, 'much handsomer than Frederick.'

He wondered if Frederick could hear her from the other room. What he had learned in his stay: that Maddy disliked Frederick, her fat, awkward younger brother, that she praised their guest as a way of damaging her brother. Earlier in the week, they brought a kitten home from a farm, and as it ran about the floor Frederick stepped on it. Maddy shouted at him, 'Oh Frederick, be more careful. Don't be stepping on the poor thing. You are clumsy. You make a botch of just everything.' But the kitten wasn't injured, it only gave a squeal and escaped, and the mother mumbled at Maddy not to be mean, but she went on saying how Frederick made a hash of things, and then she picked up the kitten and cuddled it against her breasts.

'Poor kitten,' she said. 'Poor little kitten to be stepped on by a great clumsy boy.'

It was the night before he was to return to the city, and Maddy sat on the edge of his bed, and he was afraid that she was going to do something – he didn't know what. He was stirred and uneasy.

'Yes, you are a very handsome boy,' she said. Her eyes smiled, and he had a picture in his mind of a wedding. Maddy getting married. To a tall man in a dark suit. She had turned sixteen earlier in the week, and there had been a cake. Was sixteen old enough to get married?

'Mother!' It was Frederick's voice from across the hall, in the other small bedroom. 'May we please have cocoa?'

Frederick knew that his mother would come, and then his sister would have to leave. Frederick could hear what she was saying, and he wanted to stop it. The mother called out from the kitchen of the cottage, saying that she would bring cocoa in a minute. Frederick's father had arrived yesterday. Right now he was walking down to the store for bread, and tomorrow he would drive them both to the city. He was a minister, and mostly he stayed in the city while the others came to the summer cottage. The invitation had been for a week, to be company for Frederick, they said, though he and Frederick weren't exactly friends. During that week the two boys visited with another boy named Trip Hallstrom who lived just up the lane on a small farm. The farm had chickens and geese, and they had been astonished by the size of the egg that one of the geese had laid in the grass near the barn. One day they had seen the rooster leap up behind one of the hens, and Frederick had laughed immoderately and shouted, 'He's giving her a fuck,' and Trip just looked at him and shrugged. Trip didn't like Frederick either. He thought that the only person who liked Frederick was his old father.

He couldn't tell if Maddy liked her father. Or if the father liked her. The man was very old, and he spoke only to begin serious conversations. Before Maddy came to his room, he heard her voice and her father's voice, and then the old man went out and the screen door slammed. He was tired of trying to decode all that was happening, and he was glad he was going back.

'Are you anxious to go home?' Maddy was saying, as if she'd read his mind.

'I guess so.'

'But you'll remember us.'

'Yes.'

'You're very polite. When you grow up you'll be popular with the girls. I can tell.'

She was smiling at him. He wanted to look away from her, but he couldn't. He felt the danger of it, the cat-like smile, the tiny hairs on her upper lip. She would steal his breath, like a cat stifling a baby, and he would be lost. If I die before I wake, he thought, and his breath came uneasily.

'Are you going to get married?' he said.

She laughed.

'Oh, I'm not ready for that. Some girls get married at sixteen, but I'm not one of those.'

They could hear her mother coming with the cocoa, and Maddy stood up from the bed and left the room.

When they left in the morning she was still asleep. When he met Frederick at the university reception decades later he thought to ask about his sister, but he didn't. Frederick was full of confidence and fine words that afternoon, while he himself only nodded and listened. It was his own profession to be full of smooth, suitable words, but memory stopped his lips. He tried to remember her picture in that French tabloid, an aging face frozen in maquillage. That warm summer evening when she wished to steal his breath and leave him for dead in the cottage just up the lane from a sandy beach: he could feel it now, the air pulled out of him, an emptiness sucking the ribs inward.

When he had changed planes, he feared, his bag had not changed with him. Lost now or lost earlier, it was now on its way to the limbo of vanished possessions, and he would arrive with nothing but the clothes he wore, an address book, and whatever pens and scraps of paper he carried in his briefcase. Brain and body in their mysterious contrapuntal unity all he could lay claim to. Would you like me to listen while you say your prayers? he said to himself. He did not pray, of course, though some mystery, as to what prayer might be, endured. Now and then, singing some religious piece with the community choir that rehearsed in a church hall near him – one of his regular activities, weekly rehearsal, two performances a year – he had a glimpse of a wholeness of heart that some might call prayer. He remembered a soloist who had performed movingly with the choir once or twice, when a sweetly pious woman praised his sincerity, saying, I'll believe anything if it has a good enough tune. And once on his travels he found himself in an art gallery standing behind a young couple who were studying a painting, flat fields of dark red, and as he was thinking to himself that he could make nothing of the patches of colour, the young woman turned to her companion and said, It's a prayer really. A secular prayer.

Music began to flow through the aircraft, this time not a choir but an orchestra of instruments, unfamiliar timbres, alpenhorns and ancient stringed instruments and thick-voiced reeds. Each plane was designed to produce a different kind of natural music. A small propeller-driven machine took off into heavy rain sometime in 1941. Danger awaited over the English Channel. The music of rain.

Such odd memories attacking him. Lucy hiding herself in the woods behind the hotel and challenging him to find her. Corinne's first phone call after she had left him, her voice shaking. Seeking distraction, he reached for his briefcase again to find his appointment diary, think through the next week's activities, but when he looked in the narrow black case he couldn't find the little book. The appointment diary, his map of the future, was gone to the limbo of missing possessions. Memory had to survive unprompted, and what memory most wished to do was go back into the half-forgotten, brood over certain naked moments. How sometimes in the days of their marriage Lucy would turn to him – behind the check-in desk, or sitting at a table in the dining room – and she would indicate with a lift of her head some man across the room and say, Do you think he's my type? Do you think he'd suit me? And he would always say, No, not at all, and they would laugh, and Lucy would look back and say, I'm not so sure. It was supposed to be a joke they shared.

He saw long grass blowing, heard a sound of wind. Slowly the view moves to the right, shows the edge of the grass, the sand below it, a wrack of weeds at the line of high tide. Another sound: a cricket chirps continuously. If you listen carefully you can hear them, almost hear them, children's voices in the distance, but they are far away, out of sight. The eye moves further to the right and discovers a dark, bulky figure standing at the water's edge, a thickness in silhouette against the light. Slowly the figure begins to walk across the sand, his arms at his sides, moving toward the distance where the children's voices are heard.

Beneath the desert of sunlit cloud might be anything. An ocean where a passenger liner is making its way to Europe, or to China. The voyage takes days, and the passengers must pass the time, eat and sleep, dressing themselves out of the suitcases that have been brought to their cabin, the bulk of their possessions in steamer trunks stowed in the hold. The stewards move sleekly through the library bar, the dining rooms, the narrow companionways; the engines churn the water as they drive the steel hull forward across the sea, nothing visible but the grey ocean on all sides, a horizon where the low chop of the waves meets the cap of clouds. Perhaps tomorrow the sun will shine. A famous actor is travelling on the boat, in first class. A young woman is prostrated with seasickness. On deck a woman sits in a chair reading a book to her two small boys. The two children set off into the woods, she reads. A man passing by nods to her. Many dream of shipboard adventures, but in fact there will be few such untoward occurrences. In the library bar a young man reads a novel and wonders if he will complete it before the arrival on a foreign shore. All this is in the last days of passenger travel by sea. Soon everyone will travel by plane, though expensive cruises will still be available. There is something cold and familiar about this ship, figures moving through an endless grey twilight, and below, in the cargo in the hold some mysterious thing that he must seek out, the object of his quest. The memories have the alarming sheen of an image from an old movie, or perhaps he is recalling a story he read in childhood, an adult story that he came upon before he was ready for it, so he was left with a small inexplicable scar among his thoughts. He remembers, when he was a boy living in the hotel, finding a magazine, long out of date, with a list of steamships sailings, dates and destinations.

The prow of the liner divides the sea. A man falls through the clouds, the lost aviator, colder and colder as he descends, turning to ice, and then he will plunge into the water beside the boat, and a lifeboat will be dropped to search for him, though the inertia of the great ship will carry it long past his point of entry before it can be slowed or stopped. He sees the lost aviator sailing down through the thin air, asphyxiating before he reaches the oxygen that he might have breathed.

A figure was coming down the aisle, stopped, the man lowering himself into the empty seat on his right.

'I noticed you,' the man said. 'Thought I might come back and say a few words. Often thought of it, you know, but one postpones it and nothing happens.'

He studied the man's face, which might have been familiar or might not. If you stared at a face you soon began to believe that you had seen it before.

'Do I know you?' he said.

'Just been in France,' the man said, 'dogging it around Paris on foot, looking at things, the galleries of course, and all the rest of it. I've been taking a French course on Thursday evenings, the sort of thing you do when you're on your own, trying not to get too dim and eccentric. You do that kind of thing?'

He went on without waiting for an answer.

'Aiken,' he said. 'Dr Aiken. Veterinary surgeon. Don't know if that brings anything back.'

'I don't think so.'

'Thought it might. In Paris, in that train station place, Musée d'Orsay I think they call it, what I noticed was this man copying a painting. Had his easel set up, palette, rags. I believe they get permission. Make a copy of a famous painting. Monet I think it was. You'll know about all that.'

'No, not really.'

'A good copy, nearly finished. Looked to me to be a perfect copy, or next thing to it. How would anyone know? A perfect copy. Yes, I realize there are tests, X-rays and analysis of the pigments, but just to look at it, see it the way I see you or you see me. You'd never know which was the real thing and which was the copy. Once there's a perfect copy, there is no real thing, I suppose. I was thinking about that. Saw you here, and I said to myself that we should have a talk. She's gone now. But here you are.'

'I don't think I understand.'

'No need for concealment now. She's gone, as I say. No harm to be done now.'

He waited for the man, this unknown veterinary surgeon to explain himself.

'I'm not catching your meaning.'

'She was a dancer. No doubt she told you that. It was her story. Ballet at first, then she shifted to modern dance. *La vie de bohème*, that was the way things were. Not much money, bouncing about on a filthy mattress in a loft with some bearded wonder who smelled of marijuana, all those hours bending the body into odd shapes, a few raw vegetables and a glass of red wine for dinner. Pretty. Do pretty girls get chosen to be dancers or does the dancing make them pretty? You have an opinion about that?'

'No.'

'One of those puzzles, like one hand clapping. You remember that one. When we were young.'

Once again he waited in silence. The veterinarian, whoever he was, would sooner or later explain without being asked.

'She was getting tired of it all when I came along. I adored her, you see, and I could offer her a nice house, a yard where she could grow flowers, clean sheets on the beds, a woman to come in and do housework. No more dirty mattress in a loft, no more sleeping around. Just a perfect life together. I adored her. But I always suspected it wouldn't be enough. They get used to it, you know, the loose life, easy come easy go. When she joined your choir it gave her an activity. She'd given up dancing after she was injured. Quit dancing and married me. Went out once a week to those rehearsals, and afterward.'

The choir.

'She liked to go out for a drink after rehearsals. Told me all about it. Mentioned you, in fact. She said you were a good listener. Described you so I could take a look at one of the concerts. A nice man, she said, ready to be a friend.'

He tried to remember all the people who, over the years, had gone for a beer in the pub just down the block from the church, struggled to recall a woman who was a dancer, or looked like a dancer.

'I wanted to know,' Dr Aiken was saying, 'whether the two of you had an actual affair. Bed and all that. Why should it matter now, now that she's gone and I'm old? It doesn't, doesn't matter at all, and yet I'd still like to know. Well, I cared about her, you see, and it's a missing fact, a gap in the evidence. Or like those paintings. I'd like to know which one I'm looking at. The real one or the copy. I'd never see the difference, but I'd like to know.'

As he sat listening to the man talk he wondered if he might search the little address book for a name that would identify the wife. Aiken, he supposed, was her name too. Alicia or Liz or Jane? No reason for her to be in the address book.

'I don't seem to remember her,' he said.

'Popped it into so many of them you can't remember one from another, is that it?'

'I think you have me wrong. Perhaps I knew your wife, but I can't seem to bring it back. You may have the wrong man. Stories get muddled.'

The man was staring at him, the grey eyes intense, angry.

'Well,' he said, 'if you choose to deny her, there's nothing to be said. A copy may look perfect, but it's still a fake.'

He lifted himself, pushing hard with his arms to get him upright, out of the seat, and he went off down the aisle. Dr Aiken. A dancer. One of the women who came to the pub. He could make no sense of it, but the conversation left him ill at ease. What was I doing, he wondered, that I don't remember her? He recalled some of the others, two large German men who looked like brothers but were unrelated. The conductor and his woman friend who was the regular accompanist. A husky alto with an English accent. Glimpses of other faces. Then it came to him, that perhaps the woman had been lying. She was having an affair, but with another man altogether, one who didn't sing in the choir, who sat in his car waiting for her after rehearsals. On some nights she skipped rehearsals altogether, spent the two and a half hours in her lover's apartment. The role he himself had played, without knowing it, was as a beard, a stalking horse to divert attention from the other. More than one even. A whole series of paramours for the weekly pas de deux, while she returned home with stories of the polite, innocuous baritone who befriended her in the crowded beverage room. She had selected him as available and harmless, invented a friendship between the two of them, had perhaps once or twice come to the pub so she would know where everyone went, how long they stayed. The perfect role for him, with his harmless, well-meaning ways. No doubt she thought of him as a prig, an old maid, but he served her purpose, helplessly innocent, available for use. He began to wish that the flight was over, that the earth would reclaim his body, not leave him at the mercy of these sudden incursions.

Images of fire. Flames are visible from a distance. The hotel, so recently sold, is burning down. A not uncommon fate for old hotels. The orange glow in the sky shows the shapes of the bare trees and illuminates too the dark coiling smoke. The flames grow brighter and then begin to fade. The old building burns and collapses into hot ash, and what is left is whatever survives as memory. He will call Corinne and give her the news, remarking on their luck, that this happened

196

after the sale, not before. She will suggest that the new owners have burnt it down to claim the insurance. It is the sort of idea she got from her new husband. She could, he supposed, have been correct.

How much of his life had vanished in that burning building? He was very young when they moved there, to the little apartment hidden away out of sight of the patrons, a tiny kitchen, a living room, and two small bedrooms side by side. There was an outside door through which they could come and go without entering the public rooms of the hotel. That door opened beside a clump of lilacs. A narrow cement path led to the back door of the hotel kitchen and in the other direction to the gate in the picket fence that opened on a side street, not far from the main street of the town. Mornings, he went out that door from their little kitchenette, feeling as if he was being watched by someone until he came out to the main street, and then he was part of the town's daily activity, a boy on his way to school, safe. Within the hotel anything might happen. One night a man died there, though the boy slept through it all, half-waking to hear urgent whispering voices, then dozing off again. When he asked his mother about it the next day she would tell him nothing. It was the cook who frightened him with a version of what had occurred. They lived in the building, but on sufferance somehow, as ghosts might, appearing when summoned. He didn't belong and that made him the more eager to know its secrets. He was timid, and yet the desire to poke into things was like a mosquito bite. You couldn't keep your fingernails off it. The maids knew him, and when they were cleaning a room, he might sidle in through the open door and look around. He suspected that he wasn't supposed to do this, and he was afraid of what his grandfather might say if he found him.

'Doing your rounds?' one of the maids might say to him when he appeared, and he would nod.

'Newlyweds,' one of them might say with a censorious exhalation of breath. 'The way they leave a room. You wouldn't want to know about it.' And he would leave. He didn't want to know about it.

Now and then, when the hotel was very busy, he was given errands, clothes from the Chinese laundry to be taken to one of the upstairs rooms, and the guests in the room might give him a dime or a quarter. He wasn't altogether sure whether he should accept it, but usually he did, after a battle between greed and humiliation that was like a feverish illness. He never mentioned it to his mother. Over the years he found doors that were seldom opened, quiet corners where he could sit against the wall, hearing the voices of men and women who would never see him there or be aware of what he heard.

New Year's Eve of 1949, the half century about to end. There was a costume ball being held at the hotel, organized by the Rotary Club to raise funds. The ballroom above the dining room had been opened for the occasion, the first time since before the war. He had discovered a little balcony at one end from which he could watch, not quite invisible, but knowing that no one would look up this high. The costumes. He observed his grandfather, who was wearing his military uniform and had drawn a heavy dark moustache on his face, as he danced with a blonde woman in a clinging white dress. They danced with skill and detachment. His parents were not in costume; they were both working, tending bar and making sure there was enough food on hand. He had planned to stay in his bedroom studying a new copy of *Life* magazine. Tomorrow it would be 1950. He liked the sense of history being made, and he had put on his good shoes and jacket and brushed his hair. He could hear the band, and the sound of voices. He moved quietly upstairs, along empty hallways and up more stairs to the balcony. He watched his grandfather dance, and nearby a couple in blackface, the woman short and plump, her chest bouncing, the man grinning, his teeth made whiter by the burnt cork that coloured his skin. They both wore white gloves. The local police constable and his wife were dressed as a cowboy and cowgirl, Roy Rogers and Dale Evans. A big drunken man in a grey suit and grey fedora was trying to jitterbug with a skinny girl in a short dress. He was tossing her roughly and grabbing back without much skill. Dancing past, his grandfather spoke to them, and they went and sat down. Tired of watching the dancing after a while, the boy went out the little door that led to the balcony and started down the stairs. Hearing voices below, he sat down on the stairs and listened.

'You want to frighten me.'

'Do I?'

'The things you say.'

'And ...?'

'Trying them out on me.'

'And you like it.'

'And you want me to hurt him.'

'Maybe it's what you want too.'

A door opened, and the two voices were silent, then they joined in conversation with another man and woman who were coming out of the room. The voices moved away, and he thought they had gone downstairs. The band was playing 'Pennies from Heaven.' Then he went back to his small bedroom in the apartment, got into bed and read *Life* magazine. At last he fell asleep, and in the morning the ground was covered with new snow, and the morning staff had begun to put everything back in order, serving breakfast to the guests who had stayed over. The ballroom was closed up again for years. When Lucy paid her first visit, on the occasion of the funeral, he took her round the hotel, revealing its mysteries. He found the key and showed her the tall dusty ballroom. Faded and blank in the light of a single hanging bulb.

'I'll have my wedding ball in here,' she said. And ten years later she did, the room cleaned and newly painted, paper streamers hung from the ceiling. They were married, and not long after that his father died, and his mother bought a little house nearby, more or less retired from work at the hotel. He and Lucy took over the small apartment. Until then they had lived in a suite upstairs, without cooking facilities except an electric hot plate where they could make tea or coffee or hot chocolate.

The other man became part of their life a couple of years after the wedding, a salesman who took their order for cleaning materials. A boastful man, full of stories. A coarse man, a man of cruelties. Who cheated, when he could, both his customers and the company he worked for. One day, just as the man was leaving the hotel with a new order for cleaning supplies, Lucy turned to him, where they both stood behind the front desk, said the familiar line, What do you think? Is he my type? And he had said to her No, absolutely not.

A voice was announcing something, but he couldn't make out the words. Was the flight close to its end? He believed that Lucy-Corinne would be meeting him when the plane reached its destination, but he was unable to say why he knew this, and for a moment it seemed to him dubious. It was just as likely that he would come back to earth at some anonymous airport and would have to make his own decision about what to do next. Perhaps he would have to clear customs, but to do that he must find his luggage, and he was growing convinced that the bags were lost. The shining mysterious object on the vanishing steamship contained all that he had brought with him for travel.

The light beyond the window of the aircraft had grown blindingly bright, the silver illumination raking every vein and tendon and crease and wrinkle of his pale hands as they rested in his lap. These are my fingers, the skin that touched her skin. The noise of the engines grew loud in his ears, and as the speed increased, he understood, for the first time, that there was no pilot in the cabin of this airship, no first officer assisting, that the machine was following some unknown program, recorded in strange, mathematical symbols, unreadable by the human eye.

Two figures move down the road, feet crunching on the gravel, the sound of wind. The end of the road is not visible, but he knows that they are moving toward water. The two people walking do not look toward each other. He is with his mother, tramping down a road that leads to the Great Lake. Once again she is urging him to marry, not to be alone. I am married, he says. Does she respond to this or merely listen in disapproving silence? The sound of feet walking, the two dark figures pacing toward the brightness. There is no judgment to be made.

The choir again, the sound close around him on all sides, back in his place, his thin croaky baritone doing its best, filling in a little of the sound, attentive, tuning notes to their position in each chord. His voice grown weaker, failing, he still sings with good heart, and the sound of the others lifts him. He is dressed in his tuxedo. He bought it years ago when he joined the choir, has worn it now and then on formal occasions and always for performances. The members of the choir stand tall, arranged in a curve, almost a semi-circle; he can glance to his left, see the faces of the sopranos in their black dresses, and one of them looks toward him for a second as she takes a breath before beginning the next phrase. Yes, of course, the dancer, he knows her perfectly well, tidy, stylish. How could he have forgotten? Her husband must be in the audience watching. The lights are bright on the singers, dim in the auditorium, and yet as he looks out he is certain that for a moment that he sees Lucy's face there in the darkness, quietness, observing, a man beside her, a handsome unknown man. Then he glances at the score, breathes deeply and sings out with all his heart as the piece of music reaches a moment of culmination, though his vocal cords are weakened, torn, and the sound the merest rough scratch. The wholeness of the choir's ensemble carries him on through this tumult of utterance.

4.

And Variations

La Rue du Chapeau Perdu

It is not the street you were seeking. You are not lost, you tell yourself, even though what surrounds you is unfamiliar, and the name of the street is fantastic, unlikely. Seen in the distance for dim seconds is a figure that you almost recognize, but then it is out of focus, vanished.

The geography of any city is a maze. Each hour of each day allows us to define a few details of colour and texture, residual peeling paint, rusting metal observed among the ruins. Beyond, the windows of the new constructions shine. Each street, with its particular detail, open doors, broken windows, redefines the city and the city redefines the streets through a constant flow of population, changes in fashion, the falling into disuse, the replacement of the deserted and desolate, the adaptation of the abandoned, the infilling of empty spaces. On a balcony stands a department store mannequin wrapped in chains. At night, we are told, observers trained in the Faculty of Error go about in the darkness and converse equably with the stars.

On a wall around the corner someone has painted a notice. GARDER VOS ORDURES CHEZ VOUS. Good advice, good advice always. What you might hear from an astute spiritual counsellor. But not exactly evidence.

Life here is numerous and intricate. Police and ambulance sirens shape the night. Stone steps lead up to a handsome doorway, a pillar on each side, a window above the heavy wooden door. The building is empty. Once for a few weeks in years long past the building offered a home to squatters, but the adventure failed.

A lost history speaks in desolate deserted warehouses, ruined churches, empty monasteries. Among the records: a photograph of a dark brick wall, on it a sign telling the name of the street, a fragment of an arrow indicating that cars must drive one way. But the street is not to be found on any current map. Names come and go. An obscure *ruelle*, now closed off, has vanished under the construction of a complex of offices and apartments. The maze that is every city constantly remakes itself. You enter a skyscraper, attempt to escape vertical imprisonment in the elevators; you will find yourself at a level where the elevator doesn't stop, or where a key is required to escape it. You grow confused. Outside a window you discover a decorative stone balcony at the peak of another tall building. You mime falling. The underground cities keep their secrets.

Another photograph shows an empty store, the windows covered with posters that have been pasted up over the years, one on top of another, advertising a production of *Le Misanthrope*, a political candidacy, an appearance by B. B. King, some kind of fruit juice, a rock concert long since over and forgotten, all as inapprehensible as a long mislaid fedora.

The walls of the city are inscribed with the poetry of night and abandon. Look at this one, a long wall of evenly laid bricks above a stone foundation, snow on the ground in front of it, the photograph taken in a snowstorm, the air is blurred with driven flakes, pale white letters not easy to read. VAGUES INCESSANTES DE JOIE it says: a definition of ecstasy.

The Kapitan opened his eyes. The room was not much bigger than his cabin on the ship, the only window a little square high in the wall. For a moment he thought he was in prison somewhere, but the disorder of his clothes, scattered on and under a bentwood chair, his shoes lying six feet apart, suggested a familiar drunken chaos. He tried to remember the previous night. Late in the afternoon, he had left the ship with a large package wrapped in copies of *Pravda* and tied with brown string. Yes, that part of it was clear. He was not allowed to go ashore. The local immigration and his own government forbade it, but he had made arrangements, and Papchik was a partner in his scheme. Papchik was the cargo manager, the political commissar, the crew translator, and the resident police spy, a *kagebeshnik*.

It was Papchik who handled the bribe that allowed him to find a way from the ship into the streets of the city. The Kapitan had collected his little parcel of icons from various sources – such things were a little easier in the years since the death of Comrade Stalin – during his days at home between voyages, and before setting sail he had brought them aboard and concealed them behind a panel in his cabin. As the ship steamed across the Atlantic, he thought of them there, the gold leaf dimly shining; they were of his mother's world, candles, voices singing, pussy willows at Easter. He knew the old icons were worth money in North America. The directions to find the dealer who would buy them were provided by a former seaman now retired, and written on a scrap of paper had travelled across the ocean in the hollowed out space in the heel of the Kapitan's shoe, space now filled with large denomination American bills handed to him by a fish-smelling, spherical little man, a malodorous human football, who spoke Russian with a Polish accent, and who, after he had examined each of the icons with a loupe, the glass focused on the head of the Virgin as she stared down at the little doll who was her son, took them away into a back room of his store and returned with the U.S. dollars, bills of large denominations to be split with the partners in the conspiracy, a few in smaller denominations that the Kapitan kept with him for incidental expenses.

The Polish Football brought forth also a bottle of whisky from a bottom drawer, and with two thick glass tumblers golden to the brim, they toasted the buying and selling of these outdated gods, a deal eminently satisfying to each. Polish Football recommended a small hotel and gave the Kapitan instructions on how to find his way through the streets, and the Kapitan clapped on his suede cap, then walked west, crossed a parking lot, paced up a hill, angled into a narrow alley and up to a small door near the corner of the next street. The desk clerk, as he had been told, spoke Ukrainian; they could communicate. The Kapitan examined the room, stowed the key beneath a leather insole in one of his shoes, the money in the hollow heel of the other, and set off in the cold rainy dark to find adventure.

Now, the morning after, the Kapitan stared at the ceiling of the room and tried to remember the rest of the night. Things flashed past, unexplained, fragmentary, uncertain. Tall black boots, a black cowboy hat, he thought he could remember those things. There must have been a woman attached. And perhaps voices in the night in the hall outside his room, speaking Russian, though he preferred to believe that was a dream.

He remembered going through the cold, rainy streets to find a bar. The establishment he chose lit the sidewalk with an explosion of energy from panels of light bulbs, but inside, it was so dark it was hard to make out the other drinkers. *Vodka*, the Kapitan said to the waiter who stood silently waiting by his table, and the man went to the bar and poured. The Kapitan lit a cigarette. When the drink arrived, the Kapitan downed it and indicated the glass and the cigarette that lay on the edge of a metal ashtray. The waiter returned with another drink and a package of cigarettes, and the Kapitan put one of the strange pale pieces of paper currency on the smooth black surface of the little table. *Gdye dyevushki?* he said. The waiter stared, shook his head. The Kapitan repeated the phrase, slowly and loudly this time. *Gdye dyevushki?* The man shook his head, picked up the money from the table. By the time he returned with change, the Kapitan had downed the second glass of vodka, and pointed again to the empty tumbler and held up three fingers. He couldn't quite believe the provincialism of the place, that they understood not even a phrase of Russian, and as he picked up the glass, he stared intently at the dim, unhealthy face watching his and this time whispered, *Gdye dyevushki?* When the man was once again unresponsive, the Kapitan drew himself up in his chair and let fly with the foreign phrase he had laboriously committed to memory, *Hwerr gorrls?* The man looked about the room, nodded and went away, returning with a large tumbler containing a substantial dose of white spirits. The Kapitan sat and waited.

And then? The Kapitan tried hard to summon up the rest of the night. Tall black boots. Yes. And ... did he have marks of boot heels in his back? At that point in his struggle with memory the Kapitan, searching for details of who had been, at least temporarily, attached to the black boots and hat, was seized by panic, his heart pounding as he rolled out of bed, scrabbled across the floor, grabbed his left shoe and lifted the insole. The money was still there in the hollow heel. He searched the pocket of his trousers for the remains of his funds for adventure. The pocket was empty. The Kapitan got to his feet, drew a deep growling breath and looked around the room for a place to empty his steaming bladder. No toilet, no sink, nothing. He pulled on his pants and set off down the hall where he saw an old black woman with a cleaning cart. He made a gesture and she pointed to the end of the hall. A small room with a toilet and sink. He pissed for a long time, humming with relief as the pressure in his bladder eased.

You hear stories in the street, urban legends, the old tales given shape in the haunting modal melodies of folk songs. The devil appearing in the ashes of a fireplace. La Corriveau hanging in the air in her iron cage, her bones drying in the wind and sun. There are other names for all lost places, and every language has the equivalent.

Via del capello perduto. The world-famous mafiosi speak *dialetto*, but one persistent local scholar claims to have found, expressed in a literary language based on the dialect of Tuscany, a folk narrative brought here in the past, the tale of a man growing older, who, having lost his way while seeking a cobbler, stumbled blindfold through an open door to find himself muddled and bereft in the *sous-sol* of a deserted monastery, where he sat for days or weeks in a hopeless twilight until a pretty nun discovered him and led him down the *via del capello perduto* and through the ensuing long-buried ways. They travelled through abandoned tunnels, past tumbling underground rivers, while in the darkness all around them he could hear the grinding of teeth, the howling of wolves, occasionally screams of pain. When he was exhausted and afraid, he would reach out for her hand, and though he was never able to grasp it, the attempt would draw him along, upward, past stinking lagoons, the smell of burning hair, and into a labyrinthine narrow path that would finally, after many twists and turns as he followed his guide who spoke to him in words he couldn't understand, bring them to a field of spring grass on top of Mount Royal. Perhaps you remember hearing fragments of that story, late at night in a bar, pissed on Fin du Monde, too drunk to find your way home so that you were forced to sleep in a park. You can work it out for yourself. The tale and its moral are there to be found. Search your memory or the heap of pictures on your coffee table until you find the right one, perhaps the photo of dark letters scrawled on a white-painted stucco wall, LE RIDICULE TUE ... DIEU EST MORT.

Departed in darkness on the night bus, and he had now arrived in the city of dawn with no plans, except escape and discovery, fleeing the inevitable, courting the outlandish. Once outside the terminal, Greg glanced in all directions, took in the location of the mountain, the river, stared at the light catching the tops of the high buildings. He checked out his reflection in a plate glass store window, stood still to assess the figure facing him. He couldn't make out details, a young man, faceless, a wide black hat, long hair. *This day will never happen again.* Yes, that was what he wanted, everything untoward, extraordinary.

This day will never happen again. He stood there as if drunk or stoned, high on the strangeness of travel. Greg had never walked these streets before. A young woman passed by him wearing a tie-dyed shirt, a denim mini-skirt, bare legs. He wanted to stop her, ask her name. Maybe later in the day he would do that, speak to every stranger who passed.

The university year was over, and back in Ontario a job awaited him (along with a demand that he cut his long curling hippie's hair), in the tool and equipment rental business begun by his father, but now, since the old man's second heart attack, run by Greg's older brother, Art. Greg wished and half-believed that in the course of today the future would be taken out of his hands, history would seize him and make him part of its inevitability. History. He wasn't a Marxist, but he had concluded from listening at S U P A meetings to those who thought they were – the dialectic suddenly back in fashion now when every-thing was going to ratshit in Vietnam – that he, like every individual on earth, was up to his neck in history's flood, immersed in a tumbling river of events, and Greg wanted at the least a clear consciousness of his drowning. Or so he believed, riding the night bus to a city he had never before visited. *This day will never happen again.* In between his grander thoughts he wondered about convincing his father, who now spent much of every day reading the paper, watching television game shows, to return to work at the rental yard. If Art was there, if Greg was there, the Old Man would have no need to lift or haul or do any of the things that were bad for his heart. He could meet people, spend time with his boys, what he always said he liked best. First Greg would have to convince his brother that it was a good idea.

Hungry, Greg turned a corner and entered a café. As he ordered and carried an espresso and a croissant to one of the tables, he ob-served, across the room, a plump, babyish girl in a large, soft fabric hat, a cigarette held in her fingers as she stared into nothingness, her thick legs bent, feet on the crossbar of the stool where she sat. A round, dissatisfied face.

The croissant was crisp and the dough broke into little pieces as he tore off a piece and put it in his mouth. Sipped the strong coffee. The plump girl glanced toward him then quickly looked away, sucked on her cigarette and released the smoke into the air. She had sullen lips. Why was she dressed up so early in the day? What was she seeking? Greg decided he had no time to spare for this baby-faced creature in a floppy hat. Her hat was white, his black. Would he, in fifty years, regret that he had not made some overture, spoken?

Is it true?

What? Is what true?

That your boredom is exquisite and excessive.

No, I wouldn't say that.

But you recognize the reference.

No. I don't.

The poem.

I don't know anything about poems.

What do you know about?

I'm not sure. Things.

Emotional anemia.

What?

Emotional anemia.

I suppose that's from a poem too?

From the same poem.

Are you always thinking about poems?

I looked at you, your large hat, your sullen lips, the smoke rising from your cigarette, and I thought of it, a poem I read just recently. A poem by Ezra Pound.

Who's he?

A poet. Just a poet.

What does he say?

I can't remember every word.

You seem to.

He says that you would like someone to speak to you.

Maybe I do. Want it.

I think maybe you do.

Or maybe it's you who longs for some sudden and brutal contact. Maybe it's you who is dying of boredom.

It could be that you're right.

I like your hat.

And I like yours.

As Greg was strolling along the street, he found himself entering a store selling used books, in a basement down several steps from the sidewalk. He was not searching for any book in particular, but entering a bookstore he always felt he might find something wonderful, unexpected. He moved slowly past the shelves, reading titles, stopped at the poetry shelf, looked for familiar names, as if they might offer him something. Nearby a shelf was labelled *Curiosa*, a handful of books on it, *Contes de la Capote Anglaise*, the title of one, *The Bishop's Mitre* another. The shelf below was filled with communist pamphlets. In the corner at a little table covered with books, slowly turning the pages of one of them, sat a slender man wearing a flat cap, black suede with a small brim. He had arched eyebrows, a moustache and on his chin a small, trimmed beard.

'You look familiar,' Greg said.

'Lenin,' the man said. He pointed to a poster on the wall. There was a resemblance.

'That hat. Where did you get it?'

'On a fire escape.'

'You were escaping from a fire and you stopped to pick up a hat.'

'Exactly.'

'Is this your bookstore?'

'In the mornings.'

'A good job?'

'Doesn't pay much.'

'So how did you get the hat?'

'You are persistent.'

'It's unusual.'

'Well, if you must know, I was walking down an alley, on my way to work one day. In the winter. I saw it lying on the bottom platform of a fire escape, you know, the stairs that fold down when you put your weight on them, then fold up again. You can climb down, but not back up. Proof against thieves, or supposed to be. So there was the hat, too high to reach, but it was there and I wanted it. "Raymond," I said to myself, "we must have that *casquette*." So I ran down to the store and found the pole we use to open the vent in the back wall, and I carried it along the street and poked it up through the fire escape platform until I could push the hat over the edge. Disinfected it a little and here I am.'

Greg made an appreciative noise.

'And yours, so very dark and dramatic?' Raymond was saying to him.

Greg's hat, with its wide black brim and a tall crown, had something seventeenth-century about it. Puritans come ashore.

'In a store,' Greg said. 'No great tale to tell.'

He drifted back to the poetry shelf.

'A. M. Klein,' he said, 'he's still living here somewhere, isn't he?'

'So they say. No one sees him.'

Greg took down the book and opened it, read a few lines.

'Where does he live?'

'He doesn't see visitors,' Raymond said. He tapped his forehead. 'Didn't plan to visit.'

'Somewhere in Outremont. Just another crazy old Jew.'

Greg picked up one of the pamphlets, *The Communist Manifesto*. Set it back down.

'The owner's a communist?'

'You ask a lot of questions.'

'I want to know.'

'The guy who used to run it was some kind of Red. There were stories about how people on the run from the FBI would sneak across the border and hang out here, sleep in the back room.'

Greg hadn't planned to buy anything, didn't have much money, but he took the Klein book to the table where the mock-Lenin sat in his suede cap with its tiny brim.

Late in the day Greg will pass by an old woman on the street, a woman respectably dressed, features that you would have said were probably Jewish. This woman, he will decide, is Klein's aged wife, out to visit the world before it vanished, the morose old scholar left behind in whatever mysterious silence it was he inhabited, and as Greg looks at her face, skin wrinkled and sagging, it will come upon him that the old do not experience themselves as old, that this woman, as much as any clever child, believes the existence of the world depends on her awareness and participation. She is perhaps enraged by her husband's existentially sad state, and Greg just then will understand how his father, weak of heart, walking to the corner to buy a newspaper and then walking back – all the while aware of the dreadful inadequacy of the heart muscle beating in his chest, that one day it would stop – even yet sometimes looks at the world with the same hungry eye as when he was an adolescent. The old woman will stare at Greg's black hat as she passes. Does she disapprove? No, it reminds her of her youth when men wore neckties and sharp fedoras and their hot eyes undressed her.

And many years afterward Greg will find himself on a summer afternoon sitting on the deck outside a cottage in eastern Ontario, late on in middle age, a high school teacher almost at the point of taking retirement, having lived a decent enough life, maintained a sometimes difficult marriage, and in the course of a conversation with his pretty daughter-in-law, which began with a discussion of a war in the Middle East and then went on to the sudden thinning of the atmosphere and the virulence of ultraviolet rays and the need for old men to wear baseball caps and use sunblock, he will suddenly say, *I used to have a wonderful black hat.* When he describes it, his daughter-in-law will ask him what happened to the wonderful black hat, and he will realize, with sudden astonishment and distress, that he has no idea. *I can't remember,* he will have to say. *I just can't remember.* And that vanishing will seem like a truly dire fact: that there is no photograph to show it, the tall crown, the young man's long hair hanging down below the brim. The abandonment will shake him. Life is all a saga of lost hats. As he sits on the deck above the water with his pretty daughter-in-law, he will think that there ought to be a book called *An Anthology of the Forgotten and Unintended* which would somehow explicate this bleak situation.

Sasha was scrabbling about in the big closet on her hands and knees as she heard a noise, the quiet click of a digital camera as if someone had taken her picture from across the room. Portrait of Sasha, bum in the air. Shivering, she turned. No one there, of course. Dust up her nose, she sneezed. Could she take such a naughty photograph of herself and add it to the Desirable Girl site? Maybe. Shivered. Giggled. Sneezed. Sat on the floor and stared round the large closet, almost of a size to make a separate bedroom, except that it was windowless and had only the one door opening into the wall beside her bed. She hung her day-to-day clothes on one side, exotic outfits on the other, suitcases against the wall, in front of them boxes of costume jewellery that she was saving, bits of old-style frippery, furnishings and adornments. What she was searching for was a hat she had salvaged when she was helping her mother clear out her grandmother's house, a cute little black hat with feathers and a veil, perfect for the Desirable Girl, and she was sure that it must be here somewhere. She had come into the closet when she got out of bed this morning, wearing her purple velvet dressing gown, and begun to search, but the loose sleeves of the dressing gown kept getting caught on the sharp edges of things, a tall ornamental ashtray, the standing mirror, a lamp which tipped and nearly fell, so she abandoned the offending garment and threw it back out on the bedroom floor, then began her scramble among the costumes and appointments on the floor to see if the hat had fallen among them. On a shelf above was an old hatbox, and she had taken everything out of it, a red tuque, bunny ears, a straw boater, but the hat she remembered so well was not there. Yesterday in a second-hand store she had found a black suit jacket that appeared to date back to the 1940s. Diamond-shaped black buttons. She was certain that she had seen one just like it in a movie, and as she was paying for the jacket she remembered the little hat, and pictured the two of them together, a bit of rouge, dark lipstick. It would make a perfect image to add to the Desirable Girl website. Dye her hair black with one of those dyes that washed out easily, black jacket, black hat, black hair, the look of one of those respectable murderesses.

A novel in photographs, that's what it was, the Desirable Girl site, and she had an eager desire for the linked sites that she would someday create. Complicating the plot.

She sneezed again, pushed aside the base of a brass lamp and found behind it on the floor a lacy scarf in a subtle grey-green, fallen there and lost, tied it around her neck and proceeded, her hands and knees growing grey with dust from the closet floor. She got to her feet and walked back into the bedroom, caught a glimpse of herself in the mirror, scarf round her neck, knees and hands stained with dirt. She hadn't posted such a photo yet, the beautiful naked girl with her perfect breasts; if she ever did, perhaps she would make the figure anonymous, the features invisible. A cloth bag over her head, tied at the chin. Or a mask. One of those masks of feathers. She was pretty sure that the site was secure, that it wouldn't lead anyone to her door, but still.

Did she want to lead them to her? Did she want to be found? Well yes. And of course no. She didn't especially want a man in her bed. They had such big feet. Though now and then in the darkness she would imagine one climbing in the window and kissing her fingers. And so on. She liked better to think of men finding the site and wondering about her, intoxicated with the wit and variety of the Desirable Girl.

She began to run water in the high claw-footed tub, observing herself in the bathroom mirror while the hot water poured out, and as the mirror began to vanish in steam, she witnessed her vanishing and then imagined herself magically appearing again in another mirror, the tall one in the lobby of the hotel where she worked as a desk clerk, mist thinning and the girl's image as it came in sight, to the astonishment of arriving tourists and departing businessmen, one of them with a Clark Gable moustache and a grey fedora, who tipped his hat to the doxy in the tall glass.

As the tub filled she walked into the big room, with its bare brick walls, in front of them a complex mapping of steel pipes, no longer hooked up to anything, painted a vivid gamboge that set them off against the brick. Two rice-paper blinds covering the wide windows which were remains from the days when the building was a factory. Dressed, she would pull the strings to roll them up, and the room would grow bright. In the far corner sat the sewing machine, where she adjusted the fit of her costumes. There was a plan that one day she would begin to make clothes, unique items, some of them rebuilt from garments she had picked up second hand. She had inherited the sewing machine when Lomas and Patricia moved out of their house and into a tiny basement apartment, where they spent the months of good weather, the colder months now passed in Florida. Her stepfather had sold his partnership and only worked half the year now. When Sasha was little, Lomas would sew outfits for her. He and Patricia loved to dress her up, and when she looked back on her pampered childhood, Sasha always thought that she was more their hobby than their child. Lomas, who was an optician, would bring her home a pair of glittery spectacles now and then, plain glass in the exotic frames. As she grew up they encouraged her to study fashion design at a CEGEP, and she tried it for a term, but it was too professional, too competitive.

A couple of years ago, Sasha had visited them at their winter quarters in Florida, a week in February when winter was at its most interminable. The morning after she arrived, Patricia handed her a little bag from a clothing store, a red bikini, not much to it. Lomas looked at the little garment as Sasha held it in her hand, took a sudden deep breath and turned toward his wife.

'What are you doing, Patricia,' Lomas said, 'putting the girl on sale?'

'It's cute,' Patricia said. 'She's young. She can wear these things.'

Sasha allowed herself to be sent into the guest bedroom to try it on, and she had to admit that the bits of clinging cloth looked stylish. She felt like a model in *Vanity Fair*, but she wasn't sure about wearing it in front of alien eyes.

Patricia gave a little knock on the door.

'Let's see,' she said and opened it without waiting for a reply. She stared at Sasha in the scarlet rags.

'Oh, god,' she said. 'I could never have worn that. Come and look, Lomas.'

'No,' he said. She heard the door as he went outside, not to reappear for an hour. The next day it was very bright and sunny and Sasha wore the bikini when she and her mother went for a swim in the condo's outdoor pool. She was aware of the wizened old grinders on their pool chairs gaping at her, and when she dived she thought she might come back to the surface with a bare behind, but the bikini clung where it was intended to cling, and she knew she had pleased her mother by wearing it, at least that once.

What would she have to tell her colleagues when she arrived at work today? What new vivid lies? Sasha was never sure whether Dolly and Pierre, who worked the shifts before and after hers, believed her inventions. She enjoyed shaping falsehoods, loved her deceivings, the creamy fabrications. In one of the apartments carved out of the old warehouse, she told Dolly, just down the hall from her, was a neighbour who was a holy man. He had lived under a bridge for three years to purify his soul, and now he offered lessons in the higher disciplines, double solitaire, drawing with the eyes closed, and vegetable carving. Dolly loved the bizarre, the all-but-incredible, and Sasha delighted her with her tales, how she had caught a glimpse of the holy man's face in a bright light, and noticing that he appeared to be growing horns.

It was for Dolly that Sasha invented the seventeen-year-old boy who from time to time climbed in her apartment window on Saturday nights. Dolly, though warned not to, had been known to pass on the wild tales to Pierre, the gay night clerk, but when Pierre asked Sasha about them, she denied all knowledge, insisted that Dolly had made them up. What she told Pierre was stories about an offer she had received for her costume collection from a local museum. How they had heard rumours about it and were ready to pay good money to add it to their resources. The lies helped Sasha to encompass grander days. It was like Photoshop. You could take a figure and place it in some new and unlikely environment. Thus remaking the world.

The hot water turned her skin pink, and she slithered in her own soapy hands. She had never yet photographed herself in the high black boots. They were something from the sixties, worn originally with a miniskirt, and she had never found the perfect outfit to go with them, but as she lay in the hot water, she thought she might arrange a shot from behind, the Desirable Girl seen only from the waist down, black skirt, white thighs, black boots. Yes, that could be quite delicious.

She must think of something new to tell Dolly about the holy man. Or invent something grander. In one of the studio apartments (this was true) there was an opera singer, a tall long-bodied man who could be heard rehearsing sometimes, his bass voice just audible from the cubicle near her door where the elevator rose and fell. She would tell Dolly that the holy man had written a one-act opera for the tall basso to perform, accompanied only by percussion.

The drums thumping and thumping. Yes. As the parade passed by everyone stared at her, naked on the silver plinth on a wagon drawn by white horses.

The street. It indicates a particular unit of urban geography, the way a car drives from X to Y, close to F but without passing through M, or it names the location of the building where your apartment is found, or the deconsecrated nunnery where the space is rented out for conferences, meetings, even rehearsals, and as such it has a name, say Mortlake Road or Rue du Dragon or Calle Conquista or Rue du Chapeau Perdu. You could define a street by its anecdotes and its graffiti rather than by its name, but that would lead to more uncertainty since words are often erased (vanished poems), and buildings are torn down to make way for other buildings. Now and then the names of streets are changed, but more often they maintain themselves. Certain scholars from the Faculty of Error might exposit the battle of nominalism and realism. Consider Duns Scotus.

But *the street* means, as well, a state of being, a way of life. Living on the street does not tell us that the vagrant in question occupied, let's say, Avenue A or Rue R. *On the street* means homeless, having no personal location where one can be found, where one is recurrent. To have only the street itself, with its inhospitable bareness of paved route.

The distinction between the two meanings of *the street* can be documented in various available examples of writing on the walls.

VOUS AVEZ TUÉ CETTE RUE is the cry of an inhabitant aesthetically displeased by the way things are developing in the neighbourhood, new buildings, altered sidewalks, a change of zoning.

More primal the cry of the unplaced and exhausted, the simple and peremptory rejection of how things are: FUCK LA RUE.

The Kapitan, once back in his room, assembled his clothes to begin the new day. It was still morning, he supposed. He didn't carry a watch. The chronometers on the ship gave him all the information on time that he needed. Off the ship he preferred not to know. The shape of daylight provided enough guidance, and the little square window told him it was morning. A smell that came off his lower parts before he rinsed them in the sink down the hall suggested to him that the woman in the black boots and cowboy hat had done what he sought before she had emptied his pockets and vanished. The Kapitan would have liked to punch her about the head for the theft, though he was grateful that she had not thought to explore his right shoe. He assembled himself for the trip back to the boat. As he pulled on his shirt he decided that he would not split the icon money with Papchik until they were ashore in Arkhangelsk. He had various hiding places in his cabin, and he wasn't sure what the fat little *kagebeshnik* might get up to if the split was made too early. Trust no one was the essential point of the Kapitan's creed. He lit a cigarette and sat down with it, waiting for his head to clear. The tobacco helped.

Almost ready to leave, he began to look about for his suede cap. No sign of it. He looked under the bed, beneath the cushion of the stuffed chair, pulled the bed away from the wall and looked behind it. He growled and cursed under his breath, and his fists tightened and he pictured them punishing the woman with solid and repeated blows to the face.

Through the hotel's outer door he saw snow falling. It had turned colder during the night, and the snow, blowing from the heights above, streamed through the air, and began to accumulate on the street. Outside he looked among the cars and pedestrians for a woman in black boots and hat. If he saw her he would commit an effective and determined assault. Saw no one, of course. Long gone with his money. *Da nichevo.* The snow was falling heavily and various figures sidled quickly from door to door. Cars slid in their tracks. Walking away from the hotel, he stared at the street signs and the letters above the doors of the businesses, all alien characters, incomprehensible.

He wasn't quite certain how to find his way back to the boat, but he knew he must go down the hill and toward the east. Bare-headed, still angry, snow burning his face, he set off, and when he reached the bottom of the hill, he turned left across the parking lot of an industrial site. Enough snow had accumulated that he left tracks as he walked. He must return to the boat and get it underway before this winter weather settled in. A man stood with a cigarette on a loading platform under a low roof which shielded him from the snow. Nearby a narrow alley to lead the Kapitan on his way. As he entered the alley, his feet slipping in new snow, he saw a figure standing on the pavement at the far end, black among the white streamers, a young woman in a nun's habit that hung down over the top of her shoes, a white coif covering her head, itself framed by the black habit, her fresh young face, round and scrubbed, angled toward him. Over her head, like a sign of something, she held a startling bright red umbrella.

She turned, lifted her bent head and then she was meeting his eyes, as if waiting for him to greet her, to listen to her encrypted message, to go with her, the nun's black outfit a disguise, and then she moved a step away, was out of his line of sight. He felt a burst of something in his chest, the image of the black nun with the scarlet umbrella seizing him in a queer explosion of joy and surprise. Then the Kapitan was running through the alley, his feet sliding on the snow underfoot. He gasped for breath as he ran, lost his footing on the slippery frozen surface and began to fall, his arms reaching wildly, his head knocked against the brick wall, pain jabbing into his skull. But he kept himself upright, ran on. When he reached the end of the alley and stared about him, searching the street, the high buildings close to the sidewalk on each side, looking for the black habit, the face pink in the cold, the red umbrella, she was gone.

Some of the street's graffiti are signed with three letters, PCV. It is possible that the cleverest or most intuitive of the pedestrians reading the words on the way past have been able to make some sense of the initials. Most have not cared; in their hurry to get to work on time, or to reach a tiny restaurant before all the tables are filled, or to meet at an apartment a man or woman who might or might not become a lover, or to attend a rehearsal, the passersby pass by without noticing, or if they do notice words, they do so without interest in those letters at the end. However, the street harbours a collector of such graffiti, a red-haired young woman who makes her living as a clerk in a kitchen shop, not a serious photographer, only an impulsive clicker of this and that, the momentary secrets of the street captured with a little digital affair, though she is gifted with an archivist's obsessive desire to discover and preserve and an almost philosophic fascination with the city's hurtling and abandoned poetry, and her apartment wall – she lives alone – is covered with prints documenting her explorations of the encoded fragments. It is she who discovers the solution to the little mystery one morning when she is returning from breakfast at a café, finding four words inscribed on a painted brick wall. POÈTES DU CERCLE VICIEUX. She hurries to her apartment and returns with her camera. Now and then the inscriptions are painted over within a day or two, and she is prompt to photograph each new one lest it disappear. She has the thought that someday she might make a book of them. It gives her something to imagine. She intends to mention the idea to a publisher who is an acquaintance, but so far has been too shy.

A murder victim, slashed, poisoned, but somehow still alive. The halls of the nunnery were long and bare, the windows at the end of the corridor topped with an ecclesiastical arch, and as Louisa put one foot in front of the other, slowly proceeding to her room, the length and emptiness of the corridor, the quiet, the shine of light on the wooden floor, exhausted her, made her want to close her eyes and lie down, and when she forced herself to move, she couldn't feel her legs from the knee down, and the chemical stink of something, perhaps her own body, choked her. They promised her that these things would vanish soon. They promised her that she would heal and live.

Still, mortality stood close by her, a reminder of the ultimate depletion, and it made even her best thoughts small and embattled. You said truth, you said love, and the quiet voice of fate said no, said silence.

Once inside her room, she sat in the wooden armchair by the window and closed her eyes. There was a sore on her lower gum, and she poked it with her tongue, deliberately making it hurt. What was it in the human being that made you wish to touch the source of the pain? An animal with a wound licked itself, and the enzymes in the saliva helped to cleanse and heal the wound. Perhaps it was that sane animal impulse that made you wish to poke the sore.

And then she heard or felt or maybe smelled his presence: Sonny. The funny, clever, doomed, faggoty love of her youth – maybe, though stupidly useless for it, the love of her life – was there in the room with her. It happened now and then, but the messenger from the past never spoke and she never saw him, only knew that he was with her, his travelling soul like a white bird perched on the arm of her chair. He was with her. Probably at first it was memories of things he had said that had given her the idea, things he said just before they both went away to pursue their lives, how he would talk on and on as they sat in the basement recreation room of her mother's house, couldn't talk enough to say all he had to say, and he would tell her about the Play. What he had been hearing about it. It was about the Disease, he said. She got some idea of it from what he said, some inspired but unspecific idea. But it was not ever on the list for any course she took in the following years, and perhaps she hadn't attended to him very carefully or perhaps Sonny himself only knew the rumours. In those days she often failed to listen carefully. She knew, had always known, that he was gay, though she also refused to know it and now and then would insist that he kiss her, and he would, and his lips, soft, eloquent lips, stirred her up, and she was sure that he had responded too.

Just let's try it, she wanted to say.

Maybe someday.

They sat together and laughed, and attentive, analytical listening to his words didn't seem required, and so she ended up with wild assumptions and the residue of gossip. Sonny talked about the Play, and somehow the idea she got was that everyone who died of the Disease became an Angel.

And he had and he did.

Louisa, crushed into the chair in the corner of the bare room, tried to summon enough energy to open her eyes, look about her. What if, this time, Sonny was apparent, a visible emanation? He wouldn't be, and she was ill and scarred and poisoned. She wanted to be home among her friends, but this conference on philosophical ideas in popular art had been irresistible, and she would deliver her paper. A small enough thing in the face of an empty eternity. She had enrolled months before – even though she wasn't properly recovered from her surgery or finished her chemotherapy – and she had contrived, by exerting all the discipline she was capable of, to write the paper she had planned. *Text in Motion: The Freedom and Control Songs of Leonard Cohen*. If all went well it would become one of the essays in the book she planned on twentieth century poets. *The Vivisectionists* she wanted to call it.

This morning – having managed the drive, though Janey, her closest friend, had urged her to take the train – she had on arrival passed a row of small brick houses crowded side by side and parked the car in the lot by the door of the converted nunnery, and she saw the phrase SISTERS OF MERCY written on a wall and the song began to sing itself in her head. Cohen had been brought up in the city when the streets were full of nuns moving through the days in their long black outfits, and now, as she considered that, Louisa had a sense of how someday her paper might be expanded. When she was well. She had more to say now that her experience of surgery and chemical assault had created a new state of mind in which she sensed more precisely the collocation of discourses – political, religious and sexual – in the text of the songs.

She sat, her eyes still closed, apprehending the Presence. She wished that Sonny, now he was an Angel, would speak to her. She and Sonny, she had always believed, were married under some stranger, more complicated, alternative laws of life, and he travelled everywhere with her, but as an Angel he never spoke. It appeared to be against the rules, somehow. It was odd to think of Sonny being silenced. It wasn't his style.

She ought to look through the text of her lecture. Leonard's songs:

one of the things that she and Sonny disagreed about. Late in the afternoon they sat in the two old bean bag chairs in the basement, while footsteps, those of her mother and her grandmother, moved back and forth above them, and they argued a little about Leonard, but then it wasn't worth arguing any more, and they let it go. They were too important to each other to argue. She had met Sonny in the music club at school when she was fourteen. He was a couple of years older, and within a few months they were King and Queen of the music club. Sonny's great dream was that the club would do a production of *A Chorus Line*, even though they knew it was impossible, as dancers they weren't good enough, but the two of them spent hours together talking about it.

As well as Sonny hovering like a great invisible bird, Louisa felt the ghostly presence of the vanished nuns in these corridors, in the room where she sat. She remembered Klein's poem about the nursing sisters caring for him when he was ill as a child:

> the cool wing for my fever, the hovering solace,
> the sense of angels –
> be thanked, O plumage of paradise, be praised.

Could she attain such comfort? The image of those lost nuns evoked a world of prayer, but she had no prayers. She knew the answer. Find any form of words and repeat it with sufficient concentration and it would be a prayer and would lead her to enlightenment. But the paper was to be given tomorrow morning, and it was now late afternoon, and she was too bruised to find the energy required to pray. But she was glad that Sonny was here with her in his role as invisible Angel. She wished that she could believe that if she died he would be waiting for her, in a long white gown or some such thing, but he wasn't that kind of Angel, only a protective spirit here on earth. Or something. No words for it.

Perhaps if she lay down for a while. Slept. As she stood up to walk across to the bed she caught sight of herself in the little mirror on the back of the door. Bald. She wasn't wearing the wig. Why not? She was sure it must have been anchored to her pate when she set off to the dining room half an hour before, to try and eat a little lunch. She must have lost it somewhere, but she had no memory of such a thing. I must find my wig. I am bald-headed. She would repeat that, make it her prayer. *I am bald-headed, I will find my wig. I am bald-headed, I will find my wig. I am bald-headed, I will find my wig.*

A lost wig. A lost hat. A lost or abandoned *ruelle.* There are other streets that don't exist, and not merely streets but whole cities. Where is Atlantis? Nowhere: it is a mythological city invented by Plato and once invented, with its inescapable story, a paperback heaven. Somewhere under the mid-Atlantic the radiant towers rise from the depths toward the light of the sun, fish swimming in and out of the windows, unheard-of arachnids waiting for their prey in the corners of rooms where the greatest of astronomers spy into the night and geometers analyze the characteristics of conic sections. The ghosts of wise women swim slowly past the blue murals in which the loves of the Atlantean gods are displayed. The sunken city has achieved a zone of timelessness.

Beneath every city is another city. You remember the difficult crossing of a low basement, lowering yourself through a trapdoor, scrabbling bent over toward the back where the water pipes, too close to the rock of the wall, have frozen. The building is without water, so you drag a cord behind you and in your hand is an electric paint-stripper, an electric resistance-coil heater with a little fan, and as you move it slowly up and down the pipe, waiting to hear a crackling as the ice begins to melt, you notice a pile of pamphlets in a corner of the crawl-space. When the water is running, you will crawl back to the trapdoor, taking the pamphlets with you.

They are *livrets* printed on cheap paper, the covers in two colours, the top one printed in strange green and purple. *Les Aventures Policières d'Albert Brien, détective national des Canadiens français. Éditions Police Journal.* The shadowed, whiskery green face of a corpse lies on the ground and the title in garish purple reads, *On a Rasé le Mort.* You will never know who left them behind. Words are saved or abandoned. Cities change day by day. Some disappear. The deserts of the Middle East and North Africa reveal, as the sands come and go, long-buried fragments of lost civilizations. The Street of the Potters, arenas, the sites of religious sacrifice.

Pompeii is no longer a city, but a kind of accidental museum, a documentation of the August day when the ash and lava sealed that hour from time before and after, the place lost in ash for 1,600 years. Excavated, it offers, among other things, odd bits of often scabrous graffiti, SUSPIRIUM PUELLARUM CELADUS THRAEX, it says in the barracks of the gladiators, while the wall of a brothel bears a testimony to the services of the prostitute Drauca, while LUCRUM GAUDIUM equates money and happiness, and somewhere else a scribbler complains that he has caught a cold. Not that far to the north, in the catacombs under Rome, a city of the dead is inscribed with the names of Christian apostles, PETRUS, PAULUS.

It was morning and Sasha was coming back from breakfast in a nearby café and waiting for the elevator in the lobby under the arches of silvery heating ducts which the renovation architects had left standing as decoration so that you felt as if you were in some strange modernistic arbour, shaded by mechanical trees. While she waited and the elevator didn't come, the tall handsome singer appeared at the outer door, entered and stood beside her.

'You're the singer,' she said, looking up. Close up he was even taller.

'Carlo,' he said. 'Carlo Bannigan. And you're the photographer.' He was studying the camera around her neck.

'Sasha,' she said. She was wearing the khaki pants and loose khaki jacket with big pockets which she had made for herself a few months ago partly to prove she used the sewing machine when Lomas accused her of letting it rust. With the khaki outfit, the camera and a beret on her head she looked a little like some 1930s journalist just back from a war. He looked again, checking her out.

'Just how tall are you?' she said.

'Six-four.'

'That's outrageous.'

'How tall are you?'

'Just like the old song.'

'Five foot two?'

'That's it.'

'In the opera I'm rehearsing I wear built-up boots to make me even taller.'

'Why? You're already too tall.'

'I play a ghost,' he said as the elevator doors opened and they both got in. 'A man of stone arriving to drag the villain off to hell.'

'Scary.'

'You should come and take pictures of a rehearsal. No money, but it could be interesting.'

'Yes,' she said, 'I'd like to do that.'

The elevator arrived at her floor.

'I'll be in touch,' he said.

Sasha knew nothing about opera. Lomas and Patricia, determined to bring her up properly, had taken her to concerts and art galleries now and then, but Lomas always said his taste didn't run to the hollering Fat Ladies. Sasha thought of her tall, handsome neighbour. Maybe there was more to opera than she had guessed.

She wanted such a man maybe, yet resisted, declining all that fuss, expectation, interference. The big feet. Yes, men had such big feet And she had such little white feet and hands. Sasha wondered sometimes how she came to have the pale miniature palms and fingers, as if they had stopped growing when she was twelve as the rest of her developed. Sometimes in the bathtub, she would put her little hands over her breasts and wonder how the genetic lottery had come to present her with the odd combination. Men didn't notice hands, not at first. T and A, that's what they looked at, apparently, and she had that to offer. The singer would have taken that in, of course, and perhaps it stirred him. Though she didn't really care. She had her own admiration, could live without the desires of horny boys.

Young, they were all young, those who inscribed the aphorisms. No one can prove this, of course, but it seems evident, it has the quality of truth, what you can't prove but will continue to believe. The young overflow with inspiration, rage, laughter, blood, semen. Jokes. FARN- IENTE SALON inscribed on the wall of a neighbourhood copshop. The unknown poets can't stop arriving in the night to leave their inventions. The inexplicable bits. BOOTSY FRIDAYS, it says somewhere. GUEULE D'ANGE somewhere else. An encompassing sense of mystery goes with all these brief ejaculations. The mind offers a phrase without any context except the tales of the secret city, the place where history is buried. You read the words but cannot hear the voices. Cursive swirls of paint. Little decorative gestures as delightful and unlikely as butterflies. Grinning faces. Dates. Telephone numbers. An ornamental letter H on a set of wooden doors painted robin's-egg blue. Swirls. Dancers. Bits of advice that you might even take. À DÉFAUT DE FUMER, BUVEZ. While you sleep, the rain pours down over the night's harvest of new scribbling. The older ones have begun to wear away. The tins of spray paint are lined up by the door of a rented room, a studio, or the storage room behind a restaurant kitchen. There is a convention for the shape of certain letters, learned by daylight observation, practised alone and at night.

When the sun returns, the same sun shining on the world renewed, the sociologues and philosophers go out in search of new inscriptions to collect, interpret, publish. And the day's pedestrians pass by, read them or ignore them altogether.

Morning, and the sun shone in the window of the old nunnery. While she is in the city, Louisa wonders, should she contact Lomas and Batty Patty's daughter, her young cousin Sasha? Somewhere Louisa had an address and perhaps a telephone number. Louisa was not altogether clear as to what the girl did. According to Patricia she was supposed to be a clothing designer, but no one ever saw anything she designed. Louisa's mother reported recently that her brother Lomas's spoiled stepdaughter had some kind of job in a hotel. Would the girl appreciate it if Louisa called, arriving bald-headed? Louisa and her mother had mostly fallen out of touch with that part of the family. After Louisa's father ran off with Nurse Two, they drew into themselves, a little world including only Louisa and her mother, later on admitting the widowed grandmother when she moved in. They had been abandoned, and they set up barricades to prevent dangerous incursions. Louisa's closest friend was Sonny, and her mother would invite him to stay for dinner, and he worked hard at charming her and the grandmother. Louisa's mother once tried to warn her about what he was, but Louisa just laughed and said that of course she knew perfectly well, mother, and she wasn't planning on marriage or anything stupid like that. She didn't say that they were already married in the sight of God. She knew that was too strange. As promised they both set off to live their lives, left town, she to university, Sonny to Toronto where he contracted the Disease while being careless with some infectious stranger in a bathhouse, and then with headlong rapidity he sickened and died.

Louisa continued to wonder how she could possibly have lost the wig, though she no longer really cared. The vanishing made no sense. Surely she would not have taken it off anyplace but her room, and it was not there. Perhaps some indigent cancer patient came to clean the room, and unable to afford a good quality wig had stolen Louisa's. She had searched the room a dozen times, and there was no sign of it.

Perhaps the loss was meant to teach her something. About mystery, the unaccountable. Or about humility. Or dignity. Or God. Or death. Or dogs and cats. Or chopped parsley. She sat down at the little desk and flipped through the pages of her talk, to make sure that nothing had gone missing there. In a few minutes she would stand bald-headed at the front of the auditorium that had once been the nun's chapel, and she would explain how words, as they lost literal meaning in the measured lineation of rhyme, left open the doors of Being, the Existent Majuscule. Perhaps at the end of her paper she would be granted a vision of her own death, imminent or perhaps still far off. She didn't want any such vision. She wanted to continue waking in the morning and staring out the window and starting the day.

Her runaway father had been quick to respond when he heard about her cancer. Dutiful as always, he instantly cancelled all his appointments and drove for three hours to arrive at her door. He arranged for her to see a surgeon who was an old friend of his. There was nothing she could criticize in his behaviour, except that he had abandoned her mother. In their youth, the two of them had met in a hospital where her mother was a nurse and he an intern, and then when Louisa was fifteen the doctor had gone off some other nurse, younger of course.

Louisa had not behaved well about it. She refused to go and visit her father and his new woman, and when he phoned she used to refer her mother and the new wife as Nurse One and Nurse Two. He tried to ignore the nastiness of her tone. It embarrassed her a good deal to remember that now. She knew little enough of love and sex at that age, except what she had read in books. No doubt a shrink would say she was shielding herself from it by taking up with Sonny. It wasn't until her third year in university that she decided to have adventures. Too often she thought the morning after that while she had enjoyed the lovemaking, she couldn't imagine spending much time with the man.

Luke, her lover in graduate school, was as close as she had come, but faced with a hard choice, they had chosen their careers. Now she had a circle of friends, letters from Luke, and Sonny's ghost. If still she lacked the framework of marriage and children she was none the less swimming bravely through life. *What is love?* went the Shakespeare song, and perhaps the next words summed it up. *'Tis not hereafter.* Great romance was a myth, like heaven. We can only love what is here and now. *What's to come is still unsure.*

She glanced at the pages of her lecture. The neon streetcorner romanticism of Cohen's poetry was half its appeal. She was on the schedule to talk about it later that very afternoon. As she stood in the pulpit and carefully recited the typed lines, perhaps she would look down into the audience, and there Himself would be, a dark, dramatic face, the soulful eyes studying her, taking in the hidden meanings between her words. He would be wearing a fedora, the dark face radiating a supernal calm. It was reported that Leonard still had a house here, a little place, they said, not far from the Main, and that he arrived there unheralded from time to time to be part of his city again, once more comparing mythologies. It was not utterly impossible that he might walk quietly in the back door and take his place while a bald woman in a dark grey pant suit recited her creed, psalms and proverbs.

Strange to realize that the magical Leonard Cohen had an existence offstage, that he clipped his toenails and washed his socks. Or did someone clip them for him, wash them for him? Once at a party Louisa met a woman who claimed to have slept with him. After a university concert when she was an undergraduate, the girl had sent back her phone number, and he had called, and they had compared mythologies all through that night before he returned to his wife and children.

Louisa did not have that kind of daring. As a graduate student she had believed that her thesis adviser was on offer, but while she found him moderately attractive, she had resisted temptation, though she couldn't have said exactly why. She studied dangerous men from a distance. When the cancer in her breast was first diagnosed, she had lain awake every night trying to think if this was her own fault, if she had been too sparing, too frugal with the stuff of her life. Five years ago, she and Luke – though they had been a couple all through graduate school – had taken jobs a thousand miles apart, because that was the path their careers had taken, and now they were old friends, in regular contact by e-mail, who might once have married, had children. Breast cancer was more common among women who had not borne children. They discovered that by doing statistical research on nuns.

Perhaps she would not ring her young cousin. Nor would she discover the Ladies' Man in the audience listening to her, but she would stand boldly bald (or baldly bold) in front of the group of academics and read to them her lines on what Leonard believed it meant to be free.

Greg felt a little tired, but the hunger that led him to the city was unsated. He had been walking the streets since early morning, devouring all he saw. He had a day-return ticket and not enough money to stay overnight; there was a late evening bus which he planned to catch. Now he was somewhere in Westmount, where he sat on a bench looking out over the small pond that caught the summer sun and reflected the leaves of the trees.

The book he had bought lay in his little canvas knapsack beside a paperback mystery he had been reading on the bus. There was a chocolate bar to eat sometime later on. He opened the knapsack and took out the Klein book, began to skip through it, turn over pages. There was something written in the front in green ink in small careful letters.

I don't see as I can ever trust you again – or anyone.

Beneath, by way of signature, was a kind of design of three intertwined letters. A P, an F and an O, or that was what it appeared to be. Pauline Francesca Otley. Or some such thing. He might have the letters wrong. Maybe it was an E, not an F. He would never know the meaning of the little diagram, nor of the words written above it. The handwriting, the green ink, it looked like a girl, and someone had done her wrong. It happened. Now he felt as if the book he'd bought was tainted by someone's unhappiness, the betrayal that had taken place, and he was tempted to leave it there on the bench for someone else to discover, carrying home a souvenir of pain. But in a few minutes he would put it back in the knapsack and fasten the canvas straps. However it had come to him, it was his.

He flipped through the pages, glanced at a couple of poems about the mountain, Klein's childhood paradise. After he explored the park and got something to eat, he would go up there and find the lookouts Klein wrote about, survey the city.

Greg strolled round the pond and toward a red brick building with large windows and a black roof. When he came close he discovered that it was a public library, and he went inside, saw a few people studying the shelves, an old man with thick white hair sitting at a table with a pile of books beside him and a school scribbler in which he was making notes. The whole place had that strange hushed quality, not complete silence but like a hushed whispering somewhere out of sight. At the desk was a woman with dark hair, dark lipstick and glasses with glittering frames. He walked past her and toward a hall at the north end of the building, where a corridor led to the left, beyond it sunlight, and when he opened a door he found himself in a conservatory full of tropical vegetation. An aisle that penetrated the greenery, and he saw a girl with a notebook in her hand, standing still, as if awaiting him.

She had thick, dark blond hair blunt-cut round her head in an effect that was like some artist's rendering of Joan of Arc. The face was sculpted as if in clay or silver, forceful and yet precise and delicate, fine straight nose, *hollow of cheek as if she drank the wind*, damp, intricately curving lips that might have been shaped for a rendering of some ancient and fine-boned Egyptian Pharaoh. Something illuminated about the lightly freckled skin, and the eyes were brilliant blue behind curving blond lashes. At her neck was knotted a scarf of red silk, and the almost tall body was both slender and sensual.

Here was the most beautiful woman in the world, and Greg did not believe that she was real. Her blue eyes met his for only a second, intent and daring, and then she looked away, turned from him and walked off into the brilliant green foliage and vanished. Greg stood perfectly still, compelled and disbelieving, and then he decided that he would catch up with her, that he would speak. He knew from looking at her that she was from some other place, brighter and kinder perhaps, and he was determined to know her.

He will not find her, not knowing where to look, though for years afterward there will be moments when he remembers what he saw and believes that he might meet her again. The memory demands some large bravery, foolhardiness even, on his part, and the crazed hope is part of what drives him to a number of occasions of drunken misbehaviour. Stoned, drunk, falling into the street until he comes to realize that she was an illusion, that on that afternoon he was young and brainstruck and no such girl exists. So he sets aside the memory, loses his black hat, and becomes a teacher, marries and does well enough.

She did exist of course, and for a moment in the luminous conservatory along the green leaves, she hoped that he would speak to her – she liked his outrageous black hat – but he was not quick enough, and so she turned away and went on to another life.

It had begun as only an exotic addition to her comic book collection, but Sasha had found inspiration in it. The comic book lay on the table in front of her. CHARLOT was the title at the top of a cover, which showed the figure of Charlie Chaplin as the little tramp, bowler hat, moustache, baggy pants. The little man was on a ship, hung up on a cargo hook that had caught his jacket, while beneath, a fat cook swung a frying pan at an astonished Captain, whose hat and pipe had flown into the air. She had found the comic in a junk store she'd discovered a few days before. They came and went, the junk stores, and it was often the new ones that had something surprising. On the front of the comic was a price, 2 francs. It had been brought from Paris, the date on it 1973. Ten years older than she was.

Since finding inspiration in the comic Sasha had been accumulating the necessities to disguise herself as Chaplin's tramp. She wasn't sure about the hair, perhaps butcher her own to get a wig on top. The figure in the comic had black curls with blue highlights.

Friends of the Desirable Girl. Sasha could establish a new website, and she would play all the parts. She had a little box of false hair to begin the creation of a moustache. Instructions from the internet, spirit gum and acetone close at hand, a small magnifying mirror on the shelf. Hung over the back of the straight chair, a white shirt and tie and a suit jacket. Baggy pants, oversize vest. She would search them out in her costume collection or make a trip to Friperie, her favourite second hand store, to find them.

There was a knock on her door. She knew who it was, and yet it was still a shock. No one came here. As she walked across the big room to the door, she felt naked. She looked in the narrow mirror by the door and reassured herself that she was clothed, safe.

'I'm a few minutes late,' Carlo said. 'We'll have to hurry.'

An intimacy in how he plunged into things, no shy hesitations. He was carrying an equipment bag in his left hand, as if he might be going off to play squash. Sasha picked up her camera bag, which she had packed and ready, took down a beret and jacket from the rack and put them on. He spoke as she was locking the door behind her.

'I don't know why things always come up when I'm due at a rehearsal,' he said.

'What?'

'Oh, just the arrangements for a wedding where I'm singing. She picked impossible times to rehearse and then she wanted to talk everything over three times.'

'Her big day. She only gets married once.'

Carlo turned and looked at her.

'Most people I know seem to get married two or three times.'

'But only the first time really counts.'

'Let's take the stairs,' he said. 'I can't stand to wait for the elevator.'

They flew down the stairs and out.

'It's not far from here,' he said.

'A theatre?'

'It's a warehouse. We're rehearsing and performing there. Supposed to be the first step in turning it into an arts centre with an experimental performance space.'

Sasha was jogging to keep up with his long strides. She had expected him to be charming and flirtatious, as if this was a first date, but she might have been a neighbourhood dog for all the attention he paid. At the corner was a derelict store, the sign destroyed, the word VIN the only one that could be read, the window frames empty, inside half of an upper storey fallen away, a piece of floor in front of a window remaining. A cat appeared in a doorway, fled. They turned at the corner.

Was there a name, she wondered, for the grey-green colour of the doors and window frames of the empty warehouse they were passing? The riveted metal door of a cargo chute was painted the same colour, but less worn. She might have taken a picture if allowed time to unpack her camera. Carlo checked his watch, slowed his pace just a little as he turned left though a gateway of a wire fence, into an empty lot, the ground uneven as if a building had been torn down. A couple of cars and a van were parked by the door of the warehouse at the far end. She tripped on a chunk of mud as she tried to keep up with Carlo's long paces.

As she looked across the barren lot to the metal doors, presumably once used for loading and unloading trucks, Sasha tried to imagine what this photo session would be like. The ground they crossed was bare and hopeless, as if, deserted, it had endured the disaster that must sooner or later come and wipe out our attempt at civilization. Sasha walked side by side with the tall silent man across the cracked concrete area behind the building, weeds coming up between the slabs, wherever there was a space for detritus to gather and rot into something like soil, and for the tiny thread of roots to break their way down toward earth. Inside the building something occult was taking place.

Once inside, Carlo hung his jacket over a chair, opened the equipment bag and took out a helmet and boots with tall soles. A little group was gathered around a slightly raised area with a small stairway to a platform at the back, where a large mirror was hinged in a frame so it could be turned from side to side or all the way round. Carlo led her to the little group of people, introduced her and explained she would be taking pictures.

'But you don't interfere,' said Marc-André Chose who had been introduced as the director.

'She knows what she's doing,' Carlo said. Sasha was relieved that he was prepared to defend her. Carlo was putting on his helmet, and once it was on, he made a gesture to a sound man, who nodded, made adjustments. He walked on the stage, turned and began to sing a few notes. The helmet was obviously miked, and the sound of his voice given an added reverb so it had a supernatural power. The lighting man turned on a couple of spots and Carlo looked huge in his tall helmet and high shoes.

Sasha took out the camera, set it for what she guessed the light to be. It would adapt within that range. She clicked off a couple of shots of techies carrying in a table. An accompanist sat down at the keyboard of an electric piano. A drummer stood by a tymp nearby. Carlo took his place at the back of the stage, two other performers near the front. Sasha had done some research on the opera, and she could identify the characters as the servant Leporello, the short balding one, and the sturdy man with a trimmed beard who must be playing Don Giovanni. In seconds the scene started, and the actors, out of nowhere, produced a sense of tension and involvement. Carlo stood at the back of the stage, obviously to be somehow invisible to the audience, while the others reacted to the drumbeats of someone knocking at the door. Carlo, was announced by drumbeats, demanding entry to Don Giovanni's house, Leporello quivering and preparing to flee, Don Giovanni defiant. Sasha zoomed the lens in close, hoping to get the intensity that had appeared on the faces, uncertain what the effect would be of the mouths wide open to sing. Good of Carlo to believe she knew what she was doing, but she wasn't sure herself. He was stepping forward. Into the light.

'Don Giovanni.' His first words, with the booming resonance of the reverb, chilled her. He summoned the libertine to some kind of judgment, the three deep male voices moving around the drama of the scene. When the defiant libertine gave his hand to the statue, his whole body was seized. By what? The shocking cold of death? The shocking fire of hell? Other voices sounded from offstage as the Statue dragged his quarry up to the little platform at the back, and the Don gave a howl of pain, and just at that point the director shouted OK and walked on the set. Sasha had been shooting and moving through all this.

Two other men had come in the door, and the director summoned them up to the stage. Sasha was standing close by, but she couldn't quite hear what they were saying in rapid French until suddenly the director began to curse, a whole lineup of liturgical improprieties. His gestures became large and violent, and for a moment Sasha thought he was going to attack one of the others, a rather slim man with a shaved head and a long purple scarf.

'Bien! Parfait! La machine à coudre est foutue!' Marc André Chose shouted, lifted his arms in a huge gesture of frustration.

More curses. He reached out as if he might grab the designer, who backed away.

'Foutu,' the director was screaming. 'Crisse de scénographe! Tout est foutu.'

Sasha couldn't quite understand what the big problem was with the screwed-up sewing machine. Carlo had wandered down to the front of the stage.

'I have a sewing machine,' she said to him. 'If that's all they need.'

Louisa unlocked the door of the car. The walk across the parking lot had tired her. She got into the driver's seat and sat perfectly still, her eyes closed, trying to summon up energy and focus. The drugs that had moved through her bloodstream seeking and poisoning the fast-growing cells had poisoned everything they touched. Nothing in her body functioned properly now, and existence was in question. She felt like an example from some text on existentialism, something that proved the absolute strangeness of being.

Suppose she were, even after her oncologist's best efforts, to die. No more Louisa Jeanette Palmer. She would not know her own absence, and the world, apart from her group of close friends, a few students, her mother and her father, wouldn't care. She should, perhaps, have married and bred children, thrown herself into the biological functioning of the world, sanctioned the possession of her womb by the sperm of a chosen or unchosen man, but even tumid and hot with life, she knew, death would be death. The two or three people who had spoken to her after her talk, praised it, would forget every word. It would be nothing. It was so hard to get a grip on it, well, you couldn't. It wasn't even slippery and hard to hold, it was just nothing. Not there. Later, if not sooner, she would be *not there*.

You understood why people believed that there must be something. Perhaps she could convince herself that Sonny would be waiting for her after all, in a heavenly white nightie, laughing. But for all she knew Sonny had discovered True Love in Toronto before he was infected, and that's who he awaited in the world of white nighties. But they were the best of friends. Always. In spite of everything. In the hall beside her locker on a day late in her last year of high school, one of the Three Bitches called her a fag hag. Jealous, are you? she had said in response and the Bitch had laughed and walked away. After Sonny's death Louisa had read the Play and discovered that she had got it all wrong, or Sonny had when he told her about it. It wasn't really about how every fag with AIDS would become an Angel, and strangely at a loss after this discovery, she had for a while lost touch with Sonny's presence, but in time it returned. Mattered not what the play said, she decided. The spiritual marriage had occurred.

She opened her eyes. Across the parking lot was a tall stone wall, and behind it the roof of some part of the nunnery where she had been staying. Her room was reserved for one more day, but she was finished. She had spoken her words; an arrangement had been made for their publication by the editor of a magazine who was in attendance, who looked at her, the bald head, the puffy features, and looked away, not wanting to stare at a dead woman. *Who by fire?* She had made something in her paper of Cohen's note to the song, that it was inspired by a prayer recited on the Day of Atonement. The rhetoric of prayer as an imperative discourse.

Sunlight caught the grey limestone of the wall. Its top was ragged, as if the stones up there might come loose and fall. *Who by falling stone?* She felt a longing to be a poet, to make a prayer out of the nunnery emptied of its holy women, or the wall of falling rocks. She stared at the light on the wall, the way it appeared to penetrate the rock as it might penetrate water, the limestone illuminated from within like grey glass.

Louisa breathed deeply, felt a little strength flow into her limbs. She turned to set down the small case, which she had been holding in her lap, pressing it against the steering wheel to keep herself upright, and as she was about to set the bag on the seat beside her, she saw it there, occupying the passenger seat, her wig. It faced forward, as if waiting for the head that would assume it. For a moment Louisa imagined the wig on top of a skull.

'How did you get there?' she said to the wig. They were, after all, on intimate terms. For the last few weeks the wig had created her appearance, defined her personality, but now it failed to answer her question.

'Just how,' she said, 'did we get separated?'

Once again the wig remained stubbornly silent.

'All right,' she said, 'enough of that.'

She took the wig and fitted it over her bare head, settled it in place and twisted her neck to look in the rear view mirror. Her features looked quite different, thinner, more commonplace, she thought. Once or twice in the last few weeks she had caught an accidental glimpse of herself naked in a mirror, bald, thin, her pubic hair vanished, and she had tried to imagine a man who could desire her like this, with a fierce irregular desire. She knew no one like that. Luke long gone.

The woman in the mirror smiled. Louisa wondered once again if it was a failure of some kind not to visit her cousin Sasha. No. There was something too queer about her, as there had been about her whole family. Batty Patty her family had called the girl's mother. Patricia was a loose-mouthed, prematurely sexy girl who lived in the upstairs apartment next door to Louisa's grandmother's house on a street in NDG. Louisa met her when she was five or six and on a summer visit to her Gran. Every day, it seemed, the fifteen-year-old Batty Patty arrived at the back door, impulsively launched into conversation with whoever answered, offering to share gum and candies, breasts spilling out of her blouse, a comic book stuck in the back pocket of shorts that were too tight and too short. Then she was seventeen and pregnant, no father even remotely evident, and then, when the baby was six months old, suddenly and against all likelihood, Louisa's uncle Lomas, who was twenty-three and being some kind of left-wing intellectual, married her and became stepfather to little Sasha.

In later years Louisa and her mother once discussed the marriage. Her mother believed that at seventeen Patricia, in spite of the plump new baby sucking endlessly on her big white breasts, had found time to introduce uptight Lomas to slack and easy sex and in gratitude he had taken her on.

'Probably he could have done worse,' her mother had said of her brother, and something in her tone made Louisa conclude that her mother had not been slack and easy in her sex life. Unlike Nurse Two, perhaps.

Married to Patricia, Lomas had quit his dead-end job and enrolled in a training course for opticians, and soon enough he had a full-time job, and eventually he became partner in a small business. Louisa didn't see a lot of the family after her father left and her grandmother moved in with them. From what her mother heard, Lomas was devoted to his stepdaughter. He sewed her dresses. This struck both Louisa and her mother as eccentric, but they were, Lomas and Patricia, they both were.

Strangely, Lomas, though so seldom seen, had a hand in leading Louisa toward the paper she had just delivered. It was after her grandmother's funeral. They had gone back to the house. For some reason Sasha and Patricia had not accompanied Lomas on the trip down, and Louisa observed Lomas as he did a good deal of damage to the booze that was on offer. Fitting enough, Louisa thought, after his mother's funeral. Lomas, as he grew drunk, looking a little desperate, tried to attached himself to Louisa; he was laughing too much, hysterical. Realizing he was past driving, he had arranged to stay overnight and head back in the morning. For company on the drive, he announced, he had two discs of the songs of Leonard Cohen.

'Met him at a party once,' he said, 'back in his early days.'

He looked at Louisa, his reddened eyes sparkling.

'Missed my calling,' he said. 'Should have been a backup singer for Leonard.' He paused and sipped his drink. 'In a gold lamé dress.'

He made a strange face, choked on a laugh and walked away. Louisa was left wondering whether this was some kind of bizarre confession or only alcoholic high-jinks. Thought probably the latter, but who ever knew such things? All the members of the family were half cracked. She was convinced that if she visited Sasha now while she was in the city, she would come on something unsettling. No visit. Still it was Lomas's strange remark that led her to begin listening to the Cohen songs, and to think that someday she might do a paper about them.

The overnight case she placed on the seat beside her contained a nightgown, pills, a change of underwear, the text of her talk, a very small digital notebook, her cellphone, a new sweater she had just bought and not yet worn. Once again safely bewigged, she took the car key out of her purse and inserted it. She hoped she had enough energy to drive all the way home. Stop and rest when she needed to. Possibly she should have taken the train, as Janey suggested. Before starting the car, she moved the purse, opened the suitcase to extract her cell phone, and laid it on the seat. You weren't supposed to talk on it while driving, but it was reassuring to have the cell available. It was programmed for both Janey and Elspeth, and if desperate, she could punch a button and reach one of them.

Louisa closed her eyes in an attempt to summon up courage. She felt a kind of vertigo, then noises in her ears, a voice, well, almost a voice. Words.

Phone now.

What?

Punch the button. Don't try and drive all the way yourself.

I'm OK.

No, Louisa, you're not. Phone and go back in and wait for help to reach you.

Sonny?

You mustn't make the drive alone.

Is that you?

Pick up the phone.

Sonny?

The collector who identified the initials PCV has found but not yet photographed a new inscription. Right now she is walking home to her apartment for lunch. She is wearing a baseball cap that reveals little of the red hair and makes her look appealingly boyish. She is working a split shift, off now until late afternoon, when she will go back and work through the evening. This morning, taking an unusual route, along a *ruelle* where she hadn't previously walked, she saw the new piece of graffiti. Y A T'IL UNE VIE AVANT LA MORT? it said, and that bohemian piety is now on her list of things to be photographed. A block away is another on her list. LA VIE EST AILLEURS. Being a somewhat bookish young woman she is aware that this is a quotation, and she is tempted to come back some night with a tin of spray paint, and underneath the quotation to inscribe Milan Kundera's name. She wonders, irritably, whether the quotation is deliberate or whether the hand behind the words believed that they were original.

At the next corner she turns left and this leads her past two stores, one empty, the other selling medical equipment. In the window staring toward her is a skeleton suspended from a metal frame, looking as if it might be about to begin dancing. The door beside the display window has a sign, LOGEMENT À LOUER, and the grinning skeleton seems to be beckoning her. It demands from her some act of transcendence, an escapade.

She recognizes the queer state of mind coming over her, the sense of misplacement and unease, the urge to follow some fling of insane impulse and bring about radical change: to steal enough to take off and travel the world creating a book or a documentary film about graffiti, the way the surface of the world is haunted by those brief poems, the haiku of the dispossessed. Life is all challenge and disdain, and it provokes in her a flame of defiance. Her history will be as brave as any, and there is no knowing what she might do next.

When she reaches her apartment, one storey up from the narrow lane, her neighbour across the way is once again sunbathing on the patio outside her apartment door. The warm weather has brought her out, short blond hair and a sulky spoiled face, a woman almost in middle age but well-preserved, taking the sun on a lounge in a two-piece bathing suit. This sunbathing is a new thing in recent days. She must be aware that while she is invisible from the street below, all those in the apartments above and opposite observe her.

The camera used to record the words on walls is close at hand, and moodily defiant in her fine baseball cap, the graffiti collector decides that she must record this new neighbourhood phenomenon. Brandishing the silver camera, the collector stares out her window, and then, taking courage, she carries her camera out on the tiny balcony of her apartment, the sunbather in her green two-piece looking up, shocked, scandalized as this young woman looks boldly toward her, raises the camera, and as the sunbather stumbles, trying to rise, thinking to escape or cry out, she is fixed by the other woman's eye, a contemptuous gaze that is provoking and dangerous, as if those green eyes under the St Louis Cardinals baseball cap could sublimate pale flesh, stripping it away to reveal the bones within and arousing those bones to jig, compelled and terminal.

Sasha bent over the sewing machine, the material of the banner passing through the fingers of her left hand, drawn past the needle by the right as she ran up the long seam on the edge of the red material. Little white hands: Dolly, with her wide palms and big knuckles, would sometimes compare their hands and laugh. The material Sasha was sewing was a kind of nylon with a tendency to pucker, and it had a satiny sheen that would catch the light. Or that was the intention. Each long piece had to be hemmed, a slot like a buttonhole made at the top with enough extra fabric sewn round it that it could be tied to the wire that would lift it, and without tearing.

The scene at the rehearsal had concluded with the designer in tears, threatening to quit; it emerged that the problem wasn't just the sewing machine, but that the seamstress had taken on another job and was refusing to set to work on the banners, even when offered a rented sewing machine. When Carlo suggested that Sasha could do the sewing, Marc-André Chose left it for the designer and Aimé, the producer, to settle everything, and went back to rehearsing. After a bit of discussion Sasha drove off with Aimé and the designer, whose name she had never learned, to pick up the material. As she left, Carlo came to her, and to her astonishment, kissed her on both cheeks.

'Be magic,' he said.

Remember, the designer had told her when they picked up the material, the banners have to last four rehearsals and three performances, but that's all, so make them strong enough, but mostly make them fast. She had promised to have them done tonight, had phoned Pierre and arranged to trade shifts with him, so she had until midnight. Five of the six red pieces were hemmed and hanging over a rack on wheels while she finished this last one. Then she had to sew on the long pointed slashes of a different, lighter red, which had an orange flash to it in certain lights, then the narrow highlights of bright yellow. Each of the banners would lie concealed below the level of the platform at the back of the stage, and at the moment when the Commendatore took hold of Don Giovanni's hand, two spotlights would begin to strobe as the banners were pulled quickly up on their wires, a fan at each side to ripple the fabric, two set pieces turning to reveal mirrors where Don Giovanni was multiplied as he cried out among the waves of flame, and between the flickering lights and the rippling fabric he would be surrounded by fire. Earlier in the story, the designer told her, Don Giovanni and one of the girls wore costumes made of the same red fabric.

She reached the end of the seam, nipped off the thread with the scissors that lay beside her. She gathered up the banner and took it to the rack to hang there while she sorted the slashes of light red. They didn't need to be hemmed, sewn close to the edge they were unlikely to fray. As she hung the cloth she noticed that the afternoon sun was just beginning to catch the crimson banners, and they shimmered dangerously. She couldn't resist the effect, and she grabbed her camera and tripod from the table where she had left them, set them up facing the row of banners hung one over another and quickly took off her clothes, chose a place to stand behind the red cloth, checked that the camera was looking her in the eye, then three times she set the shutter delay, moved quickly behind the banners and held the pose until the camera clicked. The last time she put one of the banners round her like a head scarf and pressed forward into the sunlight, and in the last second before the shutter clicked she felt as if her breasts and belly were swelling in the heat of the blinding afternoon sun.

There was no time to study the photos she had made. Later she would download them to the computer and see what they had become. She was becoming more daring in what she would upload to the Desirable Girl site, and she had moments when she was afraid of what was possible. She took out the lighter red slashes, looked them over, trimmed an edge here and there, then hung them on a chair while she lifted down one of the banners, spread it on the floor and tacked the added pieces into position with pins. She carried the banner to the machine, laid it in place and began to sew the two pieces together.

Sasha wasn't used to sewing for so long, and her back and shoulders were aching. Maybe when she was finished this set of patches she would make herself coffee. Or after this first one she might put on a disc. She had a recent one by *Nickelback* that she hadn't played much.

The machine hummed and ticked and she drew the fabric past the lifting and falling needle, and by the time the sun had disappeared behind the edge of the window the reds were completed. Sasha turned on the burner and filled the espresso maker with a fragrant dark Brazilian roast.

As she wandered around the studio drinking the coffee, glad to be on her feet and moving, she was tempted to look at the new pictures, but she made herself wait until there was time to dwell on them, let them sit still in her mind. When she had finished the coffee, she turned on the CD player and began the process of sorting, pinning and sewing the narrow yellow highlights. *Nickelback* drove her on.

It was late and dark by the time she finished. She found a piece of cheese in the fridge and ate it with a cracker and a glass of white wine. Sasha wondered how long she would have to wait for the money they had promised her. One by one she took the banners down from the rack, spread them and folded them carefully, then packed the six of them into her backpack and set out to the theatre on her bicycle. The night was cool, and it was good to be out of doors, feel the wind on her cheeks.

On stage in the great roomy space of the warehouse, Don Giovanni was seducing some girl. Sasha didn't understand the words, but it was clear enough what was going on. The singer wasn't especially handsome, but he concentrated his desire on the girl in a way that was making it impossible for her to say no. His eyes never left her, and there was a quiet fury in his looks. You're mine, his eyes said, you're mine.

Aimé, the producer, saw Sasha come in the door and stand quietly watching the action. He came to her and indicated a side door that led them into a hallway. She followed him out.

'T'as fini?' he said, as if unbelieving, although she had promised.

'I said I'd finish them by tonight.'

'Je t'ai pas crue.'

He took the banners as she passed them to him and unrolled them. He studied them, ran them over his hands, his fingers spread to caress the cloth.

'Parfait, chérie, c'est parfait.'

She asked him about money, and he wrote her a cheque. Sasha wondered if there was money in the bank to cover it.

'Bon,' she said. 'Je dois travailler.'

'Tu travailles la nuit?'

'Des fois.'

He held up the banners, gave them a triumphant shake.

'Mille mercis.'

Back at her apartment Sasha made a salmon sandwich, pulled the plastic curtain around the ancient bathtub to take a shower, and dressed for work. She had a few minutes to spare, so she transferred her new pictures to the computer. She almost didn't recognize what she saw, so surprised was she at what was revealed, the scarlet flames as the sunlight caught flesh and fabric. She superimposed two of the images, and it was magical, her body complex and duplicated, the face just out of alignment with itself, everything crimson and sensual. It left her breathless, wondering whatever she might do with the image, how to reveal or conceal it. She had wondered as she cycled through the streets this morning if she might reprogram the site to allow for comments. She had never done this until now, and the thought of it chilled her, and yet it seemed necessary. Links to the Desirable Girl.

The bus drove through the streets of the night city, cars and trucks around it moving in dense packs like wild creatures, hunting wolves or migrating caribou. Passing a street corner Greg saw the faces of a couple turned toward each other, some intense dialogue filling the space between them. Alone, he curled in the corner of the seat, a determined erection pressing itself against the fabric, crowding the tight jeans as if ready to burst them. He had sat here as the bus loaded, waiting for a woman to join him, a stranger who would smile, giving him permission to talk to her or pretending to sleep, to let his body touch hers. The luminous girl he had seen among the ferns. Or some other stranger. The plump girl he had seen in the café, a kind of plaid cape over her shoulders, her floppy hat, heavy eyes. But no one had joined him. Well, it was meant to be a day of solitude, and his mind was as if a little drunk with the intensity of the images that had seized him. As it began to grow dark, he had found his way back to the bus terminal. Passing a little grocery store, he saw two women leaning out windows, side by side, in adjoining apartments he supposed. The windows wide open, they turned their heads and chatted. Below them hung a sign for KIK Cola, and as he passed them by, neither one appeared to notice the figure on the sidewalk glancing up. In the course of the day he had grown invisible. More and more he had been drawn into engagement with the hundreds of thousands of men and women who surrounded him, the children, the old on the point of death, the rich and poor. His reflection was possessed by every window where it had been mirrored. He remembered a low building on a narrow street, probably once a store, the windows and walls covered with advertising posters. As he walked past, the French word came to him: *affiches*. There was a little door, standing open, and inside the door a stairway, and at the top of the stairway only the sky. Steps to nowhere.

A man was walking toward him, short, slight, a cap on his head, and in his left hand a white plastic pail. In his mouth was a long pipe, and his jaw was tightly closed to hold the pipe in place as he chugged quickly past. Greg moved on, aware that he was growing hungry again, but the hunger too, along with the strangeness and solitude, gave an edge to his perceptions. He looked down a narrow alley between two tall buildings, and on each side there were fire escapes, several sets moving off toward the vanishing point, geometrical patterns leading up to the top of the buildings where the setting sun illuminated a parallelogram on the walls of brick.

Late in the afternoon he had passed a vacant lot, rubble at the edges, and at the far side of the lot, by a low stone wall, a man was bent over, searching the ground, in his hand a felt hat held inverted like a dish, and he was finding something on the lumpy earth and dropping it into his hat. Treasure. Could it be mushrooms? What else? Dandelion leaves to be eaten as salad greens? Some other ancient and mysterious herb, which had mystical powers. Greg had grown fascinated with the old magic that turned up in literature, botanical means of transcendence.

He took his puritan black hat from the seat beside him and put it on his lap, not so much to conceal the furious erection as to allow it a certain privacy. Dear Erection, I am sorry I can do nothing for you. His sometime girlfriend, Virginia, had moved back to her home in western Ontario, and she would not be coming back. She was moving on to studies in physiotherapy at another university, and they both realized that they weren't going to keep in touch. One of the things she said to him before she left, summing him up, was 'You just want sex all the time. That's all you need from me.'

He was polite enough not to agree. He demurred a little. But she was right, of course. It was what he wanted from her. All he wanted? Well, why not? They were young, and the young were meant to be at it incessantly, afloat on seas of desire, and he felt that his eagerness was perfectly understandable.

What he had seen painted on a wall that afternoon: WE CAN'T SOLVE ALL OUR PROBLEMS IN THE BEDROOM. Perhaps that was true. It sounded as if it ought to be, but that was in part the neatness of expression. Aphorisms were like that. The illusion of wisdom.

The bus was turning onto an expressway, lights of cars racing ahead into the night. He tried to create a map of the city in his mind, to follow his footsteps and recapture the extraordinary vividness of the experience, the sense of strangeness and escape that he had sought. He recalled a moment among the trees on the mountain, looking down at the tall buildings, the river beyond, the landscape beyond the river, and then noticing in a little thicket below a couple lying side by side, holding each other. Were they going to solve all their problems or none of them? Problems. Perhaps problem was the wrong word, the wrong way to shape experience. Problem, resolution. It wasn't like that at all. You just want to do it all the time. And what is the alternative? What was to be built, apart from a house to shelter children? And children were a thing apart, the accident that revised the universe.

Was he right or wrong to think that he should try to get his father back to work? Would it kill him? His brother seemed perfectly content to let the old man watch game shows and soap operas on television. His mother too took it for granted. What was it that made Greg wish to stir the man up, make him assert his continuing claim on the surface of life.

Factories, warehouses, a curving street of small houses. The voice in his head that sometimes spoke for him said, *He will never go back to that city again.* Well, who was to know? A hundred practical reasons might cause him to take the journey, one kind of business or another, a love affair, a family contact. But he understood too that if he returned it would all be different. He would be different, and the city would as well. He would carry with him precise instructions as to where he was to go and what he was to do when he arrived. The mystery would be reduced to the pragmatic. Problem, resolution. He could not come back to the odd transcendence of following only impulse.

What, he wondered, when he was as old as his sick and weary father was now, would he think about love? He looked at the black hat in his lap covering the urgent, comic tumescence of his swollen cock, and of course he did not know that one day he would be reminded of the hat when it was gone, lost, and to his astonishment he would have no idea when or where. Not the slightest idea.

It is a cloudy afternoon, and two old men walk side by side. Through thick patriarchal beards they exchange fragments of philosophic nonsense, verse in several unknown languages. Two dons, perhaps, from the Faculty of Error, on an afternoon ramble, looking like brothers, or a matched set of clay statuettes illustrating tales from the early books of the Bible. They are in the neighbourhood of an old synagogue – no, not the one that was demolished, a smaller building. A little further on they turn a corner, laugh together at an obscure joke. A few drops of rain fall. Beside them is an old brick wall painted white, with a square metal-covered loading chute and a tightly sealed steel door. The wall is covered with scraps of writing, old words grown pale, but over them is inscribed in tall assertive black letters. PRENDS TON QUÉBEC PAR LES COUILLES. No ambiguity to this epochal imperative, with its hint of fanaticism, of male rage. Or is it only a feverish patriotic love?

One of the old men remembers the days of the Hitler war, when he was a child, when the phrase KILROY WAS HERE became ubiquitous. He has read various explanations as to how the inscription began its travels. As a boy he had believed that Kilroy was a fast-moving, shadowy but real person who might eventually be discovered, no matter how quick and clever his disappearances. Each day he read the newspapers, awaiting the discovery. While Kilroy doesn't find his place among the Pompeian inscriptions, one of his ancient brothers or sisters does. SATURA WAS HERE.

Not many blocks away is the graffiti collector's apartment, and on the wall a photo of a black-and-white cat, seated complacently, its tail wrapped round, looking out a window. On the stone window ledge one can find the words P. COB LOVES RUSSIAN GIRL. Does the cat in the window have a connection to the assertion? she wonders. In fact P. COB is a mildly famous figure in a certain neighbourhood of another city, a slightly mad Kilroy who appears on a multitude of walls, telling his garbled stories. This photograph is evidence that the crazed autobiographer has at some point gone on his travels. Down a secret street he has met a Russian girl and fallen for her. The tale, like all those told by his inscriptions, is feverish but elliptical.

Marcel, the hotel manager, disapproved of it, Sasha being left on the desk overnight, but she and Pierre had made the arrangement, and while Marcel growled and insisted she discuss with him all the possible emergencies, having phoned her at home to insist that she dress in something plain, he didn't actually forbid them to make the switch. Sasha was wearing stone-washed jeans, a white blouse, and a man's tweed jacket that turned up in a second hand store and fit her well enough that she spent hours shortening the sleeves. Thank God for small men. She looked at herself in the mirror in the hall outside the office, her hair pulled back in a ponytail held in place by a barrette, and she assumed that Marcel would approve of the plain elements of the outfit, though she herself thought it was really pretty hot, the jeans tight, the blouse emphasizing the plumpness of her breasts, and the jacket a kind of affectation that made her look all the more girlish.

As she studied herself in the mirror she remembered the fantasy girl appearing there naked out of the mist, and the man in a fedora with a moustache, someone pretending to be Clark Gable, who nodded and vanished. Outside the hotel door she saw two figures, swollen with backpacks, studying a map, then looking into the lobby, turning to speak. One of them tried the locked door, and as Sasha went toward it, tapped on the glass. They fell in through the door, grumbling at each other in German. Probably German. They would speak perfect English and decent French. All Europeans did.

Rooms?

Yes, one.

Price.

Quoted.

Silence.

Sasha told them they could find a student hostel a couple of blocks away, and they hoisted their packs and fell back out the door. The hotel website had a few unanswered queries, and she sat down at the computer keyboard and replied, recorded two bookings. The buzzer summoned her back to the door, and she let in a middle-aged couple who looked as if they had indulged in a long dinner with more than one bottle of wine. They collected their key and went up the stairs. Another man came right behind them, white hair, white beard. He stared at Sasha as she handed him the key. Turned away. Guests might continue to turn up until 2 or 3 AM, and the earliest would be up to check out by 6. In between she could doze in a chair.

Sasha considered putting a disc into the lobby DVD player, but there were only two DVDs in the drawer, one a movie she'd already seen, and one a collection of wrestling videos which, she assumed, Pierre treated as a form of gay porn. On the way here tonight, as she was wheeling her bike down the *ruelle* to the backyard where she would take off the seat and lock both wheels to a steel frame, she had seen a sentence written on a back fence. MR GAY YOU ARE LOVELY, it said in a cursive hand. She must remember to report that to Pierre. Perhaps he had seen it. She didn't intend to report to him that someone had crossed out the last word and written SICK above it. She kept forgetting to tell Pierre Patricia's story, from the days before her marriage when she worked in a restaurant, and one day when the cleaning man was sick and she was stuck with swabbing the washrooms, she found an inscription on the wall above a urinal. MY MOTHER MADE ME A

HOMOSEXUAL. Below that in a different colour of ink was the reply.
IF I SEND HER THE WOOL WILL SHE MAKE ME ONE TOO?

Sasha looked around her, found a room key left lying on the desk and hung it in place, then sat in a stuffed chair and waited for time to pass. Time. Click, click, click. But that was a debasement of the mystery. Time. All that is. Not the watery soup of expectation, not even the dark chocolate of memory but you, sitting, in your chair. Now. She is sitting in her chair. Now. Eventual events. Images. What do dreams have to do with time? Knots and tangles.

She thought she heard someone knocking on the front door. If it was a returning guest why didn't he ring the bell? That was how to summon She Who Works to serve your pleasure. She waited, and the knocking was repeated. Sasha rose from her chair and went into the wide, bright hall. She observed a figure beyond the glass. A woman. Of a certain age. Handsome, straight white hair cut to hang close around her face. She made a gesture, indicating that she wished to come in. Sasha looked into the night beyond. A cab drove away from the curb. Cars passed by. The stairs and sidewalk were empty. She hoped this was not a trap baited with an old woman, the thieves, murderers, rapists, waiting for the lock to be released. Sasha opened the door.

'Thank you,' the woman said, walked past her, sat down in an upright chair with a back and seat upholstered in a fabric of satin – pink, say the colour of a child's tongue, stuck out at a friend who had angered her.

'Did you find your hat?' she said.

Sasha stared into the observing eyes.

'What hat?'

'The little black number with feathers and a veil.'

Sasha studied the woman. Something familiar about the long oval face, but she couldn't place it. A friend of her mother's, that thought came to her mind, but nothing to carry it further toward an explanation. She imagined Patricia, but no such face came along.

'No,' she said, 'I didn't find it.' She felt an awkwardness, as if this woman, who wore an oddly cut, green-shining but not unattractive pant-suit and stared at Sasha, intent dark eyes surrounded by a fine lace of wrinkles, might have been in her apartment and watched as Sasha crawled around the floor.

'Under the sink,' the woman said. 'That's where you'll find it.'

'Why would it be under the sink?'

'One of those unanswerable questions.'

'How do you know it's under the sink?'

The woman stared at her, without speaking. Sasha noticed a small brown mole on her cheek, a tiny scar on the chin. The woman reached up and stroked her white hair as if she were petting a cat.

'Have you made up your mind about the basso?'

Sasha was beginning to grow a little annoyed by such impudence. 'No,' she said.

'But you've been giving him some consideration.'

'He's offered nothing.'

'But you can read between the lines, can't you? All you have to do is wag your tail once or twice.'

'It seems a little unsuitable. His height.'

'Comic?'

'That long body hinged like a lift bridge to a buttress.'

'Yes.'

'My fault for being petite.'

'You might find it's a pleasure serving as a fulcrum.'

Sasha laughed, and the woman looked at her slyly.

'For a cantilevered basso,' she said.

'If I allow it.'

'Say yes. Make that your rule.'

'Shall I get you the key to your room?' Sasha said.

'I don't have a room,' the woman said.

'Then why are you here?'

'Such an impatient little thing we are,' the woman said. 'The youthfulness of the young.'

Sasha studied her, determined that she would find the face somewhere in memory, that she would force some recognition.

'Look at this,' the woman said and held out a piece of paper. It was an old black-and-white photograph, a stone wall, and on it someone had written LIES AVAILABLE EVERYWHERE.

'I knew we'd like that.'

As the woman spoke her lips grew thinner, lost colour, deep wrinkles channelling the pale surface. Sasha found she was conscious of her own tongue quickly licking her own lips, young and plump and damp and red.

'Harsh words,' Sasha said.

'Surely not. You adore falsities.'

'Do I?'

'Yes.'

'What makes you so sure you know that?'

'Don't be a prig. There is a universe out there, and the idea of truth is a restriction on its plenitude and charm. You know that.'

'Yes,' Sasha said, 'I do.'

'Somewhere in the rooms of this hotel a mystery is waiting for you.'

'No, not that. She Who Works is prim and attentive.'

'Not the Desirable Girl.'

'Not tonight.'

The woman was looking across the hall. Toward the mirror, Sasha realized, where the dark eyes observed her from behind, the tweed shoulders, tightly drawn ponytail of hair.

'How many rooms are there in the establishment?'

'Twenty-one.'

'And how many people are staying in those rooms?'

'One room on the second floor is empty, the others have one or two.'

'Something between twenty and forty.'

'Yes.'

'How many dreams are pursuing their insidious ways through the spaces of the building?'

The thought made Sasha uneasy.

'No way to know.'

'And in how many dreams do you have a place, as an object of desire or perhaps something more mysterious?'

'None of these people know me.'

'Some have seen you when they checked in, or when they returned from a late engagement.'

Sasha remembered the man with the white hair and beard.

'You are present in the sub-atomic structure of the place, and the dreams can discover you.'

'I don't believe that.'

'It's something you will learn.'

'I don't think so.'

The woman stood up. Trim, though a little heavy both top and bottom. She walked toward the door, turned, put her fingers to her lips and blew a kiss.

'It will come to be,' she said. 'It will all come to be.'

Watching her go, Sasha felt faint and muddled, almost paralyzed. The woman was through the door and walking down the steps. Sasha made her way back to the office, switched off the lights, though the dimness was still penetrated by the light in the front hall, and sank in the easy chair in the corner, hoping sleep would come. When she got home she would look under the sink for her hat. And she was a little frightened, knowing that she would almost certainly find it.

Papchik stood by the rail and stared at the North Atlantic. The waves rose and fell in the strong wind, and the steel walls of the freighter were buffeted, as it repelled the force of the waves and made its passage onward, northwest. Was there a Marxist-Leninist explanation for this collision of forces? The air was cold and a few flakes of snow blew past. They would reach Arkhangelsk in another week, and then as the deep winter set in, the White Sea would freeze, and the ship would be iced in for the winter. Ships would move in and out of the Crimean ports in the south, but this one would wait until the breakup in the spring.

Papchik had not been told anything about plans for the ship or the crew. It was his business to see the tons of wheat unloaded and then report to his superiors. Perhaps they would send him to the Crimea, to one of the ships there, on its way to East Africa or Australia. He had never sailed to those places. It was coming on to summer there. Or perhaps he might arrange a transfer to Moscow or Leningrad, a different kind of work.

He felt the force of the ship's engines in the steel on the deck, as if the engineer had increased the number of revolutions. Though it was morning, the sky appeared to be darkening, and when he looked over the side of the ship, there was a sheen of blackness on the heavy waves. Somewhere underwater, in the play of the currents, the Kapitan's body rolled and tumbled. Shark meat. Perhaps the steward was standing in the corridor below, knocking on the door of the Kapitan's cabin, bringing him a mug of strong tea. The Kapitan would not answer, and sooner or later the first officer would provide a key, and someone would enter the empty room, which stank of tobacco smoke. A package of Canadian cigarettes lay on the bed, but it would disappear. An empty vodka bottle lay in a corner. Someone would tidy it away.

Papchik had sat in there with the Kapitan last night, watching the man crouched on his bunk drinking glass after glass, his face growing red and dark, his voice at the edge of incoherence. Early in the conversation Papchik had asked about the money, the American dollars that the Kapitan had brought on the boat after his adventure in the city. The Kapitan smiled with a certain affected slyness and said they would discuss it later. But his eyes moved, signalling the location of the money by the way they avoided certain parts of the cabin. He gave a throaty chuckle as he told Papchik about the hollow in the heel of his shoe. Papchik poured him more vodka, and as the Kapitan grew drunk his eyes could no longer avoid the hiding places, though he would shift his glance there, then look away. He began to mumble incoherently, something about his mother and an icon. How when he was young she had encouraged him to join the militant atheists of the Party, but then in her old age a wooden icon had appeared from somewhere, and he would catch her with it when she thought she was alone. How she stared at the gold surface, the leaning head with its wide eyes focused on the little god-man as all her old superstitions came back. Once begun on this story the Kapitan kept mumbling, *tsaritsa nebesnaya*, it was the old woman's phrase, and as the man repeated it Papchik almost believed that in the muddle of his intoxication, the Kapitan was saying his old mother's prayers. The hoarse voice would whisper, grow silent, whisper again, *tsaritsa nebesnaya, tsaritsa nebesnaya*, and then he looked up at Papchik, suspicious and afraid, and he grew silent. More vodka until the man was barely able to stand, but Papchik convinced him that he ought to go up to the bridge and check the speed and course with the helmsman and first officer. The Kapitan was very careful to lock the door of his cabin behind him. He fell twice against the bulkhead, struggled up the ladder, and when they reached the deck, he stumbled against the rail. Papchik waited on deck near the bridge, a cold rain blowing in his face. In the pocket of his jacket was the little *dubinka*, and when the captain lurched back out, slipping on the wet deck and grabbing for the rail, Papchik took his arm and led him toward the stern. The first officer, and the helmsman who steered the ship into the night had seen how drunk the man was, staggering and incoherent. They would not be surprised when it was discovered that the Kapitan had gone over in the rain and wind.

Halfway to the stern, as they passed a heavy winch, the Kapitan turned his head, as if confused and suspicious. Drunk as he was, some self-protective instinct survived, but it was too late. Papchik stepped back as he took out the flexible *dubinka*, and a single sharp blow behind the ear brought him down. He reached into the jacket pocket where the Kapitan kept the key to his cabin, and when Papchik had the key, he bent to lift the inert figure from the wet deck. The Kapitan was heavy, but Papchik was strong, and he got his upper body over the rail, then lifted the legs and the body went to its resting place under the north Atlantic. Papchik quickly and silently made his way to the empty cabin on the lower deck, locked the door and rifled the small room, found the money. He heard voices in the passage outside the cabin, the watch changing, and he kept very still, and when they were quiet, he made his way back on deck, tossed the stolen keys overboard and returned to his own cabin.

He slept fitfully, rose and ate, and now he paced the afterdeck, checked the storage of some machine parts that were lashed there under heavy canvas. He had a week to make his plan. Did he tell his superiors the whole story and hand over the cash? Or did he contrive some way to keep it. Very dangerous to hold American dollars. When Comrade Stalin died things changed a little, but still one must be very careful. While Stalin was alive, one did not speak his name, not even in the ultimate privacy of the mind; thinking was almost as dangerous as speech, for the Georgian was God and God could read thoughts.

But Comrade Stalin was gone and there was a new General Secretary, a short, bald man, a little like Papchik himself. Papchik's wife thought this boded well for his career, but Papchik himself was less certain. History had many cunning ways. You must never let your concentration slip, see everything, hear everything, remember it all, except what must be forgotten. Like the Kapitan's unfortunate accident.

Carlo stared at the screen of his computer. He wasn't sure what came next. After the final dress rehearsal he invited Sasha, who was there again with her camera, to come with them for a drink, but she shook her head, indicated that she had something to whisper to him and when he bent his head said, 'Google the Desirable Girl.' When he looked puzzled, she smiled at him, packed her camera into her backpack and walked away. By the time he got back from a long conversation in the bar last night it was late enough that he only wanted to sleep, and it was only this morning once he was up and had made coffee that he remembered. So he fired up the computer and typed in the phrase, and there she was.

It was, he supposed, some kind of invitation. The earliest pictures in the photo file were more or less comic, Sasha in various outfits, odd combinations of old-fashioned hats and dresses, with bare feet or a long formal gown with rubber boots, but as the series went on, they were more daring. Then a series without her figure, pieces of clothing hung in front of a rice-paper blind and against a high white wall, a jacket, a skirt, a hat, as if the personality had been disassembled into these garments. Then a collection of lacy brassieres hanging from their straps, oranges and apples in each pouch, one hung high up from which bulged two grapefruit.

Moving on, he came upon the red banners, the fire into which he led Don Giovanni, but here draped over, around, the shapely body, they were another kind of flame. The double exposure, one image superimposed on another gave a sense of complexity and sensuality at once, a round breast half revealed, doubled, undefined. Comic again the version of Sasha as Charlie Chaplin's little tramp. She had a complete fictional life created here. Perhaps no mere reality could compete with it.

Then came a title, Her Perfect Body, but it was locked. He looked at the empty frame, the place for the password to be typed in. *Clue: Stoner.* Twelve letters. Had he mentioned to her his weakness for crosswords? Or was this just a general challenge to any man who wanted her that badly. Carlo stared for a minute at the screen, then he suddenly knew it was addressed to him and was typing in the twelve letters. c.o.m.m.e.n.d.a.t.o.r.e. Clicked on Enter. The picture came up. Her Perfect Body. A triumph of daring, the sensuous pale body photographed from behind, posed in the torque of contrapposto, feet leftward, shoulders pivoting right, the head, wearing a little black hat with feather and a veil, turned toward the camera, eyes almost hidden behind the veil, but meeting the lens. It was dramatically lit from one side, and the directional illumination outlined the plump and shapely tush. A curve of spine led the eye upward to the ridiculous little hat. The photo was sensual, a little absurd, and deliberately inviting. He couldn't keep his eyes off her. Her Perfect Body. The perfect lover asking him in. Would he accept the invitation? He had been so careful for years. A little tidy sex, no involvement. He was still aware of the scars.

The child would be seventeen now. He had never seen her. It had all begun to fade and sometimes when he recalled it, the pain was like something suffered in a dream or a story. Sometimes. Equally often it was bare and wretched and close.

He was attending C E G E P, and Alicia was in a couple of his classes, a tall, skinny girl with long black hair that she usually wore in a braid, sometimes with the braid wrapped around her head. They had spoken once or twice, and the night he was performing at the student bar he was pleased to see her in the audience, another familiar face to catch his eyes as he plucked the guitar and sang this and that. He sang one set of Old Left songs that no one else knew any more; they were popular with the students there. They weren't going to hear anyone else singing about Joe Hill. It had been out of date for a lifetime.

Then he was finished, and he was sitting at a table with Alicia and some others, and then she took him home to the basement apartment, with its low ceilings and damp walls, and she was all black hair and swarming appetite. They spent most of the weekend in bed, insatiable. He went home Monday morning. They got together again sometimes. Carlo assumed she was on the pill until two months later when one night she turned over in bed, and lying on her stomach, looking away from him, told him she was pregnant.

They had never before discussed their families, and only now did he hear the story of how Alicia's mother had been unmarried when she was born, impregnated by a married man who wasn't about to leave his wife. And now Alicia had got herself knocked up. They sat in silence, mumbled. They never said the word abortion, partly because it was clear that Alicia had no thought of any such thing. Aborted was what she herself might have been, but wasn't. In a moment of crazed abandon they married, in an office with two strangers as witnesses, and Carlo moved his few possessions into the dim basement. For a while they made love night and day, and then the anger began.

Whose anger was it? Hers, Carlo thought at the time, though now he was less sure. When he thought of her now he saw the unshaven armpits, the untidy black mat on her belly, the hair of the braid undone and hanging down her back. There was a rank smell in the apartment, and though they both showered regularly it clung to their skin. Even in the worst arguments, Carlo never once accused her of entrapping him – it was the one decent thing he could remember – and even now he didn't quite believe she had. In some kind of desperation she had trapped herself. This was her punishment for her intense hungers. Daughter of a whore, she would be one herself, was that it? He never understood.

Now and then he would try to imagine how he might have risen above it, have claimed for them some kind of dignity and calm. She had started to smoke and wouldn't give up drinking, and he remembered his rage, how he thought he might seize her, tie her up, keep the child safe. Or so he said. Perhaps he only wanted to punish her for something. For a while they made love avidly even when they could no longer speak to each other. Then that ended. They proceeded around the ugly little rooms as if drugged, unspeaking, untouching.

She was eight months pregnant when she vanished. Weeks before, she had been through the usual ultrasound and had told him that the child was a daughter. He tried to accommodate himself to that. Then she was gone. He phoned her mother, who hung up the phone. The next time he tried the number the phone had been disconnected. It was five years later that he received a letter from a lawyer who represented her, asking for his co-operation in divorce proceedings. He did what was asked, assumed that she was wishing to remarry. Good luck to her.

So somewhere out there he had a seventeen-year-old daughter. And here on the computer screen was a naked woman nine or ten years younger than he was, offering herself. What difference in age was acceptable? Did age have anything to do with it?

He felt a strange sense of presence behind him, over his right shoulder. If he turned he believed he would see the girl, his daughter, long slender arms and legs, hair the colour of his, a face like a mask, forehead, straight nose descending straight from the bone of the skull, almost without a bridge, the cheekbones very high, then a long jaw. Skinnybones, he thought, I would call her Skinnybones.

You don't dare call me that.

No?

You were never there. Don't try to be affectionate now.

All right.

You deserve nothing.

I could make an argument about that.

I hope you won't.

All right. I won't.

My stepfather was everything I needed.

That's good.

Now you're being pious.

If you say so.

I don't suppose you know my name.

Skinnybones. Your name is Skinnybones and you are seventeen years old.

That woman in the picture.

Yes.

She has a fat ass.

Do you think so?

Yes.

I suppose you could say so.

Are you going to bed with her?

I don't know. Maybe.

Give her a baby?

I don't know.

You don't know very much.

So it appears.

What do you know?

I know how to sing.

The snow is falling heavily, piling up on the curving iron staircases that lead down from the upper floors of apartments, and the cars are moving slowly through the streets following their headlights, the illumination reflected from every snowflake so that there is a certain haze of brightness in the air. To walk you must push your feet through the piles of snow that accumulate from the recurrent waves of frozen particles, not yet removed by the snowploughs or the shovels of the storekeepers.

If you examined photographs of this night they would show the heavy snow piled up in odd shapes on the top of the cars. The lights of a *dépanneur* illuminate with sidewalk, though there are few people out in the streets. Down a long lane, each of the round glass lamps creates a haze of whiteness around it, and as the eye moves, reaches into the distance, the lamplit circles grow smaller, everything, including the figure of a solitary man walking away from you, recedes toward the vanishing point.

The man is a waiter at a good restaurant a few blocks away. He works until after midnight, and then he likes to walk home, observing the lights of the long streets, the automobiles slowly making their way along the narrow ways, to find their place or to go on to another destination. Most nights he walks by a little house which he would like to own, though it is not for sale. He is saving his money to buy something, a little house or an apartment. Some nights when he gets home he pours himself a snifter of brandy and sits with it for a long time, reading or thinking. But not tonight. One of the things he does to make a little extra money is act as a sperm donor. His health is excellent, his IQ satisfactory, no genetic weaknesses that anyone has ever discovered, and on the occasions when he is to donate he tries to get a good night's sleep, and to make sure that there is no alcohol in his blood. He gives his best to it. The children he will never know must be offered all the best chance of happiness.

Though there is an aura of reflected light all through the air, the blackness of dark walls resists vision, and the inscriptions on the walls are in many cases almost impossible for the eye to read. In the winter night, you might think, the only wisdom is wordless, silent, but words are there all the same. At the corner of a *ruelle*, where it meets a slightly wider street, on the back of a building, unnoticed in the storm but still present, these words. RECRÉER LE RÉEL SOUS UN MÊME SOLEIL.

Lomas stood inside the small passenger cabin of the ferry and looked at his sick old father standing on the lower deck. A strong west wind was blowing, and the water of the channel was running in low heavy waves, spray tossed off the foaming tips. It was cold out, but Leo, his father, chose to stay on the deck, leaning on the side between the parked cars and the bow, the brim of his tweed flat cap pointed ahead into the gusts of air, as if his eyes must be fixed on the dock in order to guide the boat to its landing.

Lomas stared out the window at the old man, his back slightly hunched, his hands on the rail, and as he watched his father from above, through glass, he imagined a higher, more impersonal point of view, a detached and analytical eye observing the family and its fragmented, distant ways, Lomas in the cabin, his father at the rail, Sasha waiting for them in the car. And of course there was Patricia back at home with his mother, having chosen not to come on the outing at all.

After the visit to the old family farm on the island, his father had decided they should cross to New York State for lunch, but when they parked near the ferry dock, Sasha announced from the back seat that she preferred to wait in the car, pulled a comic book out of her bag and began to read. Perhaps Lomas ought to have insisted, created a scene, dragged her from the car, but that was not his way. He pointed out that she would be hungry, and she announced that she had a peanut-butter and banana sandwich in her bag. Her grandfather suggested it might be dangerous to leave her there for an hour or more, and she calmly said that as soon as they were on their way she would lock the car doors, and besides there was a house a hundred feet away and soon cars would be lined up for the next ferry.

Patricia was back at the house, probably trying on some old clothes that she'd found stored in a trunk in the basement, Sasha was locked in the car, his father, whose days were numbered, though no one said that aloud, stared over the rail of the ferry, and Lomas sheltered in the cabin. They were disparate, untouching, yet Lomas found he couldn't take his eyes off the thin, hunched figure of the old man, couldn't stop wondering what he was thinking. Perhaps he worried about Sasha and wished to hurry the boat to shore. Lomas perhaps didn't worry about the girl as much as he should.

> *The child that's born on the Sabbath day*
> *is bonny and blithe and good and gay.*

Counting on that, Patricia had insisted that the child be called Sabbatha, and Lomas had more or less consented, but she had, from the beginning, been called Sasha for everyday use, and though he wasn't sure now which of them began it, Sasha was now her name.

The boat shuddered and swayed a little as the captain changed direction, and while Lomas watched, the wind coming at a new angle seized the hat from his father-in-law's head, the arm that flew up to catch it too slow, and it sailed a few feet through the air and then fell into the water. His head, balding, pale above the tanned face, spots of keratosis in the pallor, was naked and queer. He looked older, sicker, without the hat. His features were grim and angry.

They could buy a new cap of some sort at the general store. The ferry was approaching the dock, and the rhythm of the engine had changed. The boat would pull in beside the concrete loading ramp, sheltered from the heavy swell.

The cap had vanished into the deep channel where perhaps it would become wedged between two limestone plates and gradually over the years be worn to fragments, shreds, threads, molecules, return in the metaphysical river to nothingness and then back into creation. Or perhaps it will tumble along in the current, flowing northwest, carried a little further day by day, swaying and tumbling, until through some whimsy of wind and current it is driven up one stormy night on a patch of stone shoreline at the west end of Nun's Island below a little park where a ten-year-old boy who has skipped school on a sunny May morning finds it and though it is faded and shapeless, claps it on his head and laughs.

Acknowledgements

These stories have also been published in *Journal of Canadian Fiction, Atlantica: Stories from the Maritimes and Newfoundland, Queen's Quarterly, 98: Best Canadian Stories, 03: Best Canadian Stories, 05: Best Canadian Stories, 06: Best Canadian Stories.*

In 'La Rue du Chapeau Perdu', most of the contemporary graffiti quoted in the text are recorded in photographs taken by the author 1992–96. A few are recorded in photographs in *Montréal Graffiti, VLB Éditeur, 1987.*

About David Helwig

Born in Toronto in 1938, David Helwig attended the University of Toronto and the University of Liverpool. His first stories were published in *Canadian Forum* and *The Montrealer* while he was still an undergraduate. He then went on to teach at Queen's University. He worked in summer stock with the Straw Hat Players, mostly as a business manager and technician, rubbing elbows with such actors as Gordon Pinsent, Jackie Burroughs and Timothy Findley.

While at Queen's University, Helwig did some informal teaching in Collins Bay Penitentiary and subsequently wrote *A Book about Billie* with a former inmate.

Helwig has also served as literary manager of CBC Television Drama, working under John Hirsch, supervising the work of story editors and the department's relations with writers.

In 1980, he gave up teaching and became a full-time freelance writer. He has done a wide range of writing – fiction, poetry, essays. Helwig is also the founder and long-time editor of the *Best Canadian Stories* annual. In 2009 he was named as a member of the Order of Canada.

David Helwig lives in the village of Eldon on Prince Edward Island where he gardens and plays golf. He was the third poet laureate on the Island in 2008 and 2009. For many years he indulged his passion for music by singing in choirs in Kingston, Montreal and Charlottetown. He has appeared as bass soloist in Handel's *Messiah*, Bach's St Matthew *Passion* and Mozart's *Requiem*.

His website is www.davidhelwig.com.